<u>BAKING</u>

Have fun trying
all these things.
Opa & Oma

Christmas 2019

BAKING

HAMLYN

Baking — practise tested techniques and achieve perfection

Published 1986 by
The Hamlyn Publishing Group Limited
Bridge House, 69 London Road, Twickenham, Middlesex, England.

ISBN 0 600 32646 2

Set in 9/10pt Gill Sans by Servis Filmsetting Ltd, Manchester

Printed in Spain

This book . . .

. . . brings something new to the world of cookery. It is not a recipe book in the usual sense, but is more in the style of a textbook. But don't worry it is not full of boring instructions but provides baking information using over a thousand appetising colour photos.

To help beginners to baking every chapter starts with a basic recipe. Precise step-by-step photos take you through every stage. Every type of mixture is described exactly. Helpful tips show the easy way to guaranteed success each time. So if you have any problems when preparing or baking a mixture, always turn to the 'basic recipe' page.

When you have mastered the basic recipe you will have the necessary knowledge to move on to the next level in the art of baking. The following pages build on each basic recipe providing variations and specialities leading you gradually to particular masterpieces which sometimes call for skill and practice. To be tried out by the more experienced cook in fact.

Each chapter includes plenty of variations and ideas which you can combine to enjoy the pleasures of creative baking. There is one thing you should always bear in mind, never try to judge quantities by eye, but always weigh and measure precisely. This is the absolute must of any type of baking or you will just not be successful. But feel free to combine the various building blocks that make up our system in any way you like to make your own completely individual creations. And one more thing, don't try to take on too much at a first attempt. You will succeed better if you gradually build up to the more difficult things. And if things do go wrong sometimes, don't give up, for practice makes perfect.

Useful Facts and Figures

Notes on metrication

In this book quantities are given in metric and Imperial measures. Exact conversion from Imperial to metric measures does not usually give very convenient working quantities and so the metric measures have been rounded off into units of 25 grams. The table below shows the recommended equivalents.

Ounces	Approx g to nearest whole figure	Recommended conversion to nearest unit of 25
1	28	25
2	57	50
3	85	75
4	113	100
5	142	150
6	170	175
7	198	200
8	227	225
9	255	250
10	283	275
11	312	300
12	340	350
13	368	375
14	396	400
15	425	425
16 (1 lb)	454	450
17	482	475
18	510	500
19	539	550
20 ($1\frac{1}{4}$ lb)	567	575

Note: When converting quantities over 20 oz first add the appropriate figures in the centure column, then adjust to the nearest unit of 25. As a general guide, 1 kg (1000 g) equals 2.2 lb or about 2 lb 3 oz. This method of conversion gives good results in nearly all cases, although in certain pastry and cake recipes a more accurate conversion is necessary to produce a balanced recipe.

Liquid measures. The millilitre has been used in this book and the following table gives a few examples.

Imperial	Approx ml to nearest whole figure	Recommended ml
$\frac{1}{4}$ pint	142	150 ml
$\frac{1}{2}$ pint	283	300 ml
$\frac{3}{4}$ pint	425	450 ml
1 pint	567	600 ml
$1\frac{1}{2}$ pints	851	900 ml
$1\frac{3}{4}$ pints	992	1000 ml (1 litre)

Spoon measures. All spoon measures given in this book are level unless otherwise stated.

Can sizes. At present, cans are marked with the exact (usually to the nearest whole number) metric equivalent of the Imperial weight of the contents, so we have followed this practice when giving can sizes.

Oven temperatures

The table below gives recommended equivalents.

	°C	°F	Gas Mark
Very cool	110	225	$\frac{1}{4}$
	120	250	$\frac{1}{2}$
Cool	140	275	1
	150	300	2
Moderate	160	325	3
	180	350	4
Moderately hot	190	375	5
	200	400	6
Hot	220	425	7
	230	450	8
Very hot	240	475	9

Notes for American and Australian users

In America the 8 fl oz measuring cup is used. In Australia metric measures are now used in conjunction with the standard 250-ml measuring cup. The Imperial pint, used in Britain and Australia, is 20 fl oz, while the American pint is 16 fl oz. It is important to remember that the Australian tablespoon differs from both the British and American tablespoons; the table right gives a comparison. The British standard tablespoon, which has been used throughout this book, holds 17.7 ml, the American 14.2 ml, and the Australian 20 ml. A teaspoon holds approximately 5 ml in all three countries.

British	American	Australian
1 teaspoon	1 teaspoon	1 teaspoon
1 tablespoon	1 tablespoon	1 tablespoon
2 tablespoons	3 tablespoons	2 tablespoons
$3\frac{1}{2}$ tablespoons	4 tablespoons	3 tablespoons
4 tablespoons	5 tablespoons	$3\frac{1}{2}$ tablespoons

An Imperial/American guide to solid and liquid measures

Solid measures

Imperial	American
1 lb butter or margarine	2 cups
1 lb flour	4 cups
1 lb granulated or caster sugar	2 cups
1 lb icing sugar	3 cups
8 oz rice	1 cup

Liquid measures

Imperial	American
$\frac{1}{4}$ pint liquid	$\frac{2}{3}$ cup liquid
$\frac{1}{2}$ pint	$1\frac{1}{4}$ cups
$\frac{3}{4}$ pint	2 cups
1 pint	$2\frac{1}{2}$ cups
$1\frac{1}{2}$ pints	$3\frac{3}{4}$ cups
2 pints	5 cups ($2\frac{1}{2}$ pints)

Note: When making any of the recipes in this book, only follow one set of measures as they are not interchangeable.

Contents

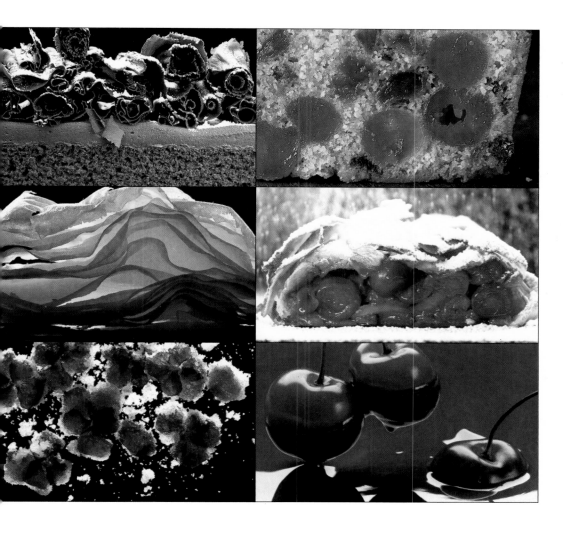

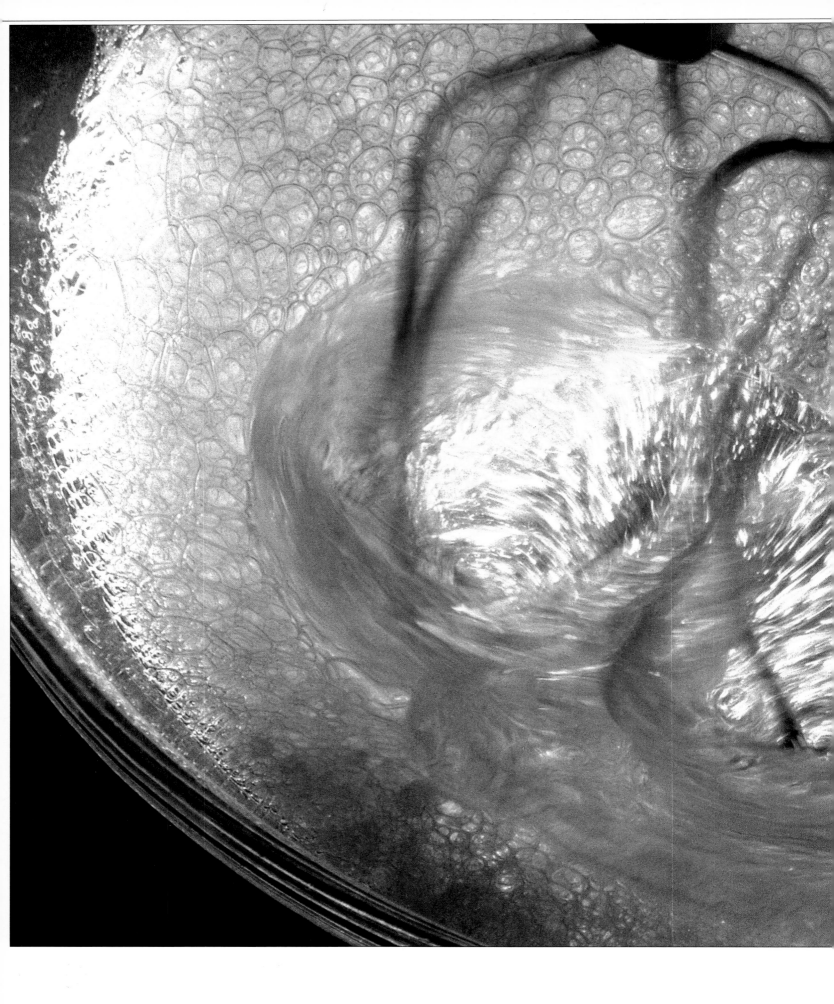

Baking techniques –
making the job easier

Get the right measures!

The basic difference between baking and other forms of cooking is that quantities in baking have to be precise. In other forms of cooking the best dishes are often produced when the cook decides to vary the recipe, adding a pinch of this or a dash of that, but in baking you cannot do this and need to stick strictly to the recipe or you may end up with a disaster!

Once the mixture is in the oven there is nothing more you can do. And if the proportions of ingredients are wrong, or you have added them in the wrong order, you can expect something to go wrong. Don't ever try to judge quantities by eye, it just doesn't work and your baking will never improve!

Scales – the most important tool

If you ever get the chance to peep into the kitchen of a professional baker you will see that everything centres around the *scales*. You will never see a professional estimating weights by the spoonful, as ingredients must be weighed exactly.

Good kitchen scales are not cheap. They must be able to weigh small quantities as well as heavy weights with precision. They must also be stable so that they do not tip under the weight. A *measuring jug* is really only useful for measuring liquids and it needs to be graduated for small measures of less than 6 tablespoons. Don't use a measuring jug for solid ingredients like flour or sugar unless you absolutely have to as measuring in this way is just not precise enough.

Eggs play an important part

It is normal in baking recipes to indicate the number of eggs required. This would not, however, be precise enough for the professional pastry chef. Eggs range from the very large at over 75 g/3 oz each (class 1) to tiny ones at 40–50 g/1½–2 oz (class 6) with a variety of weights in between. It is obvious that this variation can affect your baking – in fact in professional recipes the quantity of egg is always given as an overall weight. The eggs easily found in the shops are class 3 and 4 (between 50 g/2 oz and 65 g/2½ oz each). These are the sizes that should be used in our recipes.

Always use fresh eggs – you can tell when an egg is fresh by the white which should form a thick layer around the yolk. If you are not sure of the freshness of your eggs, break them one at a time into a cup or on to a plate. The runnier the egg white, the older the egg. Be very careful when you separate eggs since the tiniest bit of yolk in the white will prevent it whisking up properly.

Measuring small quantities

When a recipe in a new cookbook mentions a tablespoonful, this refers to a modern type of spoon, not one of the old-fashioned deep tablespoons which hold much more. Here you can see at a glance what a *level* table- or teaspoon normally holds:

Flour:

1 tablespoon	=	10 g/⅓ oz
1 teaspoon	=	3 g/⅛ oz

Caster sugar:

1 tablespoon	=	20 g/¾ oz
1 teaspoon	=	7 g/¼ oz

Cornflour:

1 tablespoon	=	10 g/⅓ oz
1 teaspoon	=	3 g/⅛ oz

Butter:

1 tablespoon	=	15 g/½ oz
1 teaspoon	=	5 g/⅙ oz

Icing sugar:

1 tablespoon	=	10 g/⅓ oz
1 teaspoon	=	3 g/⅛ oz

Cocoa powder:

1 tablespoon	=	10 g/⅓ oz
1 teaspoon	=	3 g/⅛ oz

Ground nuts:

1 tablespoon	=	10 g/⅓ oz
1 teaspoon	=	7 g/¼ oz

Baking powder:

1 tablespoon	=	10 g/⅓ oz
1 teaspoon	=	7 g/¼ oz

Tried and tested

All the recipes in this book have been tried and tested in our own kitchens using a conventional electric oven. At the beginning of each basic recipe you will find a list of the equipment required. Exact preparation, baking and cooling times are given. The ingredients are always listed in the order in which they are used. When extra ingredients are needed like: 'flour to sprinkle on the worktop' or 'butter to grease the tin', they have been given in the basic recipes but omitted from most of the recipe variations.

On which shelf should you bake?

As a general rule, the middle of the cake should really be in the middle of the oven, so that a deep fruit cake, for example, should go on the bottom shelf or, in a large oven, the next to bottom shelf. Flat pastry bases or biscuits should go on the middle shelf.

Another point to remember is that a cake tin should never be put on a baking tray but always directly on to the shelf, otherwise the tin gets overheated where it is in contact with the baking tray because the heat is prevented from circulating properly.

Never put the cake on the bottom of the oven either, or the base of the cake will burn. The shelf height is less important in a convection oven where the circulating air allows you to put two or three baking trays one above the other.

Check the baking time

Never follow this part of the instructions too blindly as the exact baking time depends on so many different factors – the type and age of the oven, the type of tin, the room temperature in which the cake is made – to name a few.

As a cake gets near the end of the recommended baking time keep a careful eye on it and when it looks done, test it with a skewer. Stick a thin wooden or metal skewer vertically into the deepest part of the cake. If crumbs, or some uncooked mixture, stick to it, the cake still needs a little longer to cook. The cake is completely cooked only when the skewer comes out absolutely clean.

Getting the right temperature

In our recipes the baking temperature is given in centigrade, fahrenheit and with a regulo number for gas ovens. So whatever type of oven you have you should easily be able to set the right temperature and achieve successful results each time.

A convection oven works on a different principle from the normal electric oven and is very efficient, so always follow the manufacturer's instructions. You will always need about 10 to 20 per cent less heat than in a conventional oven. If you really find it difficult to get the temperature right with your oven, buy yourself a thermometer. They are inexpensive and will tell you exactly what temperature your oven has reached.

Basic equipment

1. *Whisk.* In two sizes, for whisking egg whites, custards and cream and delicate mixtures. They are available in stainless steel or can be plastic-coated. When buying check that the grip is comfortable.
2. *Steel cake base.* A thin round metal plate, useful for moving delicate gâteaux or lifting sponge bases or cakes.
3. *Stainless steel mixing bowls.* You should have at least two sizes. These metal ones conduct heat and are ideal when you need to warm a mixture over a pan of hot water or for melting chocolate.
4. *Pastry brush.* With long, soft, natural bristles. This is useful for glazing, brushing with cream, milk or egg yolk. Always wash out well and the brush should last a long time.

5. *Kitchen scissors.* Choose a steel pair with a comfortable grip. For cutting pastry strips and general kitchen tasks.
6. *Rubber spatula.* For scraping creams or cake mixtures out of the mixing bowl. Also useful for smoothing the tops of cakes or gently stirring in.
7. *Mixing spoons.* In plastic which do not get discoloured by acids (eg fruit juice). In wood for beating creams and cake mixtures.
8. *Pastry wheels.* Featuring a zig-zag edge to cut out patterned pieces of pastry.
9. *Pastry cutter.* This type has a sharp edge for cutting pastry and flat sponges.
10. *Zest knife.* This special knife is useful for cutting thin strips of orange, lemon or cucumber skin (zest).
11. *Kitchen knife.* A finely serrated knife for even cutting of sponge cakes.

The right tools for the job

No one can work without the right tools. This is just as true of the home cook as of the professional chef. Take your kitchen equipment seriously. Buy solidly-made equipment which will stand up to regular use. And buy several of the regularly-used items – you can't manage with only one mixing bowl and there are some specialised items that you can't afford to be without.
Not all the items you may see in a kitchen shop are really practical, so try going to a professional catering shop to buy top quality equipment. The following list gives the basic equipment you will need.

12. *Palette knife*. A wide, blunt knife which is an all-purpose tool useful for smoothing cake mixtures, cream, icing, etc. It is also used for lifting cake bases and cakes.

13 and 14. *Pastry scrapers*. Plastic with smooth or zig-zag edge. For spreading pastry or cake mixtures and for decorating or smoothing gâteaux. They are used wherever the palette knife would be too long and unwieldy.

15. *Wire rack*. Essential for cooling any baked items. It allows the air to circulate round a freshly baked cake and prevent it sweating.

16. *Paper icing bag*. Used to pipe lines, ornaments and patterns with icing.

17. *Piping bag with assorted nozzles*. Used to shape and decorate soft doughs, creams and cake mixtures.

18. *Piping tube*. A solid piping bag, but it is more difficult to use as you have less control over the flow of the mixture.

19. *Cake ring*. Shown here in plastic, but more solid ones are also available in stainless steel. They can be adjusted for size. Place them on a baking tray and fill with the mixture for baking. A useful item as you can vary the size of the cake.

20. *Scoops*. Available in plastic, wood, aluminium or stainless steel. They are useful for measuring flour, sugar, salt, etc.

21. *Sieve*. Buy a selection of different sizes. Particularly good for sifting flour, dusting with icing sugar, etc. Use a plastic type when there is contact with acids –

straining lemon juice, for example – and a metal one for hot or more solid ingredients.

22. *Rolling pin*. For rolling out all types of pastry and for crushing solid ingredients like spices or nuts.

23. *Plastic mixing bowls*. These are used for making pastry or whisking custards, creams or egg whites. They should not be too thin a plastic and should have a firm, even base.

24. *Measuring jug*. Available in heat-resistant glass, plastic or porcelain. Ideal for measuring liquids.

As well as all the equipment listed here you will need a number of other kitchen tools for baking, which should already be in your kitchen: a variety of knives, ranging from small vegetable knives to heavy, long-bladed all-purpose knives; lemon squeezer; grater; saucepans in an assortment of sizes; ladles in two sizes; food processor or mixer, liquidiser, hand mixer with pastry hooks and beaters or grinders. None of these electric gadgets can do everything so, depending on how often you bake, a choice of gadgets will always be useful.

A choice of tins

Having the right tin to cook a particular type of cake is extremely important. If you bake a cake in an old-fashioned ceramic mould or in the pretty ring mould brought back as a holiday souvenir you will find that the cakes will take up to one-third longer to cook. In this section details are given on what to look out for when you are buying baking tins or moulds.

The different types available

The photograph detailed includes a sample of the many baking tins and moulds that are available in a variety of shapes and materials (for a further selection see pages 88–9). Tins in *black sheet-iron* or *dark-coloured sheet-steel* (not illustrated) are the most useful. They absorb the heat and pass it directly to the cake mixture (page 88–9). These good old-fashioned tins that our grandmothers used to use give good results but are difficult to look after as they have to be dried immediately and then left in a warm place to dry completely.

Tinware (see items 2 and 7) reflects the heat back into the oven rather than conducting it to the cake mixture so that the cake browns on the outside long before it is cooked through. Cakes cooked in tinware will take 10 to 20 per cent longer to bake (see pages 20–1). For the best results use them in gas or convection ovens in which the heat is more direct.

Non-stick tins with inner coating (6) are the most modern baking tins. Cakes will simply slide out of them even when they have only been lightly greased. They are also very easy to clean and give the best results as regards consistency and browning (see pages 20–1).

Copper moulds (5) look good and are excellent to use. But they are expensive to buy and to maintain as they will need recoating from time to time. They can also be difficult to clean!

Paper cases (8) are practical for cooking small cakes and buns, particularly for children. They need no preparing but are very easy to peel off cooked buns and can then be thrown away.

Cast-iron containers (4). These are very heavy but do absorb and retain the heat well and the cake cooks evenly in them. They will continue to retain heat so that cooking will continue after the oven has been turned off, so make sure you allow for this in your cooking time.

Ovenproof glass baking dishes (3) are poor conductors of heat so baking will take longer. They are good, however, for seeing how the cake is cooking.

Ceramic moulds (11), like glass ones, are poor conductors of heat and you may need to increase the baking time by up to a third. However, they are decorative dishes.

Ovenproof porcelain dishes (13) are again poor conductors of heat, but these are what you need for pies with lids. They are also suitable for microwaves.

Cardboard moulds (14). Disposable tins usually sold in mixed packs. These are practical to use as they require no greasing or washing up.

Cake ring in stainless steel (10). This is a professional piece of equipment which can be adjusted to any size and stands directly on a baking tray so that you can vary the cake size to suit. It also makes it easier to remove the cake.

Heart mould without base (12). This is used exactly the same way. The cooked cake pushes out easily.

Biscuit cutters (9) for cutting out biscuits and pastry shapes.

Tartlet tins (15), round or boat-shaped. These are used to bake individual tartlets. To bake several

The basic cake tin in various forms

Every household should have some sort of *spring tin* with a removable rim. These usually come with a ring mould which saves having to buy a savarin tin. Spring tins come in several sizes: from 15–25 cm/6–10 in diameter, 30 cm/12 in diameter and sometimes even 33 cm/13 in, they have an outward-sloping rim suitable for flans.

A *fluted ring mould* is another popular container. The size of the fluting may vary, but all feature a chimney through the centre which distributes the heat evenly to the centre of these deep cakes.

A *loaf tin* of 450–900-g/ 1–2-lb capacity, or even more for close-textured loaves, has many uses. It can be used to cook sweet loaves and bread of all kinds, but is also very good for pies and terrines.

A *baking tray* is usually supplied with the oven. If you need an extra one when making biscuits, for example, try covering the oven shelf with extra-strong aluminium foil.

A good idea for single people or couples are *miniature format baking tins*. They are just the right size for a small cake.

at a time, line them with pastry and stack them up to six deep. Then you only need to fill the top one with dried beans when baking blind (see pages 24–5). The ones underneath are sufficiently weighted to hold down the pastry.

Aluminium foil tins (1). These are intended to be disposable. Like tinware they reflect heat so need more cooking time but save on washing up. *Plastic moulds* (not illustrated) are easy to use, as the cakes slide out every time without sticking. With use they become cloudy and unattractive and can only be used in electric or microwave ovens and never in a gas oven.

What makes a good baking tin?

In the ideal baking tin the cake should cook evenly and in a reasonable time, and should come out easily when cooked. The tin should also be easy to clean. What the tin is made out of also has an effect on the consistency of the cake. If it is the wrong material and the cake has to stay longer than usual in the oven because of it, the cake is bound to be dry.

You can see how the various materials affect baking in different sorts of oven in the chart detailed (explained in the last column). The chart highlights that there is no point economising on baking tins for cheap tins will not prove to be as successful as good-quality ones.

Preparing the tin

As a basic rule all tins must be greased, even non-stick ones. Exceptions to this are for puff pastry which needs a moistened baking tray so that the steam helps the pastry rise.

You can get away without greasing a tin only if you line the tin with greaseproof paper. There is no problem with a baking tray, but in loaf and cake tins the paper can wrinkle at the edges, so make sure that the mixture does not come into direct contact with the tin.

Ideally use melted butter or margarine for greasing. If you brush it on you can get right into the corners.

Grease the tin before you start making the cake

and keep it in the refrigerator so that the fat sets and becomes visible. Then you can go over any bits you may have missed.

Transfer the mixture to the chilled tin and bake immediately. If the butter has set firmly enough the cake mixture won't fuse with it.

Many recipes, especially for delicate sponges, tell you to sprinkle the greased tin with flour, ground nuts or breadcrumbs. Obviously, this must be done before the tin goes into the refrigerator as they will not stick to the fat once it has set.

Choosing the best

The price difference between the cheapest tinware and professional baking tins can be extremely high. But the expense is well worth it. A good-quality baking tin like this will last you a lifetime. A good compromise for price is to buy solid black sheet-iron or teflon-coated tins which lie somewhere between the two.

The right tin and how to use it

Tinware tin

Black sheet-iron tin

	Electric oven	Convection oven	Gas oven
Baking time	517	524	515
Energy used	7,56	5,89	7,34
Sticking	2,75	2,75	2,67
Browning	3,83	2,08	2,33
Cleaning	3,00	3,00	3,00

	Electric oven	Convection oven	Gas oven
Baking time	480	483	488
Energy used	6,91	5,46	6,84
Sticking	2,33	2,42	2,33
Browning	2,17	1,83	2,92
Cleaning	2,58	2,58	2,58

You carefully weigh the ingredients, mix them as instructed, put the mixture in the right sort of tin, bake it exactly as the recipe says, and still that wonderful cake you were anticipating sticks firmly to the tin and refuses to come out. Alternatively that appetising brown colour you were expecting doesn't materialise and a pale and wan cake emerges from the tin. If this hasn't happened to you, you've been lucky! Anyway, here are some basic cooking instructions to help ensure that you have success every time – whatever you bake!

Teflon-coated tin

Silicon-coated tin

	Electric oven	Convection oven	Gas oven
Baking time	481	494	504
Energy used	6,77	5,87	6,92
Sticking	2,17	2,17	2,08
Browning	2,33	1,92	3,00
Cleaning	1,92	1,92	1,92

	Electric oven	Convection oven	Gas oven
Baking time	453	460	478
Energy used	6,27	5,49	6,31
Sticking	1,17	1,17	1,17
Browning	1,75	1,75	2,25
Cleaning	1,08	1,08	1,08

Getting the cake out of the tin

Never take the cake out of the tin the minute it comes out of the oven. The cooked mixture needs between 1 and 3 minutes, depending on the type of cake, to firm up.

Every cake will contract slightly as it cools and this makes a narrow gap between the cake and the tin which makes it easier to turn out the cake.

Time it carefully – don't leave it too late to turn out the cake. If you leave the cake on the baking tray or in the tin until completely cold, it will probably stick fast. This is especially true of sweet shortcrust pastry containing a lot of sugar where the condensation produced as it cools crystallises with the sugar.

Always loosen delicate sponges from the base of the tin using a cake slice or palette knife (see pages 16–17).

Always completely cool cakes on a wire rack. This will keep them light as there is no condensation to make them soggy.

Which tins for which oven?

Tinware tins normally give the best results in a gas or convection oven. Use on the bottom shelf to get full advantage of the heat. In an electric oven with separate controls for top and bottom heat, reduce the top heat and increase the bottom heat. If the top of the cake still browns too quickly cover it with damp non-stick baking parchment or aluminium foil.

Black sheet-iron tins conduct heat well. With the bottom heat too high the cake can become dry, so use a high shelf (especially with gas) and try placing a baking tray beneath it as a protective barrier. In electric ovens with separate controls for top and bottom heat, reduce the bottom heat. *Teflon-coated tins* are most suitable in electric ovens, and the best results of all, with more even and faster baking, are achieved in convection ovens. *Silicon-coated tins* are ideal, giving the best possible results in any type of oven.

Cleaning the tins

It is not a good idea to leave cake tins standing around for long after use. They are much easier to clean in hot soapy water while they are still warm. A brief soaking will also help to remove any encrusted remains. Never scrape the tin with a sharp object for this will damage both the metal and its coating. This will also make the cake stick even more next time you use the tin.

Notes on the chart

Baking time: total of all baking tests in minutes. Energy used: total of all baking tests in kwh. Sticking, Browning, Cleaning: marked on the scale 1 (very good) to 6 (very poor).

The new generation

Gas or electric?

At one time baking with gas was unpopular. It was felt to be difficult to work with a naked flame. At low temperatures especially, in drying out meringues for instance, there were usually problems. But those days are gone. Technological advances have even caught up with the gas oven. The latest models look exactly like electric ovens. The flame works invisibly with a fan to provide an even temperature and the right degree of browning.

Modern gas ovens now have all the latest features.

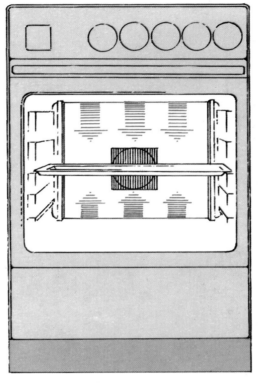 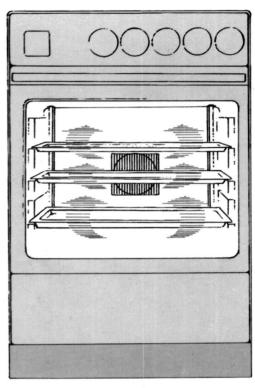

The market for ovens is large today and the choice can be very confusing. Anyone buying a new oven today is spoilt for choice, but first you have to choose between gas and electric. Then there are the individual features of each model: convection or conventional (i.e. with top and bottom heat), with grill, built-in microwave, self-cleaning facilities. They can be built into a kitchen unit or go under the worktop – there are so many differences. The advantages and disadvantages of different types are detailed here.

Conventional oven

This term covers the classic form of heating with both top and bottom heat. The heating elements are positioned under the floor of the oven and on or above the top. They work on radiated heat, i.e. the heat reaches the food in a straight line from above and below. *Advantage*: direct heat penetrates more quickly. *Disadvantage*: the temperature is not uniform throughout the oven. It is lower near the door, for instance, so it often happens that sponges or biscuits at the back of a baking tray are often cooked while those at the front have yet to brown.

Times and temperatures in the recipes in this book are based on this type of oven.

Convection or fan oven

A few years ago this type of oven was considered to be the technology of the future. A fan on the back of the oven swirls the hot air around the oven. The heat comes from elements behind the side walls. *Advantage*: an even temperature which cooks the food from all round, even with several baking trays one above the other. *Disadvantage*: the circulating air tends to dry out the baking and some mixtures refuse to brown.

Nevertheless, even with these drawbacks most bakeries have now switched to convection ovens. It is quite difficult to convert the temperatures given in the recipes to this type of oven. With the heat in the oven absolutely even, lower temperatures are required than with a conventional oven, but for a longer baking time. Convection ovens, however, do not need preheating, so this compensates for the extra energy used for the actual baking.

A basic rule to follow is to allow 15 to 20 per cent less temperature and to allow 10 per cent longer for the baking time.

A new generation of ovens

Lessons have been learned about the good and bad features of both types of oven, so that combination ovens are now gaining in popularity. These have both top and bottom elements as well as circulated heat which allow you to choose the right sort of heat for whatever you are cooking. Luxury models even have a built-in microwave, and these can be used to save time with certain types of baking. Microwaves are normally unsuitable for baking because, although the cake cooks, it will not brown or rise.

In a combination oven you can use the microwave to cook a cake quickly and then switch to circulated or conventional heat to brown it. These up-to-date ovens have another great advantage; they are self-cleaning. They work on the basis that very high temperatures burn off the dirt and just leave it as ash in the bottom of the oven. Alternatively, the enamel walls are specially treated so that dirt won't stick to them in the first place.

Do you need to preheat?

This has become an important question with the rising costs of energy and one which has given rise to some degree of experimentation. It is now often said that you can get just as good results without preheating. The problem is that very few types of mixtures will tolerate waiting in a cold oven for the right temperature to be reached, especially when this can take 20 minutes or more for some older models of oven. So preheating is necessary. The newer the stove, the less energy will be wasted. A convection oven doesn't need preheating because the circulating air warms it immediately.

Baking without an oven

This can be possible, but only for a few specialised items. All you need for deep-frying is a deep, heavy-based pan on the hob. Waffles are baked in a waffle iron and a number of simple doughs, sponges and flan bases can even be cooked on the hob in a normal saucepan. Nevertheless, to cover most baking techniques, you will need an oven. Mini ovens are available which can be used in very limited areas like a bed-sit.

How to avoid disasters

Sometimes you can see a disaster coming. Here are a few tips to help you avoid it:

Cream refuses to thicken
This could be caused by the cream, the room or the bowl being too warm; the sugar being added too soon.

This can be solved if you stop whisking at once, before the cream separates, or if you transfer the mixture to a metal bowl. Alternatively you can chill in the freezer or refrigerator and then whip slowly.

Egg white refuses to whisk
This is often because some egg yolk has been included with the white; there is fat on the utensils; the sugar has been added too soon. There is no solution unfortunately. Take fresh egg whites and add a little salt before whisking.

The cake is soggy
This could be caused by not enough baking powder, yeast or whisked egg white having been included or the mixture having been too heavy; the cake was beaten for too long; the mixture was too tacky.

You can use the cake for crumbs or in a trifle (see page 227).

Cake won't come out of tin
This could be because the tin was not greased enough, or you didn't leave the cake to stand for a few minutes when it came out of the oven, or the coating of the tin is damaged.

To solve this, wrap the tin in a hot, damp cloth for a few minutes.

What is baking blind?

This term is used to describe prebaking an empty pastry case to prevent the filling making it soggy. Line the tins with pastry, then with greaseproof paper and fill with dried beans. This keeps the base flat and stops the sides collapsing. You can use the beans over and over again for baking blind.

Rolling a square of pastry

Make the pastry into a roll rather than a ball for rolling out. Alternatively always roll the pastry at an angle from the centre outwards.

Six at a time

Lining a lot of small tartlet tins individually with pastry is extremely time-consuming. Here is a quick and easy way of doing it. Group the greased tins close together and spread the sheet of pastry over them. Using your fingers or a pastry brush gently press the pastry into the tins. Now run the rolling pin firmly over the tins to cut the edges.

Getting the pastry on to the baking tray

Wrap the pastry round the rolling pin to lift it, then unroll it on to the baking tray.

Cutting down a cake

If a cake is too wide for your purposes or if the edge has got burnt, you will need to cut it down. Use an adjustable cake ring (see page 19) for this and then use the off-cuts in a trifle (see page 227).

Decorating the edge with flaked almonds

Take a generous tablespoon of toasted flaked almonds in the palm of your hand and press them on to the buttercream or cream on the side of the cake. Brush any that fall off the plate and use again. Finally press the almonds on firmly with a spatula.

Use a bain-marie for gelatine

Try this quick and easy way of melting gelatine. Soak the powder in a large soup ladle and place in a pan of gently simmering water. The metal ladle conducts the heat quickly and melts the gelatine, but make sure that no water splashes into the ladle!

Cake ring

When you get used to making cakes, adjust the ring to the size of the sponge rounds, sandwich them together with cream inside the ring and then top with fruit.

Use the ring when you want to cover with glaze. It holds everything firmly together and prevents the layers slipping. When the buttercream and glaze have set, cut inside the ring and lift it off.

Keeping piped cakes in shape

Pipe whirls of choux pastry on to oiled baking parchment and then slide them one at a time into the hot fat.

Preventing splashing with whipped cream

To prevent cream splashing when you whip it hold a tea-towel loosely over the bowl.

Vanilla sugar

This is very easy to make: just fill a glass jar with sugar and add a vanilla pod split along its length.

Using a piping bag

1. Fold over half the bag. Put in the nozzle and press firmly into place.
2. Hold the bag underneath the part you have turned over and carefully fill with the mixture.
3. Unfold the bag, smooth out any creases and twist the top to prevent spillage. Hold the bag at the top with one hand squeezing the mixture towards the nozzle, hold the nozzle in your other hand.
4. To change nozzles, simply place the new nozzle over the original one and press into place. With heavy mixtures you will have to hold this new nozzle in place as you pipe.

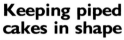

Covering a cake with marzipan

Roll out the marzipan 5–6 cm/2–2¼ in larger than the cake. Press the marzipan on the cake.

Decorating with zig-zags

A zig-zag pattern on the sides of a cake is both attractive to look at and easy to do. Spread the cake with a thick layer of buttercream or cream. Smooth it down with a zig-zag spatula (see page 17), turning the cake as you go around it, then use a palette knife to lift the cake on to the plate.

Using a zest knife

Zest (thin strips of citrus fruit peel) can be easily removed with a special zest knife.

Shopping – the secret
of the right ingredients

Flour types, crushed and whole grain

Wheat – the raw material for flour

Flour is normally made from wheat. If the packet does not detail otherwise, you can presume it contains wheat flour.

The wheat grain is made up of three main parts: the outer layer made up of vitamins, minerals and cellulose, the fat-containing germ-bud and the main body of the grain made up of starch and gluten.

From grain to flour

It is the fineness to which the grain is ground that determines how it will be used. First the grain is peeled, so that it loses most of its vitamins and fibre, and then the germ is removed – for too much fat would soon make the flour go rancid. The remaining grain is then cleaned before undergoing what can be up to twenty stages of grinding.

First it is coarsely chopped into 'meal', then ground more finely into 'semolina'. Further grinding produces a fine dust and eventually superfine flour. Semolina and meal are similar products in themselves as well as being intermediary stages in the milling of flour.

Different types of flour

The best-known flours are obtained from grain, which needs to be ground and then winnowed to separate the outer husk from the inner kernel.

Flour normally refers to that made from wheat but other cereals such as rye, buckwheat, oats, barley, rice and millet, and pulses like chick peas can be used for making flour.

Flour varies in colour from brown to a light white. Wholewheat flour contains the whole of the wheat grain and is quite dark in colour. With white flour the outer layers of the wheat grain are mostly removed during the milling process leaving the starchy white endosperm which gives the flour its light colour.

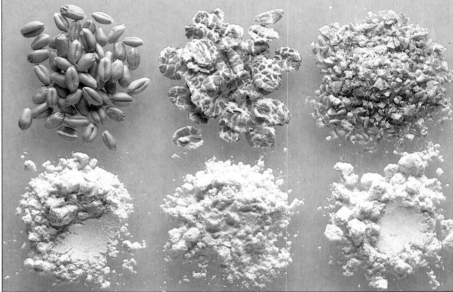

1. *Whole grain wheat*, natural and uncleaned.

2. *Crushed wheat*. Made from whole grain by a special method. Can be used for bread if mixed with flour.

3. *Wheatmeal*. The first stage of milling. Made from either whole grain or shelled wheat.

7. *Wholemeal flour*. For wholemeal bread, must be used in a sour dough.

8. *Wheatmeal flour*. For coarse brown bread. The gluten content makes it suitable with yeast or baking powder. Sour dough is not essential.

9. *Brown flour*. Milled until slightly whiter. For coarse almost white bread.

1. *Rye*. Available in various types. Little gluten, but contains a similar substance, so it should be mixed with a certain amount of wheat flour.

2. *Oats*. Available as coarse or instant crushed oats as well as flour. Little gluten, so mix with rye or wheat flour.

3. *Barley*. Low in gluten. Gives bread an earthy flavour.

Everybody knows that you can't bake without
flour, but when you first take up baking, you
should also know that there are different flours
available for baking.

4. *Wholewheat or wholemeal.* Contains all wheat grain and vitamin E from the wheatgerm.

5. *Bran.* The chopped husk of the grain together with the germ.

6. *Semolina.* Intermediary stage in milling of refined grain.

10. *Strong white flour.* Ideal for rolls and white bread.

11. *Self-raising flour.* Specially treated household flour that absorbs moisture better and won't lump.

12. *Plain white flour.* The whitest of the types available.

4. *Corn (maize).* Hardly any gluten, but you can compensate for this by adding whisked egg whites to corn doughs.

5. *Millet.* Cereal known in prehistoric times. Low gluten, so always mix with other flour.

6. *Buckwheat.* Because of its aromatic, slightly bitter flavour it should always be mixed with wheat flour.

What is gluten?

This is the protein in flour which swells in the moist mixture during baking and begins to act as a sort of adhesive, giving the baking firmness and solidity. This is most marked in normal self-raising flour. This makes a cake that is light and fine-grained without requiring any other raising agent. Whisked egg whites or beating in air is usually sufficient.

In wholemeal flour, on the other hand, the gluten from the outer layer of the grain is so binding that it requires a strong raising agent.

Special flours

Flour can also be milled from other types of grain besides wheat, the most important of these being rye. Here again the entire grain is not always used. These other types of grain contain little or no gluten and so have to be mixed with a flour rich in gluten. The bottom series of photographs show different types of grain and below them the flour which they produce.

What is wholemeal flour?

As the name suggests wholemeal flour is made from the whole grain, including the outer layer and germ. The minerals in the outer layer are not lost and the flour contains all the cellulose which provides roughage, an important part of the diet. The fat contained in the germ can turn rancid when exposed to air so the flour should be used as soon as possible.

Baking with oatmeal

Baking with oatmeal is another way of using all the goodness of the grain, for here too the whole grain is used. Meal (from the whole grain), flake (milled from chopped grain) or instant-flake forms are available and all are suitable for baking and produce cakes and biscuits with the typical nutty flavour of oats.

Fats used in baking

Without fat, pastry would just not hold together and be a crumbly, fragile mixture. Fat helps to make it flexible and the pastry moist or light, depending on the type. In either case fat gives baking most of its flavour, forming a base to bring out all the other flavourings.

Fat is always needed to grease baking trays and tins to prevent cakes sticking or sheets of pastry sticking together.

As you can see fat has a lot of different uses and there are also various types. Fats, for instance, have different smoking points (the temperature at which the heated fat begins to smoke). It is at this point that the fat separates and can become harmful. This temperature is quite low for butter. In all of our recipes we recommend butter as this gives the best results, but margarine can be substituted.

Illustrated (top to bottom):

Butter

There is nothing to beat the flavour of butter. But use a top-quality butter. The best butter for baking is unsalted butter (which must be so marked) but since salted butter keeps longer this is the one most shops stock, however both types should be readily available.

Dripping

This is the rendered fat from beef or mutton. May be used for deep-frying but is better used for roasting and shallow-frying.

Clarified butter

Made from pure butter but is expensive to make. It is used for frying and grilling.

Beef suet

This is used in a few special recipes such as Christmas pudding.

Margarine

The great rival to butter – it can be substituted in most recipes. Many prefer the polyunsaturated types for health reasons, cost or flavour. It is up to you to decide which type you prefer. Hard margarines are often still the best for baking.

Lard

This is often used in shallow- and deep-frying and to make some cakes and flaky pastry, for instance.

Oils

Many different types are available, both saturated and polyunsaturated and can be made from vegetables, cereals, nuts and seeds. They can be used for both shallow- and deep-frying.

. . . Butter and other fats sugar and honey . . .

Sugar

Believe it or not, two hundred years ago only the nobles could afford sugar! It was made from sugar cane and imported from the West Indies which made it expensive. It was kept in special gold or silver cannisters with strong locks. The ordinary people had to make do with honey for sweetening. It was only at the beginning of the last century that it was discovered how to extract sugar from beet.

Sugar is needed in baking not only for its sweetness but to give the mixture solidity and structure. Attempts at baking with artificial sweeteners have not given the same results. The chemical composition of cane and beet sugar is identical – but amazingly you can actually taste the difference. A useful tip whenever you use sugar in baking is to add a pinch of salt as this improves the flavour.

Illustrated (top to bottom):

Granulated sugar

The usual white household sugar, suitable for most purposes. This is refined further to make caster sugar for use in delicate sponges.

Icing sugar

This is sugar which is finely ground to a dust. It is very good where it is essential for sugar to dissolve quickly, especially when making marzipan and icing.

Crystallised sugar

This is coarse-grained sugar used chiefly for decorating. You can use it in baking and it won't melt in the heat of the oven.

Cube sugar

This is high-quality caster sugar, moistened slightly and pressed into cubes. It is very practical to sweeten a cup of tea or coffee.

Cane sugar

White or brown – demerara – is available. The sugar is not completely purified so it has a slightly malty taste. It is made from sugar cane.

White candy sugar

Large, white crystals of sugar. This sugar dissolves slowly, but is nevertheless popular in coffee.

Brown candy sugar

Sugar colour is added to make the sugar brown. Again used in coffee but also to make honey cakes and crunchy biscuits.

Honey

A pure, natural product. It is liquid when fresh but crystallises and becomes solid when kept. When it is like this, it can be gently warmed to make it runny again.

Baking success depends on using the right ingredients, more so in baking than in other types of cooking. The various fats behave in entirely different ways and sugar does more than simply sweeten. Here at a glance you can see the main types available.

How to turn heavy doughs into light cakes

Which doughs need raising agents?

It is obvious that cakes with a dense structure need no raising agent in the dough. This is also true of shortcrust, puff pastry or pasta dough which are meant to be solid in structure.

Crumbly cakes, such as a Genoese or Victoria sponge, are on the borderline. They need to be light and airy which usually means incorporating some kind of raising agent, but you will rarely need to add baking powder for enough air is worked in by lengthy beating in the case of a Victoria sponge or by the whisked egg white in a Genoese sponge. A generous pinch of baking powder can be added to be on the safe side, but this is not essential.

On the other hand heavy doughs which contain a lot of fat such as a rich yeast dough, or high-gluten flour such as a wholemeal dough, will need a raising agent. The rule here is – the heavier the dough, the stronger the raising agent. But be careful with quantities, too much air from the raising agent can 'suffocate' the dough and make it fall.

Chemical and biological raising agents

There are two basic types of raising agent: chemical ones such as baking powder and biological raising agents such as yeast. Yeast consists of living organisms which, with sufficient supplies of food, causes fermentation and produces air.

Baking powder

Baking powder consists of bicarbonate of soda and the acid, cream of tartar. These substances interact in the dough to produce carbon dioxide which makes it rise.

Fresh yeast

This must be pale grey in colour, with a pleasantly, slightly sour smell and firm consistency. Old yeast which has become oily and soft will no longer work and the dough will not rise. For further tips on yeast see right-hand column and page 118.

Dried yeast

This is extremely useful since you can keep a stock of it for months. Available in small cans or packets. Also as dried easy-blend yeast which is mixed with dry ingredients. Follow the instructions on the packet and nothing should go wrong.

You can't make a dough with just flour, fat, sugar and eggs. If you merely mix these together the end result will be either a very heavy or a glutinous mass, depending on the proportion of the ingredients.
To get a light, crumbly cake you need to get air into the mixture. This can be achieved by beating thoroughly but this won't work with all kinds of dough. For some you will need raising agents. These react in the dough, making it expand so that it becomes light and airy.

What happens when the raising agent works?

Basically all raising agents work in the same way. The dough is moist and warm and is an ideal environment for the chemical and biological agents which produce carbon dioxide. The gas makes millions of tiny bubbles in the dough which fill up with air and make the dough rise.

To prevent the dough being spoiled by too much air it has to be beaten or kneaded vigorously just before baking, and in many cases even while it is still rising. This distributes the air and helps give a more solid consistency.

Tips on using yeast

Most people have a healthy respect for yeast, and, to a certain extent, they are right. For yeast is actually the most delicate of the raising agents. Unless conditions are absolutely right it either goes on working for too long or just never gets started.

The main problem is getting the right temperature. Yeast will just not work if it is either too cold or too hot. An ideal temperature is around 35 C/95 F. Yeast also needs added sugar for fermentation, so you will need a pinch of this even in a savoury dough. The speed with which the yeast works depends on the room temperature. The warmer the room, the quicker the yeast works; at cooler temperatures it works much more slowly. You can take advantage of this fact when baking. If you want fresh rolls for Sunday breakfast simply leave the dough to rise in the refrigerator overnight.

Bicarbonate of Soda

One of the ingredients used in baking powder, bicarbonate of soda can be used on its own to react with an acid ingredient such as sour milk. For breads and certain fruit cakes.

Cream of tartar

This reacts with bicarbonate of soda to have a raising effect (see Baking powder, left). Used to make Scones.

Brewer's yeast

Used in making beers and wine, this is a form of dried yeast.

Even doughs need flavourings

The strange and enticing smell that wafts from the baked cake on the tea table is not produced by flour, sugar or eggs – it is the seductive smell of spices, essences and flavourings. But they need to be used sparingly for adding too much can turn the best cake into a disaster.

I. Vanilla pod

The dried fruit of a species of orchid. It has a delicate, unmistakable flavour. You use only the pith from inside the pod which leaves tiny black dots in the dough or custard – a sign that real vanilla has been used rather than an artificially produced vanilla essence.

2. Fennel seeds

Highly flavoured spices similar to aniseed. Used mainly in brown bread, exotic cakes or Indian cookery.

3. Allspice

Also known as Jamaican pepper. Used ground in various Christmas items, and for biscuits like gingernuts.

4. Nutmeg

Inner seed of a tropical tree. Always use freshly grated (nutmeg mill, nutmeg grater) as it does not retain its flavour well. Use in spicy biscuits and some gingerbreads.

5. Mace

Dried tendrils covering the outside of the nutmeg. Sold in the piece and must be finely crushed in a mortar.

6. Star aniseed

(illustrated pages 26–7, 30–1) The seed of a tropical tree. For baking remove the small brown seeds from the pod and use ground or crushed. To flavour stocks or stews add the whole pod.

7. Aniseed

Seeds of an umbelliferous flower. Have a distinctive sweetish-sharp flavour. For spicy biscuits.

8. Cardamom

Highly aromatic spice, the seeds of a tropical reed. The straw-like covering should be removed before using. Crush the small, dark seeds in a mortar.

9. Cinnamon stick

Pieces of the dried inner bark of the tropical cinnamon tree. The sticks are used whole to infuse in liquids but for baking they have to be ground or crushed.

10. Saffron

The most expensive spice in the world, for these delicate stamens of the saffron crocus are not easy to collect. Adds intensive colour and flavour to food.

11. Ginger

The root of a tropical reed with a hot, fruity flavour. Try keeping the roots buried in a pot of damp soil. It is also sold ready ground.

12. Caraway

The traditional spice used for bread, both in the dough and to decorate the top of the loaf. Like most seasonings its full flavour comes out only when freshly ground.

Flavouring with spirits

A dash of spirits in the cake mixture, cream or custard gives everything an extra special flavour. One of the most popular for cooking is a dark, aromatic rum, for this goes with anything and will not dominate other ingredients. Alternatively arrak (a spirit made from rice, palm wine and molasses), Cognac, Armagnac or any fruit brandy or liqueur will give your baking an unforgettable flavour. But always use a spirit that you would willingly drink. Poor quality spirits will give a poor flavour.

Other important flavourings for baking include orange blossom water, rose oil or rose water and bitter almond flavouring. These are so concentrated that you will only need to use a few drops at a time.

Measuring the dose

Spices are like perfumes – it is very easy to use too much. Too many different spices together will clash with one another giving no distinct flavour, while too much of one spice can be overpowering. So you need top-quality fresh spices and the right judgement. Be prepared to pay a few pence more, for quality does not come cheap where spices are concerned. If you can't find certain spices in the supermarket, try a delicatessen or well-stocked Indian shop.

Making use of nuts and preserved fruit

Nuts

These contain a lot of fat so they won't keep for long. They will soon go rancid in a warm room, and one bad nut will spoil the whole cake. So always buy fresh nuts and freeze any that are left over rather than keeping them in the kitchen cupboard.

Nuts are sold whole in the shell, shelled, flaked, chopped or ground, but it is best to prepare your own nuts, for chopped nuts can soon go dry. They do stay moist and fresh, however, in vacuum-packed plastic bags.

Brazil nuts

These are sold whole and shelled. They have a distinctive flavour and are rich in protein and fat.

Bitter almonds and pine nuts

Bitter almonds are thoroughly sorted and sold only in small quantities. The seeds of the pine cone are mild in flavour.

Walnuts

These grow in the milder parts of northern Europe. The bitter skin can be peeled off young nuts.

Pecans

The American relative of the walnut, but with a smooth shell. The nut too is smoother and narrower.

Almonds

These are all-purpose nuts which go with everything. They have a mild flavour with a slightly crunchy consistency.

Hazelnuts

These are sold roasted and shelled which gives them a flavour like nougat. They are also sold in the shell, and are often used ground with the skin.

Pistachios

These can be bought with or without the shell, roasted and salted if liked. They retain their bright green colour even after baking. They are quite expensive to buy.

Peanuts and coconuts

Roasted peanuts can be bought in the shell or shelled, also salted. Coconuts can be bought whole, grated or desiccated.

Including nuts like hazelnuts and almonds in your cakes will give them bite, flavour, moisture and texture. Our grandmothers knew this well and filled their cakes with nuts, raisins and dried fruit. For rich cakes like these stay moist and fresh for much longer.

Candied rose petals

These are used only to decorate cooked cakes (e.g. wedding cakes). They are not intended to be included in cake mixtures as they tend to melt.

Prunes and dried pears

These are used in baking and for making desserts.

Candied fruit

Used finely chopped in fruit cake or loaves.

Raisins

These can vary in quality but all are grapes dried in the air or in special ovens.

Dried fruits

Always store in a cool, dry place, otherwise the fruit will absorb moisture and get mildewed. They are best kept in storage jars with loose-fitting lids which allow the air to circulate.

If you want to try making glacé fruit you will need a sugar thermometer (available from kitchen shops) for you need exactly the right concentration of sugar. The fruit must be left to soak in the sugar solution until it has soaked right through.

Sugar-coated fruit is easier to make. Brush the fruit with egg white and then coat generously in icing sugar. Dry in the air. Do not keep for too long before eating because the sugar coating does not preserve the fruit.

Dried figs, crystallised ginger

Both are used in exotic baking or cakes. They make cakes sweet, moist and full of flavour.

Dried banana and dates

These are good for heavy sponges and also used for decoration. Stone and peel dates before use. Less sugar can be added as they are both very sweet.

Candied peel and glacé cherries

Both essential ingredients in traditional fruit cakes.

Dried fruit

Top to bottom: Greek raisins, sultanas, California raisins and Greek currants.

Keeping ingredients and foods fresh . . .

Fresh things must stay fresh

It is obvious that perishable foodstuffs such as *milk and milk products* (cream, butter, yogurt) need to go into the refrigerator as soon as you get them home. The use-by date and correct storage temperature should be printed on the wrapper.

Eggs, however, are usually taken out of their boxes and stored in a special compartment in the refrigerator. If there is a packing date on the box copy it on to a slip of paper to help you remember how long you have had the eggs. Eggs that you have had for more than three weeks should not be used in baking.

Yeast must be fresh to work properly. Fresh yeast smells pleasantly sour, is creamy-grey and of a firm consistency (see pages 32–3 and 118). Always store in the refrigerator, or, for longer periods, in the freezer.

Always use *fruit* as soon as possible after buying, especially delicate berries. If you do have to store them, keep them on a dry cloth in the salad drawer of the refrigerator. When you are ready to use them you can wash, sort and thoroughly dry them.

Dried products don't last for ever!

Dried fruit and peel are never completely dry, so they should not be stored in airtight containers or they will go musty and mildewed. Keep them in containers with loose-fitting lids or in a small linen bags.

Nuts contain a lot of fat and will go rancid if stored for too long or at too high a temperature, so use them up as soon as you can. Keep any that are left over in the freezer rather than the kitchen cupboard.

Baking powder and spices should be kept in storage jars in the cupboard.

Chocolate is another item that keeps well, between six months and a year, depending on the quality (the better the quality, the more cocoa butter it contains). Don't store it in too warm a place or the cocoa fat will form a white coating, but don't keep it in the refrigerator either, unless it is to be eaten quickly and it is a very hot day!

Where to keep other ingredients

Always keep *flour* dry, preferably in an airtight container to keep out insects. Use a tin, plastic or glass container with a close-fitting lid.

Keep *sugar* too in a cool, close-fitting container.

Keep *spices* out of the light or they will lose their colour and flavour. Put them in containers that keep out the light or in a dark cupboard.

To achieve baking success you must look after all the ingredients. They must be stored when you get them home with the same care that went into choosing and buying them. For even the best and most expensive ingredients will lose their quality unless properly handled. Bear in mind too that the finished cakes, biscuits and pastries that look so delicious and that you have made with such care will lose their flavour and freshness if they are stored in the wrong container, at the wrong temperature or for the wrong length of time.

Keeping your baking fresh

Different types of cakes, pastries and biscuits need to be stored in different ways:
Cakes and pastries made from rich doughs with a lot of fat, which contain dried fruit or peel or which have been soaked in a liquid or filled with something to keep them moist, will keep for about two to three days. These include yeast plaits, fruit cakes, buttercream cakes, cheese cakes, savarins and babas. Store them well wrapped in aluminium foil or in a plastic container to prevent them absorbing outside smells. If you keep them in the salad drawer of the refrigerator they won't sweat.

Drier cakes such as choux pastries, Genoese sponge or macaroons can be stored at room temperature in a tin or plastic container with a close-fitting lid.

All other types of cakes and pastries are best eaten fresh!

Specialities – biscuits and confectionery

A word here about the storage of Christmas baking. Certain types of cake such as the traditional Christmas cake or stollen need to be stored for three to four weeks before they are eaten to allow the flavour to develop. They should be tightly wrapped, preferably in a double layer of aluminium foil, to keep them moist.

Biscuits, like gingerbread, which are hard when they come out of the oven, but which have to soften up before eating, should be stored with a few slices of apple in a tin with a close-fitting lid. Other types of biscuits should be stored in cardboard boxes or tins between layers of tissue paper.
Pralines should be stored in paper cases to prevent them breaking against one another. Keep in a cool place but definitely not in the refrigerator, where they would begin to sweat and lose their flavour. Eat sweets within ten to fourteen days at the latest.

Tips on freezing

With the exception of meringues and similar items which become too fragile in the cold, most cakes can be frozen. You can give a cake its original fresh-baked taste if you thaw it for a short time and then reheat it gently in a moderate oven (160C, 325F, gas 3). Obviously coverings of buttercream, chocolate or icing should not be added until after defrosting for they will not tolerate heat and cold. Freeze flan cases and fruit separately, and when making up the flan pour the hot glaze on to the frozen fruit. This will both thaw the fruit and set the glaze quicker. Large cakes or baking-tray sponges are best frozen in individual portions as this will help them to defrost quicker. Most cake mixtures also freeze well and if you freeze them in the tin this will save a lot of time when you come to bake them.

Cake mixes and ready-made pastry

Food manufacturers offer a lot of choice in this area. It is a good idea to keep a selection of ready-made or powdered mixes in stock. These can then be made up and baked very quickly.

Cake mixes (illustrated top right). These come in a variety of flavours as well as basic sponges. Most require you to add fat and eggs and some manufacturers include a foil baking tin.

Canned pastry (illustrated centre left). This is a continental idea, only available from a limited number of delicatessens. Again various types available ranging from dough for rolls, croissant and pizza to shortcrust pastry. These are easy to use and are soon ready.

Frozen pastry (illustrated top left). As well as puff pastry (illustrated) you can also get shortcrust. Both must be allowed to thaw before using, so allow time for this. Most useful of all is puff pastry. A simple trick will make it taste more like home-made puff pastry. Brush all the sheets (or rolled-out dough) except one with butter. Place one on top of the other with the unbuttered sheet on the top. Roll out together on a floured board. If you have time butter it again and turn it (fold together and reroll). This will make the pastry even lighter and will give it a buttery flavour.

Modern time-savers

There is really nothing to be ashamed of in taking advantage of ready-made products. By using frozen pastry or packet mixes, ready-chopped candied peel or ready-flaked or chopped almonds, you can save yourself a lot of work and have more time to devote to your family or guests.

Ready for filling

Stored in a cool, dry place, ready-baked sponge or shortcrust flan cases and individual tart cases (illustrated centre and bottom right) will keep for months. (The use-by date should be stamped on the wrapper.) They are extremely versatile to use – you can fill them with fresh fruit and top with glaze or apricot jam and decorate with cream to make a beautiful fruit flan that looks as if it took hours to prepare.

Sponges (illustrated bottom) can not only be used for a quick gâteau, but also to make desserts. Cut into rounds, soaked in liqueur, fruit juice or coffee and sandwiched together with whipped cream, they make a delicious dessert. They can also be delicious in a trifle.

Sponge fingers (illustrated bottom left) are also excellent to use in trifles and custards. And for

Charlottes too (see page 64).

Meringues (illustrated centre left). These can be bought from any baker, grocery store or supermarket. They keep well in a close-fitting cake tin. Make a delicious last-minute dessert by crumbling meringues into whipped cream with fresh or stewed fruit or, failing all else, jam. (Meringues, see pages 222–3, 224–5).

Last-minute life-saver: sliced bread

(illustrated centre top) With a few other ingredients such as milk, eggs, a little jam or stewed fruit, you can always whip up a quick dessert with sliced bread (see page 146 for a few ideas). Layers of bread and custard (canned or from custard powder) decorated with cream and fruit make a quick, but impressive dessert.

Sliced bread is also practical and versatile for savoury dishes. Dice and fry in butter to make croûtons to go in soups. Cut into larger pieces and dip in a mixture of egg and milk with plenty of seasoning (paprika, salt and pepper) and fry until golden brown. This is delicious as a light snack.

Other practical bought items

Buy *almonds and hazelnuts* ready-flaked, chopped or ground. Make sure that chopped nuts are vacuum packed or they will dry out and become mildewed. Ready-made *sugar, praline or chocolate icings*. You can buy small tubes of coloured icing for making delicate patterns straight from the tube.

Sugar flowers and hundreds and thousands are available in a choice of colours and sizes. The variety of ready-made cake decorations is enormous with something for every taste. You can even buy ready-made marzipan roses, chocolate leaves or the old favourite chocolate vermicelli in a variety of sizes.

At the table – tempting
baking for every occasion

At the table

From a filling Sunday brunch to Christmas delicacies, from breakfast to a midnight snack, from starter to dessert – there are a host of opportunities for you to serve home-baked items right through the year and right through the day. This chapter includes a variety of suggestions on what you can serve and when.

Breakfast

The day is only as good as breakfast! Although you can't always enjoy the luxury of a rich spread for weekday breakfasts, the memory of a delicious, leisurely Sunday breakfast will stay with you all week long. Here are a few ideas to make your Sunday breakfast something really special.

Croissants

(illustrated top left)
These are crisp and buttery and are best served warm from the oven. They should not be cut and buttered like rolls. Just break bits off and put a little butter and honey on each piece. Or you could try dunking the croissant in your coffee. The recipe for croissants is on page 183.

Madeira cake

(illustrated left, second from top)
Although not normally breakfast fare Madeira cake can be an interesting addition. Eat it on its own or with fresh fruit for breakfast (see page 87). If you like, you can cover it with icing or chocolate and have it with a cup of coffee mid-morning.

Churros

(illustrated left, third from top)
Piped cakes deep-fried until crisp. They are a Spanish delicacy served with strong, bitter-sweet chocolate to pep you up after a night out (see page 204).

Poppyseed rolls

(illustrated bottom left)
These are delicious with either a sweet or savoury filling. Try them with honey or jam, ham or cheese. Made from the basic recipe for ring rolls (see page 150–1).

Yeast dough snails

(illustrated top right)
Wonderfully crumbly yeast dough with plenty of raisins and almonds. Made from the recipe on page 121. Cover with icing and serve warm or cold.

Toast and scrambled egg

(illustrated right, second from top)
If you get very hungry at breakfast time you will need something quite filling for breakfast. Try creamy scrambled eggs with lightly toasted bread, home-baked of course (see page 146–7).

Danish pastries

(illustrated right, third from top)
Filled with custard and decorated with a cherry to give a spot of colour. Instead of cherries you can use any seasonal fruit, or a dab of jam in winter (see pages 183 and 187).

Panettone

(illustrated bottom right)
This cake is eaten in Italy for Christmas breakfast. Panettone is particularly good spread with butter. Eat it with a strong espresso coffee (see page 157).

45

Tasty snacks to fill that gap

When you are not hungry enough or haven't the time for a full meal, or when you don't feel like spending hours in the kitchen, that is the time for an appetising snack. Maybe you are having a glass of wine with friends and suddenly feel like a bite of something tasty to eat. Here are a few suggestions for suitable snacks that are quick and easy to serve.

Sausage rolls

(illustrated top left)
These are extremely quick to make and wrapped in a paper serviette these can be eaten with the fingers, at a buffet or office party, for instance. Wrap Frankfurter sausages in a sheet of puff pastry (see page 167), brush with egg yolk and bake.

Canapés

(illustrated centre top)
These are ideal for drinks parties or as appetisers when friends are round for dinner. Cover pieces of toasting bread (see page 146) with lettuce leaves and cut into rounds with a serrated pastry cutter. Pipe on hard-boiled egg yolks creamed with butter and garnish with fresh herbs, capers or ham.

Sandwiches

(illustrated top right)
Make up with any filling you have in stock and if you like, add mixed salad for fuller sandwiches. Further suggestions on pages 146–7.

Hawaiian toast

(illustrated centre left)
When you try making it you will appreciate why this snack became world famous. Freshly-made with top quality ingredients, Hawaiian toast is really delicious. See also page 146.

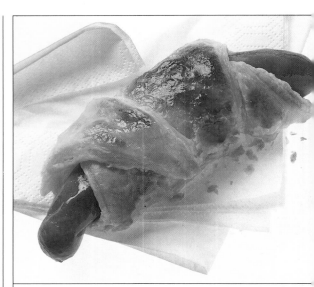

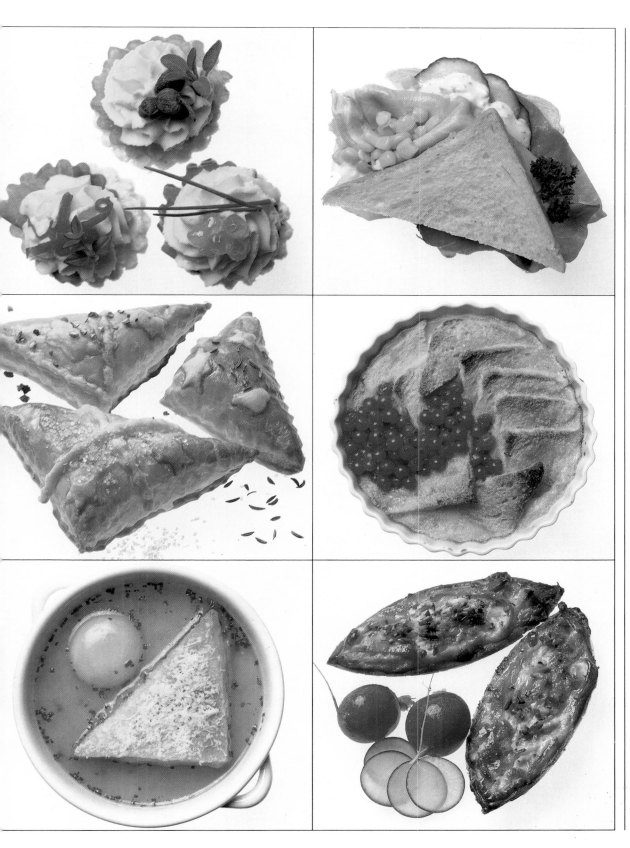

Hot puff-pastry pasties

(illustrated centre)
These are ideal to eat with a glass of wine and are delicious with aperitifs. They can be made in advance and can be eaten with the fingers. For various filling suggestions see page 172.

Bread and currant pudding

(illustrated centre right)
A variation on bread and butter pudding, this will appeal to children or anyone with a sweet tooth. Made with bread, fruit and egg custard (see page 146).

Raisin doughnuts

(illustrated bottom left)
These are best served warm. Again, these can be eaten with the fingers, just on their own or with added butter or jam (see page 143).

Zuppa Pavese

(illustrated centre bottom)
This soup is a good lunch for a hot summer's day. It is filling without being heavy (see page 146).

Individual tarts

(illustrated bottom right)
A suitable snack again for a drinks party or a simple hors d'oeuvre for a light menu. The tart cases can be made from dough, puff pastry or a savoury shortcrust and kept in stock. They can be simply filled with egg custard. For alternative fillings see page 173.

Tantalising desserts

Babas Make individual portions as described on page 133. Serve as illustrated, with stewed rhubarb and a caramel sauce. Dust with icing sugar and decorate, if liked, with a sprig of lemon balm.

Strawberry ice cake (see page 216) Pipe on the cream just before serving and decorate with ground pistachios.

Pineapple Tatin tart An adaptation of the classic recipe (see page 111) but served with thick slices of fresh pineapple instead of apple. Serve this tart hot.

Puff pastry tartlets Individual tartlets served on a strawberry sauce. Pile fresh or defrosted raspberries and blackberries into crisp puff pastry tartlet cases (see page 167) and cover with a currant glaze (see page 248).

Meringues with red currant cream These make a delicious light summer dessert. Make the meringues (see pages 222–3) and fill with piped red currant cream (see page 238–9). Serve the meringues in paper cases.

Filled almond wafer cases Bake and shape the almond cases as in the recipe (see page 224). Fill the wafers with a ball of vanilla ice cream and raspberries. Decorate with crystallised sugar, toasted flaked almonds and icing sugar.

Savarin with red currants From the recipe on pages 132–3 make individual savarins, then soak and ice them. Fill with a vanilla cream (stir the pith of a vanilla pod into double cream and whisk until thick) and fresh red currants.

Apple Charlotte A rich but refreshing dessert. Ideal as part of lunch on a warm autumn day (see page 146).

Smorgåsbord

(illustrated top left)
Take a slice of coarse
wholemeal bread like the
barley loaf on page 161,
thickly butter it and top
with lettuce, sliced egg
and plenty of fresh
prawns.

Pizza

(illustrated centre left)
A savoury dish for two or
more persons. The one
illustrated is a colourful
pizza topped with
pizzaiola, salami, red
pepper, broccoli and
cheese. For more ideas
see pages 140–1.

Puff-pastry pasties with curry filling

(illustrated bottom left)
These are ideal for party
snacks or for pre-dinner
drinks. You will find the
recipe and a number of
different fillings on pages
172–3.

Quiche Lorraine

(illustrated centre top)
Serve this quiche with a
fresh salad to make a light
meal for four. Larger ones
can be made on a baking
tray (pages 138–9).

Pitta bread

(illustrated centre)
This is the famous Greek
bread that goes with
everything: taramasalata,
Greek salad, meat kebabs
or steak. Always serve hot
(see page 157).

Savoury baking

Spinach flan

(illustrated centre bottom)
One of an endless variety of savoury flans. This is an ideal party dish as you can make several flans on a few large baking trays. Recipe and other suggestions on page 137.

Garlic bread

(illustrated top right)
Ideal with soup or grilled fish or just on its own as a savoury snack with a glass of wine. Slice a French loaf halfway through (see pages 148–9), spread with butter and sprinkle with thin slices of garlic and finely chopped parsley. Bake on a baking tray until crisp. Serve hot.

Prague ham

(illustrated centre right)
The dish is suitable for a real celebration with a lot of guests and it is much simpler to make than it looks! (See page 156).

Meat pie

(illustrated bottom right)
An excellent way of using up left-over stew or casseroled meat. Simply bake in an ovenproof dish beneath a savoury shortcrust top (see page 110) to make a filling pie.

Afternoon tea

Light fruit cake

(illustrated top left)
A fruity cake which is moist and not too sweet. The cake pictured has added cherries and pistachios for colour. Make the cake in advance as it keeps well (see page 97).

Raisin buns

(illustrated top right)
Buns made with raisins and candied peel (add 50 g/2 oz of each to the ingredients in the recipe on page 87). Bake as small buns in paper cases and no one will be able to resist them.

Oatmeal and date biscuits

(illustrated bottom left)
These are made with a light shortcrust pastry. Use the recipe on page 106 but replace the raisins with chopped dates.

Marble cake

(illustrated bottom right)
Instead of using a ring mould as in the recipe on page 92, bake in a loaf tin. Serve the cake covered in icing or chocolate or simply dusted with icing sugar.

For a lot of people afternoon tea is an important meal of the day. Here are a few suggestions to brighten up those long, grey autumn or winter afternoons. As the light fades outside, switch on the lights and sip a cup of tea and enjoy a delicious cake.

Pig's ears

(illustrated top left)
These puff-pastry cakes are assembled as shown on pages 170–1, but made to the size of a tea plate rather than the smaller ones shown. Double the ingredients to make ten of these large ones.

Filled wafer horns

(illustrated top right)
Bake wafer horns from the recipe on pages 224–5. Fill them with sweetened whipped cream or with fresh fruit and cream. Serve at once or the wafers will go soft.

Fine tea biscuits

(illustrated bottom left)
Delicate shortcrust biscuits which are made using a piping bag (see page 114). Try filling with nougat or jam and decorate with chocolate, or crystallised sugar. For other decorating ideas see pages 246 and 254–5.

Butter cakes

(illustrated bottom right)
These are made from butter, sugar and almonds spread on to bread. They are quick to make when you fancy something sweet (see page 146).

Coffee time

One thing is certain, coffee and cake will never go out of fashion, they just go together so well. Try making one of the cakes described here to liven up those coffee mornings.

Madeira ring

(large photograph left)
A Madeira cake baked in a ring, filled and covered with buttercream and thickly coated with a nutty topping. An ideal cake for a birthday coffee party when you can top the whirls of cream with candles rather than cherries (see page 87).

Lemon cake

(large photograph right)
A basic sponge cake (see page 87) flavoured with lemon rind. For a moister cake with more bite, replace half the flour with oat flakes.

Strawberry and orange flan

(illustrated left of middle row)
Fill a sponge flan case (see page 71) generously with strawberries and cover the edge with slices of peeled oranges (see page 256-7). Cover with red currant or apricot glaze and serve with whipped cream.

Cream slices

(illustrated second from left middle row)
These are made from layers of puff pastry (see page 177) filled with vanilla cream.

Sunken apple cake

(illustrated second from right middle row)
Peel apple and cut into quarters, cut into slices and arrange on top of sponge mixture (see page 94). During baking the sponge rises and the apple disappears into the sponge giving it a fruity and moist flavour.

Buttercream slices

(illustrated right of middle row)
Sandwich two pieces of Genoese sponge (see page 82) together with buttercream (see page 240). Chill well and then cut into slices. Decorate with more buttercream and glacé cherries.

Nutty slices

(illustrated left of bottom row)
Dough mixture with vanilla cream and topped with almond praline (see page 121).

Apricot curd cake

(illustrated second from left bottom row)
This cake has a sponge base (see page 71) and is topped with apricots and curd cream (see pages 238-9). An excellent cake for summer days!

Cheesecake with crumb base

(illustrated second from right bottom row)
The base of the cheesecake is made from biscuit crumbs and oat flakes, kneaded together with butter (see page 226). This is topped with a lemon cheese filling and a red currant glaze (see page 248).

Danish pastry

(illustrated right of bottom row)
Make the pastry (see page 121), but bake in a cake tin rather than on a baking tray. Cut the pastry for the whirls 2.5 cm/1 in thick and place close together in the tin.

Balmoral cake

(illustrated top left)
An impressive-looking cake which is really easy to make. It is made with a basic sponge mixture (see page 87) with 100 g/4 oz ground almonds and 200 g/7 oz melted plain chocolate added. Bake it in a special Balmoral tin (see page 88), cover in chocolate and spike with almonds.

Mini St Honoré

(illustrated bottom left)
This is ideal to make as a small cake when you have only two or three guests for tea. Halve the ingredients in the basic recipe (see pages 206–7) for a cake of 18 cm/7 in diameter. Decorate with whipped cream, candied orange and a glacé cherry.

Mocha cream gâteau

(illustrated centre top)
A classic cake made with a light chocolate Genoese sponge (see pages 74–5), thickly coated in a bitter-sweet mocha cream. It is decorated with whirls of cream and cocoa powder.

Super cakes for special occasions

Chocolate and orange gâteau

(illustrated bottom centre)

This is made from an orange Genoese sponge (see pages 74–5) with chocolate buttercream (see pages 232–3) filling and coated, very evenly, with more chocolate buttercream. Use the same buttercream to pipe whirls for decoration, and put a cherry on each portion and sugared orange rind in the centre.

Chocolate log

(illustrated top right)

Make a chocolate roll (see page 82) from a chocolate Genoese sponge (see pages 74–5) and fill with chocolate buttercream (see page 232–3). Cover the log with more chocolate buttercream and rolls of chocolate and dust lightly with icing sugar.

Cream heart

(illustrated bottom right)

Bake a basic sponge (see page 87) or Genoese sponge (see page 71) in a heart-shaped tin (see page 89 or 19). Slice the cake in two and fill with red currant cream (see page 239), then decorate lavishly with the same piped cream.

Birthdays, wedding anniversaries, christenings – there are so many important occasions which call for a special cake. When family and friends are gathered around the table, even the most cautious of us will want to try something ambitious. Here are a few suggestions on how to choose a memorable cake to suit the occasion.

The wedding cake – white for purity, green for hope and red for love

Here is an idea for those who are ambitious enough to make a wedding cake. For success, plan well in advance and allow plenty of time for perfecting the decoration as well as for maturing the cake.

The cake itself

A wedding cake needs to be very firm, especially if it is to support several tiers, for the bottom tier must not collapse under the weight of the other tiers above it. It also needs to keep well, as a wedding cake is not something that can be produced at a moment's notice. It will need to be completely finished at least one day in advance. The best cake to choose is the rich fruit cake on page 97, soaked in 6 tablespoons brandy, rum or orange juice to keep it moist.

Icing

Bake two cakes, about 25 cm/10 in and 18 cm/7 in in diameter, at least one day before you plan to make up the cake. Cut the tops absolutely flat and join the two tiers together with apricot jam. To make the icing, whisk 2 egg whites until stiff and then work in 2 kg/4¼ lb icing sugar. The icing should be thick but still easy to spread. Use half the icing to cover the two tiers of the cake and smooth evenly. Using a fine fluted nozzle on a piping bag decorate with garlands and whirls of icing. Add red marzipan roses (see page 247) and leaves of green marzipan. As a final touch add a few silver balls.

Cutting the cake

Always a great moment for the family's photograph album. Use a long, sharp, saw-edged knife which will cut the hard royal icing better than a smooth knife which will tend to crack it.

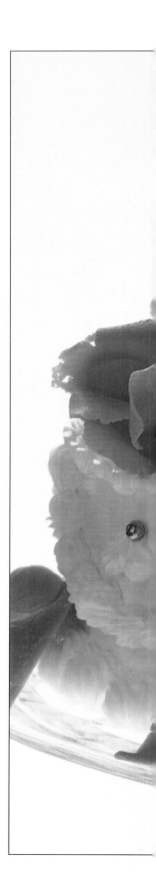

Christmas baking

Our own survey has shown that very little of the Christmas baking, made in advance with such loving care, actually survives through to Christmas Day. Much of it seems to get eaten long before the great day especially in families with inquisitive and hungry children, leaving only a stack of empty biscuit and cake tins. Perhaps the only answer is to hide everything away until the big day! Try making these different cakes and biscuits to tempt your family and friends.

Fruit cake

(illustrated top left) This should be baked some time before Christmas to allow the spices to really flavour the cake. Wrap in cling film or aluminium foil and store in an airtight tin or plastic container to prevent the fruit cake drying out (see page 97).

Basle-style gingerbread

(illustrated centre left) These should be baked in thin layers so that they are crisp when they come out of the oven. Store in a tin with a piece of sliced apple to soften them up (see page 191).

Gingerbread buns

(illustrated bottom left) These are again made from gingerbread, made with marzipan, raisins and almonds added. They should soon soften up after baking, so cover in chocolate and keep in a cool, airy place until Christmas. Store them between layers of tissue paper in a cardboard box in a cool room (see page 191).

Biscuit horses

(illustrated top)
Make the dough as in the recipe (see page 106), press into a mould and turn the horses out on to a baking tray that you have greased, floured or sprinkled with flaked almonds.

Yeast-dough heart

(illustrated centre)
Make two thin rolls of dough (see pages 134–5) and twist. Shape into a heart on a baking tray, brush with egg yolk and sprinkle with crystallised sugar. Leave to rise and bake as in the basic recipe.

Dundee cake

(illustrated centre right)
A rich, fruity cake (see page 97). Dust the top of the cake with a mixture of cocoa powder and icing sugar.

Honey cake

(illustrated bottom centre)
Make a basic dough (see pages 190–1) and bake on a greased baking tray scattered with raisins, almonds, walnuts, candied peel and crystallised sugar. Cut into squares and serve.

Spice cake

(illustrated bottom right)
Bake the cake as the normal recipe (see page 97) and then cover with apricot jam and scatter with flaked almonds. Serve with whipped cream, if liked.

Pretty shapes and colours

It seems a shame to eat these miniature works of art made from sweet pastry and sugar icing. They make good presents and delightful – but fragile – Christmas tree decorations. If you want to hang them on the tree, remember to make a hole for the string before you bake them.

Biscuits with a difference

Start by making a firm shortcrust pastry (see page 103). Roll it out thinly (3 mm/$\frac{1}{8}$ in) on a floured board and cut out shapes using cutters or cardboard patterns. You can trace the illustrations here to get your patterns. Bake as in the recipe and then decorate as you wish with icing and other decorations (see pages 248–9 and 254–5). Let the icing dry completely before storing in airtight tins between layers of tissue paper.

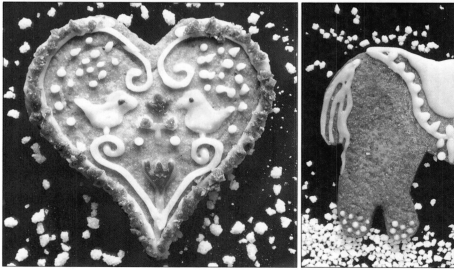

Breakfast, dessert and gift ideas . . .

1. Easter Day dessert – Raspberry Charlotte

Make the sponge fingers and custard (see page 83) the day before and allow to set in a suitable dish. Turn out before serving, dust with icing sugar and decorate with tender young lemon balm leaves. You can replace the raspberries (frozen at Easter time) with a different fruit like strawberries.

2. Easter brunch – Dough rabbit

The rabbit is made from two tapering rolls of yeast dough (see pages 118–9). Cut part way along from the thinner end to make the ears and then place one roll of dough inside the other, which is shaped like a horseshoe, pressing them together. Use currants or raisins for eyes and brush all over with beaten egg yolk.

3. Gift idea – Praline egg

A decorative half-egg container made from cardboard, pottery, porcelain or glass, with a colourful mixture of home-made praline sweets (see pages 262–3), petits fours (see pages 270–1) and cellophane-wrapped sweets (see pages 272–3).

4. Sweet and sour – Orange cream slice

On a baking tray make an orange Genoese sponge (see pages 74–5), cut it into squares and then diagonally in half. Sandwich the halves together with orange marmalade, cover them thickly in whipped cream and garnish with thin strips or orange rind.

Something special for Easter

5. Quick fruit flans

Bake the flan cases (see pages 88–9) from shortcrust pastry (see pages 102–3) or sponge (see pages 86–7) in small, shallow flan tins. Fill with any fruit you have available and cover with an apricot glaze (see page 248).

6. Crisp and light – Strawberry gâteau

Bake five thin rounds of shortcrust pastry (see pages 102–3). Make a strawberry cream (see pages 238–9) and use this to sandwich the pastry together. Cover the sides with strawberry cream. Dust the top with icing sugar and decorate with strawberry halves. For an extra touch of colour leave the stalks on the strawberries.

7. Easter lamb

You will need a special tin (page 89) in which to bake a basic sponge (see pages 86–7). Leave until completely cool and then dust generously with icing sugar.

8. White chocolate gâteau

Bake two Genoese sponges (see pages 70–1) in sandwich tins (23 cm/9 in in diameter). Sandwich together and cover with buttercream (see pages 230–1). Cover with large thin leaves (see pages 250–1) of white chocolate. Decorate with the thinnest possible lines of dark chocolate (see pages 254–5).

Gifts to please everyone

You can't buy anything like them, for they are unique, home-produced sweets, which have been prepared with loving care. Pack the sweets in see-through boxes, gift boxes or an attractive shell, but in every case first pop each sweet into a small paper case (available from stationers or supermarkets) to protect them from damage.

1. Rum truffles

Make the truffle mixture from the basic recipe (see pages 262–3). Shape into rough rolls and cover in dark chocolate and cocoa powder.

2. Cognac truffles

Make the truffles (see page 268), cover in white chocolate and roll in sugar.

3. Petits fours

Make the petits fours (see pages 270–1), cover with icing coloured with a little saffron. Decorate with walnut halves, crystallised violets and rose petals or candied orange or cherries.

4. Chocolate-coated truffles

Make the truffles (see pages 268–9), cover in dark chocolate and then dip in icing sugar.

5. Almond biscuits

Make the biscuits as the recipe on page 107.

6. Profiterolles

Make these walnut-sized profiterolles following the instructions on pages 210–1.

Genoese sponge – the finest sponge for the finest gâteaux

The dough that needs a thorough whisking

Strictly speaking there is no such thing as a sponge 'dough' – the experts refer to it as a mixture – because it is beaten and whisked until it is fluffy, as opposed to a dough mixture which has to be kneaded and stretched. Very rich types of dough made with yeast, for making brioches, for example (see pages 130–1), are beaten well but are not called mixtures. So as you can see there are no hard and fast rules.

Whisking in air

Air plays an important part in the making of a sponge, it is incorporated into the mixture by patient beating of the eggs and makes the cake particularly soft and light. In the oven the air expands and the mixture grows to three times its original size, without any other raising agent such as baking powder. Even when the sponge is cooked, it is still not the final cake – it is just the basis to make special gâteaux, slices and petits fours, by filling it with jam or cream.

Tips for making the mixture

☐ If you whisk the eggs in a bowl over a saucepan of warm water until they become fluffy they will bind more readily and the mixture will expand and become firmer. But remember – the bowl should only be warm, not hot, otherwise the yolk will curdle and separate.

☐ Use caster sugar rather than granulated and beat it together with the eggs until it is completely dissolved. Otherwise it will be 'gritty' afterwards.
☐ The best way to add the flour to the egg mixture is with the aid of a sieve so that it is light and powdery and you can be sure it won't form lumps.
☐ Put the sponge mixture straight into the oven and don't let it stand around, otherwise the air escapes and the mixture will collapse.

Baking tips

☐ Grease the cake tin carefully with butter and dust with flour – that way you can be sure the cake will come out easily without sticking.
☐ If you want to play really safe, and save time and effort on washing up afterwards, line the tin with a piece of non-stick baking parchment or greaseproof paper cut exactly to the right size.

☐ To ensure that the surface of the cake stays nice and smooth and does not crack you must remove the paper from the hot cake as soon as you have turned it out of its tin. Then place it lightly back on top of the cake to stop it from drying out.
☐ Sponges should be baked in a moderate oven (180C, 350F, gas 4). The mixture should never have to wait for the oven to reach the right temperature, so always preheat the oven.
☐ You can tell when the sponge is cooked through because it starts to shrink from the side of the cake tin.
☐ Always turn the cake out on to a wire rack to cool. This ensures it gets air from all sides so that it stays dry on the outside and does not stick.

Equipment
Mixing bowls
Small pan and a pan for
heating the hot water
Pastry brush for greasing
the cake tin
Cake tin or 25-cm/10-in
springform tin
Wire rack

Ingredients:
90 g/3½ oz butter	
6 eggs	
175 g/6 oz caster sugar	
150 g/5 oz self-raising flour	

Cooking time:
Preparation time:

30 minutes

Baking time:

40 minutes

Oven temperature:

180C, 350F, gas 4

Cooling time:

1–2 hours

Storing

Sponge is ideally suited to
be frozen. Obviously, you
have to first allow the
cake to cool properly
before wrapping it in
aluminium foil, and it is
better to defrost it at
room temperature rather
than in the oven,
otherwise it can get too
dry.

Preparation

1. Weigh the ingredients according to the recipe and put them ready.

2. Grease the cake tin with butter and dust with flour.

3. Melt the butter in a small pan over a gentle heat.

4. Separate the yolks from the egg whites and put into two bowls.

5. Add the sugar to the yolks.

6. Whisk the yolks and sugar over the saucepan of hot water until thick.

7. Remove the bowl of thick, whitish creamy mixture.

8. Sift the flour on to the creamy egg mixture. Do not stir in.

9. Pour on the lukewarm melted butter.

10. Using a different bowl, whisk the egg white until stiff.

11. Mix one-third of the whisked egg white with the yolk mixture.

12. Add the remaining whisked egg white to the fluffy mixture.

13. Mix together carefully, folding gently as you do so.

14. Place the sponge mixture in the cake tin and smooth the surface.

15. Place the tin in the preheated oven.

16. After approximately 40 minutes the sponge should be ready.

17. Use a knife to separate the cake from the tin.

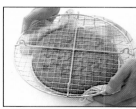

18. Put the wire rack on top of the cake while it is still warm.

19. Turn the sponge over. Remove the base of the cake tin.

20. Leave the cake to cool for at least 1 hour.

Turning a sponge into a gâteau

1. Cut the cake across into three layers of equal thickness.

2. Spread the jam thinly over the bottom layer.

3. Place the second layer on top, cover first with fruit and then with cream.

A Genoese sponge is the basis for the finest gâteaux. Here we show you how to turn a simple sponge into a magnificent strawberry gâteau. You can of course use any other type of fruit, depending on your taste, the time of year or what you have available. In each case you will need: fruit (fresh or canned), a jam which goes with the fruit, whipped cream or buttercream, a sponge base (see page 71) – which you can either make yourself or buy ready-made – and about 15 minutes preparation time. That's all the time you need before you can put this magnificent gâteau before your guests.

Strawberry gâteau

1 (23-cm/10-in) sponge base
(page 71)
3 tablespoons jam (eg blackcurrant jelly)
800 g/1¾ lb strawberries
750 ml/1¼ pints whipped cream
1 teaspoon chopped pistachio nuts

Getting the layers right

The hardest thing when making a gâteau is splitting the base into layers of equal thickness, but this is something you can easily learn. This is how the experts do it: take a knife with a long, thin, sharp serrated edge and cut into the base along the side. Then, keeping the knife absolutely level, continue cutting, gradually revolving the sponge. Cut all the layers in this way.

Gâteaux made easy

4. Cut the last layer to the centre and place on top to form a dome.

5. Cover the cake with a layer of cream, making fluffy peaks.

6. Decorate the gâteau with strawberries and chopped pistachio nuts.

Tips for layer cakes

It is more difficult to make layer cakes in the usual flat shape rather than the dome shape we have shown here. It is possible, though, if you remember the following tricks:

☐ The filling must be firm enough to cut, otherwise it will ooze out when you cut the cake or the pieces of the cake will just fall apart.

☐ If you add dissolved gelatine to the cream filling it will become firmer (see page 220).

☐ Spread the filling evenly between the individual layers so that they can be sandwiched firmly together, they do not slip and the first slice looks attractive.

☐ Use a knife with a long blade for spreading the filling or, even better, a palette knife like the experts use (see pages 16–7).

☐ When you are sandwiching together the layers of a gâteau like this, it is useful to have what is called a cake ring, which is a smooth ring made of plastic or metal where the diameter can be adjusted. Place the individual layers in this ring and it will hold them together and prevent the filling from spilling out. Before the cake is finally completed you simply remove the ring.

☐ The final touch is to decorate the edge of the gâteau: cover with buttercream or whipped cream. Then either smooth the edges, make a ripple effect with a serrated spatula or scatter with praline, chopped nuts or coloured sugar.

Sponge is an ordinary cake. It only displays its versatile qualities when it is used in conjunction with decorative creams or fruit. This makes it an ideal cake for more elaborate gâteaux.

Genoese sponge

Sponge can be made to have different textures and tastes just by adding bits of chocolate, grated nuts, more butter or ground poppy seeds to the mixture. These ingredients add more fat to the mixture and the cake then becomes moister and richer. It also becomes firmer so that you can use it to make a multi-layer gâteau without worrying that the bottom layer is going to collapse under the weight!

Chocolate sponge to Viennese sponge

Here you can see the classic sponge variations. They are made in the same way as the basic recipe (see page 71). All the additional ingredients mentioned here are stirred into the mixture with the first portion of whisked egg whites, i.e. before the main egg whites are carefully folded in (see Fig 11 on page 71).

Nutty sponge

(illustrated top right)
Because of the fat content of the nuts the sponge becomes firmer and acquires a nutty flavour if the nuts have not been ground to a fine powder. Use the basic recipe (see page 71) and add 100 g/ 4 oz nuts – praline, walnuts, hazelnuts, pistachios or almonds, whichever you prefer.

Viennese sponge

(illustrated right, second from top)
This rich sponge has a delicate and more intense taste than the basic recipe. The addition of more butter gives it a rich, moist consistency. On top of the 90 g/3½ oz butter in the basic recipe add a further 40–60 g/1½– 2½ oz butter to make the Viennese sponge mixture. It must be melted and lukewarm when added to the other ingredients.

Chocolate chip sponge

(illustrated centre right)
Add 100 g/4 oz chocolate to the basic recipe (see page 71). Grate coarsely on a cheese grater or chop in an electric grinder. It is best to mix the chocolate chips in with the flour before this is added to the mixture.

Orange sponge

(illustrated right, second from bottom)
Stir the finely grated peel of two oranges into the ingredients of the basic recipe (see page 71).

Chocolate sponge

(illustrated bottom right)
Use good plain chocolate or a top quality dessert chocolate for this sponge. The cake will then be rich and pleasantly moist. Melt 150 g/5 oz chocolate over a gentle heat and add this to the mixture before the egg whites are folded in.

Making use of fillings

Praline sponge

1 Praline sponge (see pages 74–5)
750 ml/1¼ pints vanilla buttercream (see page 231)
200 g/7 oz praline, bought or homemade (see pages 272–3)

Cut the sponge into three layers. Keep 4 tablespoons of the buttercream on one side to use as decoration. Mix the remainder with praline and rum. Spread evenly over two of the layers and press them together. Spread the reserved buttercream over the top and decorate with praline.

Apricot cream gâteau

1 Viennese sponge base (see pages 74–5)
450 g/1 lb apricots, cooked and stones removed
750 ml/1¼ pints stiffly whipped, sweetened cream
2 tablespoons apricot jam
1 tablespoon finely chopped pistachio nuts

Split the sponge base across once. Cut one-third of the apricots into large chunks and mix with the cream. Spread the jam across the lower sponge layer and add the cream mixture. Place the second sponge layer on top and spread the remaining apricots evenly on it and add the pistachios.

Preparation

The sponge you wish to use for a gâteau should always be baked the day before. A cake which is too fresh crumbles when you cut it and you do not get even layers. As a sponge always forms a dome in the middle after it has been baked, cut this level so that the gâteau can be layered properly. Use these extra sponge pieces to make a trifle, for example.

Filling with jam

This is the easiest way to make a gâteau out of a sponge. Stir the jam until it is smooth. Add a small glass of liqueur if you wish for extra flavour. Jam tastes fresher and less sweet if you add fresh fruit to it, for example, 100 g/4 oz fresh raspberries to 200 g/7 oz raspberry jam.

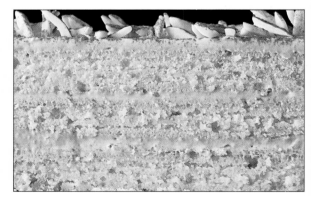

Bilberry gâteau

1 Viennese sponge (see pages 74–5)
400 g/14 oz bilberry jam
600 ml/1 pint whipped cream
2 tablespoons sugar
15 g/½ oz powdered gelatine

Cut the sponge across once. Mix half the bilberry jam with the cream and sugar. Dissolve the gelatine in 2 tablespoons hot water over a pan of simmering water, then add this to the bilberry mixture and beat well with a whisk. Spread this thickly over the lower layer. Place the upper layer on top and spread with the remaining bilberry jam.

Mocha gâteau

1 sponge base (see page 71)
3 tablespoons Cognac
2 tablespoons instant coffee powder
750 ml/1¼ pints vanilla buttercream (see page 231)
100 g/4 oz roasted almonds, chopped

Cut the sponge into three layers. Heat the Cognac gently in a saucepan over a low heat and dissolve the coffee powder in it. Take off the heat and cool, then mix with the buttercream. Spread the cream over the layers of sponge and finish with a top layer. Decorate with the roasted almonds.

Chocolate gâteau

I thin shortcrust pastry base (made with half the
ingredients given on page 103)
4 tablespoons blackcurrant jelly
I chocolate sponge (made with half the ingredients
given on pages 74–5)
750 ml/1¼ pints Canache cream (see page 236)
4 tablespoons grated chocolate

Spread the blackcurrant jelly on the shortcrust pastry
base. Place the chocolate sponge on top of this and
spread the Canache cream over the chocolate sponge.
Decorate the finished cake with the grated chocolate.

Raspberry gâteau

I chocolate sponge base (see pages 74–5)
750 ml/1¼ pints vanilla buttercream (see page 231)
4 tablespoons raspberry liqueur
500 g/18 oz raspberries

Split the sponge once and sandwich the two halves
together with half the buttercream. Sprinkle the
raspberry liqueur over the top layer and then cover
with the remainder of the buttercream. Place a thick
layer of raspberries over the top.

Stewed fruit filling

For a gâteau filling you
have to first briefly boil
approximately 500–675 g/
18 oz–1½ lb fruit. Try using
Morello cherries or
gooseberries. Sweeten the
fruit with about
100–175 g/4–6 oz sugar
and if it contains a lot of
juice, bind it with about 3
tablespoons cornflour
mixed with some fruit
juice. Bring the mixture
to the boil once to allow
the juice to thicken.
Allow to cool before
using.

Marzipan filling

This will give the normal
sponge base an almond
taste. Mix together 200 g/
7 oz marzipan, 6
tablespoons milk and 2
tablespoons rum and bind
until smooth.

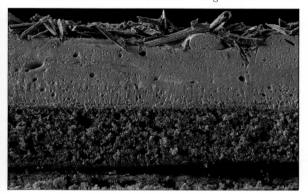

Dobos torte

I sponge base (see page 75)
750 ml/1¼ pints vanilla buttercream (see page 231)
100 g/4 oz nougat, dissolved
6 tablespoons sugar
I tablespoon butter
oil for greasing

Cut the sponge into six thin slices. Mix the vanilla
buttercream with the melted nougat. Spread each of
the layers with the mixture and then place these one on
top of the other. Heat the sugar slowly in a small
saucepan until it forms a golden caramel, then add the
butter, stirring all the time. Rub a little oil on to a knife
and then spread the caramel on the top sponge layer
with this knife. Before the caramel sets and becomes
stiff, mark the slices of cake on the surface using the
oiled knife.

Chocolate and cherry gâteau

I chocolate sponge (see pages 74–5)
2 tablespoons Kirsch (optional)
450 g/1 lb Morello cherry jam
3 tablespoons icing sugar

Cut the sponge into three layers. Whisk the Kirsch, if
using, into the jam and then spread this mixture over
two of the layers. Sandwich the layers together again
and dust the top with the icing sugar.

Adding some decoration

To ensure that a cake manages to look attractive to the end of a lively coffee or tea party, it is as well to decorate it. A glaze or frosting will help to stop the delicate cream on the outside from drying out. It tastes good and it looks good too.

Red currant glaze

(first slice, top of page)
1. Cover the top of the sponge with whipped cream and give a smooth finish.
2. Place briefly in the refrigerator till it sets.
3. Make up 250 ml/8 fl oz cake glaze (see page 248).
4. Spread red currants over the top of the cake. Then add the glaze once it has cooled a little.

Cream glaze with sponge crumbs

(second slice)
1. Cover the top of the sponge with whipped cream.
2. Dry sponge crumbs briefly in a very cool oven (110C, 225F, gas ¼).
3. Press the sponge crumbs through a coarse sieve and scatter on the gâteau.
4. Decorate with swirls of whipped cream and walnut halves.

Cocoa powder topping

(third slice)
1. Cover the sponge all round with chocolate-buttercream (see pages 232–3) or chocolate-flavoured whipped cream (see pages 76–7)
2. Sift cocoa powder over the top to decorate.

Edge made of sponge fingers. top covered with grated chocolate

(fourth slice)
1. Cover the sponge all round with whipped cream.
2. Trim 10 to 15 sponge fingers (see pages 82–3) and place round the cake so that they stand out about 2.5 cm/1 in over the edge. Press them on firmly all round.
3. Scatter a thick layer of grated chocolate over the top to decorate.

Kiwi glaze

(fifth slice)
1. Spread whipped cream over the sponge.
2. Place a thick layer of thinly-sliced kiwi fruit across the top and chill.
3. Prepare 250 ml/8 fl oz cake glaze (see page 248). Cover the top of the sponge with this once it has cooled a little.
4. Decorate the cake with swirls of whipped cream.

Chocolate cloud

(sixth slice)
1. Cover the sponge with chocolate buttercream (see pages 231–2). Using the back of a spoon, make the cream into peaks.
2. Dust the iced cake with cocoa powder.

Strawberry cream

(seventh slice)
1. Cover the gâteau with whipped cream.

2. Decorate the edge with peaks of whipped cream and praline.
3. Place the strawberries in the middle of the cake and cover with apricot glaze (see pages 248–9).

Lemon glaze

(eighth slice)
1. Mix 150 g/5 oz icing sugar and 2 tablespoons lemon juice to make a lemon icing glaze and stir until smooth. Colour yellow.
2. Cover the sponge with a layer of marzipan (see pages 24–5).
3. Cover the cake with the lemon glaze and scatter with pistachio nuts.

Chocolate glaze

(ninth slice)
1. Melt 225 g/8 oz chocolate (see pages 246–7).
2. Cover the sponge with a layer of marzipan (see pages 24–5).
3. Pour the melted chocolate into the centre of the cake and spread with a large palette knife.
4. As soon as the chocolate has set, warm a knife and mark in the slices of gâteau.
5. Decorate the top with almonds, swirls of whipped cream and small chocolate biscuits.

Crumble

(tenth slice)
1. Prepare the crumble mixture (see page 107). Spread a thin layer on a baking tray and bake.
2. Once the crumbs have cooled spread them all over the sponge.

A cake to tempt everyone

Looks simply fantastic and is guaranteed to win genuine admiration from any guest. And yet this kind of gâteau is really not so difficult to make. Of course you need a little patience – but it does pay off . . .!

Black Forest gâteau

6 eggs

175 g/6 oz caster sugar

150 g/5 oz self-raising flour

90 g/3½ oz butter

150 g/5 oz plain chocolate

For the filling:

1 (750-g/1-lb 10-oz) can or jar Morello cherries, stones removed

100 g/4 oz sugar

½ teaspoon ground cinnamon

2 heaped tablespoons cornflour

1 tablespoon water

6 tablespoons Morello cherry jam

3 tablespoons Kirsch

750 ml/1¼ pints double cream

1–2 tablespoons sugar

grated chocolate to decorate

1. Make the sponge as in the basic recipe (see page 71) with the ingredients given here.

2. Put the Morello cherries and juice with 75 g/3 oz of the sugar and cinnamon in a saucepan and bring to the boil. Mix the cornflour with the water and add to the fruit and bring to the boil, stirring all the time. Remove from the heat.

3. Cut the sponge into four layers.

4. Mix the jam and Kirsch together and stir until smooth. Spread on one of the four layers.

5. Place the second sponge layer on top and cover with Morello cherries. Keep a few on one side for decoration.

6. Whip the cream until it is stiff and sweeten with remaining sugar to taste. Spread half on the third layer.

7. Place the last layer on the top. Spread the remaining cream all round the outside of the gâteau.

8. Decorate the gâteau with grated chocolate, swirls of cream and the remaining Morello cherries.

Small cakes made on the baking tray

A sponge made on a baking tray does not always have to be used for cream-filled slices of Swiss roll. You can also make different shapes from a sponge cooked on the baking tray. You can cut it into any shape you like, for example:
1. Diamonds
2. Rectangles
3. Squares
4. Circles
5. Triangles
6. Hearts

You then spread jam or whipped cream over these different shapes and sandwich them together. Sprinkle icing sugar over the top or coat with an icing made from 2 egg whites and 225 g/8 oz icing sugar (see also the decorations on pages 246–54 and petits fours on pages 270–1).

Sponge bases

You do not have to use a springform tin to make sponge bases – you can also bake the mixture in a round shape on the baking tray. Divide the mixture (see basic recipe, page 71) on to two trays and then using a palette knife spread it thinly on each tray so that it forms a circle. A cake ring (see pages 18–9) is handy to ensure that the shape is exactly round. Bake in a moderate oven (180C, 350F, gas 4) for about 10 minutes.

As a sponge base for a fruit gâteau you will only need half the amount given in the basic recipe (see page 71). Use a flan tin and grease well, sprinkle with flour and bake for about 20 to 25 minutes in a moderate oven (180C, 350F, gas 4).

Sponge in all shapes and sizes

This section deals with little shapes, slices, petits fours – in fact, small Genoese sponge cakes. Try making the famous Swiss roll: a light sponge cake with filling which is rolled up and then cut into slices.

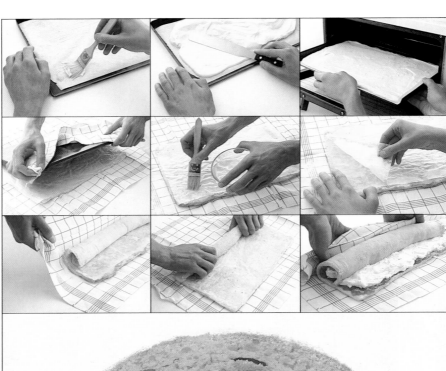

Swiss roll

melted butter for greasing
4 eggs
100 g/4 oz caster sugar
75 g/3 oz self-raising flour
50 g/2 oz butter
sugar for sprinkling
For the filling:
350 g/12 oz apricot jam
450 ml/¾ pint whipping cream
icing sugar to decorate

(step-by-step photographs from left to right)
1. Line a baking tin 23 cm/9 in by 30 cm/12 in with greaseproof paper or baking parchment and brush with melted butter.
2. Make up the sponge mixture (see basic recipe, page 71) and spread evenly over the baking tray.
3. Bake the roll in a moderate oven (180C, 350F, gas 4) for 15 to 20 minutes until light brown.
4. Turn the hot sponge out on to a tea-towel sprinkled with sugar.
5. Brush all the greaseproof paper with cold water so that it does not stick at all to the sponge.
6. Remove the greaseproof paper carefully.
7. Roll up the sponge immediately while it is still warm and elastic. Lift up the tea-towel lengthways so that the sponge will virtually roll itself up on its own. Leave it to cool down.
8. Roll the sponge out again to fill it. Do this carefully so it does not crack.
9. Spread with jam, then a thick layer of cream on top and roll up again carefully. Sprinkle with icing sugar and cut into thick slices for serving.

Sponge fingers

Makes 40

4 eggs, separated

225 g / 8 oz caster sugar

225 g / 8 oz self-raising flour

icing sugar to decorate

(step-by-step photographs from left to right)

1. Using an electric whisk beat the egg yolks with 100 g/4 oz sugar in a bowl standing in hot water until they become thick enough to leave a trail.
2. It takes about 6 to 8 minutes until the cream is white and thick.
3. Whisk the egg whites in a separate bowl until they are stiff.
4. Whisk in the remaining sugar a little at a time.
5. Mix a third of the stiff egg white and the flour into the yolk mixture.
6. Fold in the remaining egg white.
7. Put the sponge mixture into a piping bag fitted with a 1-cm/½-in plain nozzle.
8. Grease a baking tray and pipe the sponge fingers on to it. Bake for 8 to 10 minutes in a moderately hot oven (200 C, 400 F, gas 6) until cooked.
9. Sprinkle the sponge fingers with icing sugar.

Tips for desserts

To make Tirami su, the Italian speciality, use sponge fingers, or sponge off-cuts, soaked first in strong coffee, and place them in layers alternately with a Mascarpone cream in a flat tin. The top layer should be cream which is decorated with a thick layer of cocoa powder. Trifle is, of course, one of the favourite desserts using sponge fingers. Soak them in sweet sherry, then add a layer of jam and custard and leave to stand.

Sponge fingers

Sponge fingers taste good just eaten on their own or sprinkled with icing sugar. Try having them with a coffee, some ice cream or as part of a cream dessert.

Raspberry Charlotte

250 ml / 8 fl oz milk

600 ml / 1 pint double cream

½ vanilla pod

4 egg yolks

100 g / 4 oz caster sugar

15 g / ½ oz powdered gelatine

10–15 sponge fingers (depending on size)

250 g / 9 oz raspberries, hulled

1 tablespoon icing sugar to decorate

1. Put the milk in a saucepan with half of the cream, and bring to the boil with the vanilla pod and simmer for a few minutes.
2. Beat the yolks and sugar until thick. Add the boiling milk and the vanilla pulp scraped out of the pod.
3. Put everything back into the saucepan. Warm slowly, stirring constantly, until the cream sauce thickens. Do not boil or it will curdle.
4. Pour the cream sauce through a sieve and cool in a bowl standing in cold water. Dissolve the gelatine in 2 tablespoons hot water, then mix into the warm cream sauce.
5. Whip the remaining cream until it is stiff. As soon as the vanilla cream sauce begins to set, fold in.
6. Place a layer of sponge fingers closely round the edge of a greased 1.5-litre/2¾-pint Charlotte mould. Trim the fingers along the edge to fit.
7. Place the layers of cream sauce and raspberries in the dish.
8. Stand in a cold place until it sets. After about 3 hours it can be turned out. Sprinkle with icing sugar to decorate.

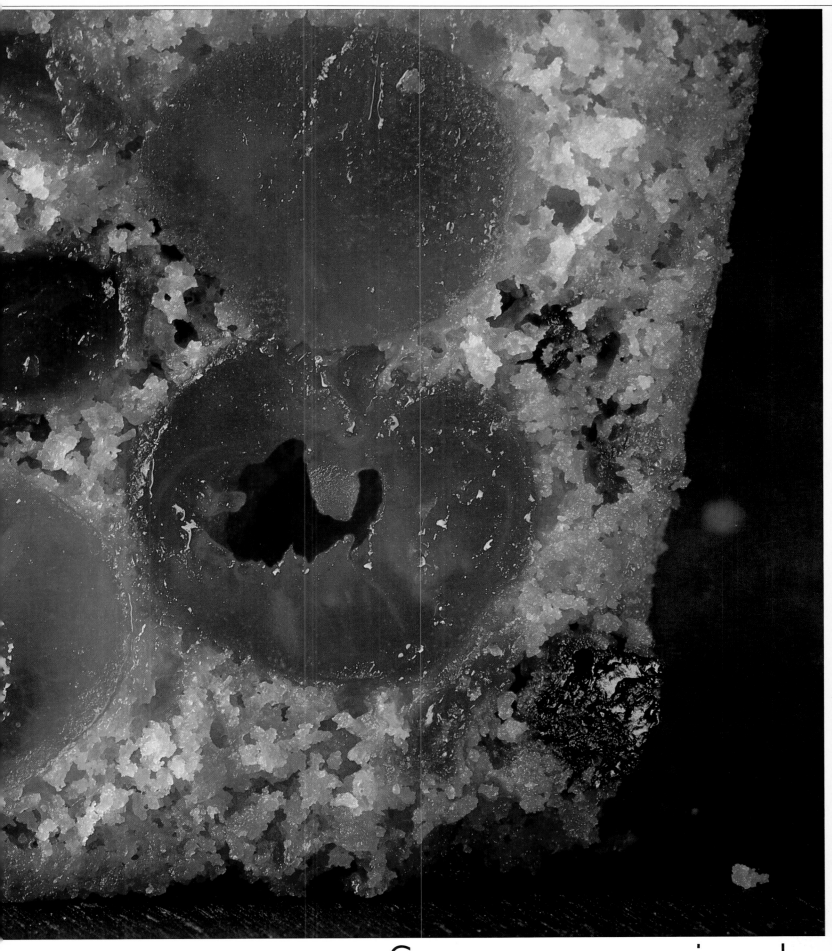

Sponge – so simple,
but simply irresistible

Tips on the mixture

As we have said it is the beating which is the important part in making this sponge. It is this that makes it lighter and moist and gives it its crumbly texture.

☐ The whisked egg white makes it lighter still, adding air to the mixture which expands during baking and makes the cake rise.

☐ The lightness of the sponge also depends on what order the ingredients are added. For a really light cake which rises well, first beat the egg yolks with sugar, then the butter.

☐ For a cake with a finer grain, beat the butter and sugar first, then the egg yolks. In each case you should stop beating when the flour is added or the mixture will become too elastic.

☐ Another method is to beat all the ingredients together for a short time – this gives a very moist, rich, firm cake.

☐ To be on the safe side it is also a good idea to add a teaspoon of baking powder for this should guarantee a light cake.

The mixture that needs plenty of beating

Like Genoese sponge, sponges that are beaten to incorporate air are mixtures rather than doughs, but whereas Genoese sponges are very light, these tend to be firmer, because of the high fat content which makes a very rich mixture. These sponge

mixtures are sometimes referred to as 'egg-weight mixtures' for the weight of ingredients depends on the weight of egg. For the traditional pound cake each pound of eggs (around 6 eggs) required 450 g/1 lb each of butter, sugar and flour. This was an extremely useful measure to know as it meant you didn't need a cookery book or kitchen scales to make this kind of sponge. There is very little that can go wrong with these heavier sponges. It is also very easy to vary the basic recipe and produce an entirely different sponge by just adding an extra ingredient.

Tips on preparation

☐ All the ingredients should be brought to room temperature so that they will mix properly together, so remember to get everything ready in advance. If you forget:
– stand the eggs in warm water for a short time.
— cut the butter into cubes and place in a bowl near a radiator or near the open door of a heated oven.

☐ Fold in flour very lightly.

☐ If the mixture is too thick – because the eggs were too small – stir in 2 or 3 tablespoons milk until it becomes smooth again.

☐ Bake in a moderate oven (180 C, 350 F, gas 4) or, at the most, in a moderately hot oven (200 C, 400 F, gas 6).

☐ To check whether the cake is completely cooked, stick a wooden or metal skewer into the centre of the cake. If there is any mixture on it when you pull it out, the cake still needs a bit more time. Only when it comes out completely clean can you take the cake out of the oven and leave it to cool.

Equipment

Mixing bowl
900-g/2-lb loaf tin
Hand or electric whisk
Spatula
Wire rack

Ingredients:

300 g/11 oz self-raising
flour

300 g/11 oz butter

300 g/11 oz caster sugar

5 eggs

Cooking time:

Preparation time:

35 minutes

Baking time:

1 hour

Oven temperature:

180C, 350F, gas 4

Cooling time:

1 hour

Madeira cake

An extremely fine-grained
sponge which melts in the
mouth. It is made with a
mixture of cornflour and
flour which gives the cake
something of the
consistency (but not the
grittiness) of sand, hence
it is also called 'sand cake'.

Madeira ring

(See pages 54–5)
The same sponge baked in
a ring mould. It is cut
across and the two pieces
are sandwiched together
and coated with
buttercream (see pages
230–1). Decorate with
praline, whirls of cream
and red maraschino
cherries.

Preparation

1. Get all the ingredients out to bring them to room temperature.

2. Brush the cake tin with melted butter.

3. Dust the tin with flour and shake off any excess.

4. Tip the soft butter into a large mixing bowl.

5. Using an electric whisk beat the butter until fluffy.

6. Beat in two-thirds of the sugar until it has dissolved.

7. Separate the eggs, letting the whites fall into a second mixing bowl.

8. Place the egg yolks on top of the beaten butter in the bowl.

9. Beat together the butter, sugar and egg yolks until thick.

10. Sift the flour on to the mixture to avoid lumps.

11. Use the mixer slowly to just fold in the flour.

12. Whisk the egg whites until stiff with the remaining sugar.

13. Stir a little of the egg white into the mixture to make it lighter.

14. Now gently fold in the remaining whisked egg white.

15. Pour the mixture into the prepared tin and smooth the top.

16. Place the tin in the moderately hot oven (180C, 350F, gas 4).

17. After about 50 minutes, test the cake with a skewer.

18. After about 1 hour the cake should be completely cooked.

19. Turn the cooked cake out of the tin on to a wire rack.

20. Leave to cool for an hour before cutting into slices ready to serve.

Getting the cake out of the tin

What use is there having the most attractive tin, if the cooked cake sticks to its corners and flutes, flatly refusing to come out in one piece. To prevent this happening tins must be carefully prepared before the mixture goes in them. (See pages 20–1) *Plain tins*, such as loaf or springform tins or baking sheets can simply be lined with non-stick baking parchment to save time and effort.
All others need greasing and ideally sprinkling with flour too.
For greasing use the same fat that goes into the cake, preferably butter but possibly margarine or oil.

Using different tins

You can make the most varied cakes from the same mixture just by cooking it in different shapes of tins. Many cakes even get their names from the type of tin in which they are baked. A ring cake can only be baked in a ring tin. And a flan can only be cooked in a flan tin.

Sprinkle with flour, semolina or fine breadcrumbs. These are neutral in flavour and go with everything. For special cakes try chopped nuts – almonds, peanuts, hazelnuts or walnuts, depending on the type and flavour of the cake.
One final tip: cakes that take a long time to cook may start to burn around the edge. You can prevent this by lining the edge of the tin with a double layer of non-stick baking parchment.

Photographs
 1. Flan tin
 2. Paper bun cases
 3. Tartlet tins
 4. Loaf tin
 5. Ring tin
 6. Easter rabbit
 7. Heart-shaped tin
 8. Balmoral tin
 9. Springform tin
 10. Fluted ring mould

All tins come in various sizes and finishes (see pages 18–9).

Decorative ways to dress up a sponge

The finished sponge will be an appetising golden brown, but you can decorate it in different ways to make it even more tempting. The simplest way is to dust it with icing sugar, but a coating of chocolate, icing or jam helps to keep the cake, so that it will last longer. Here are a few ideas you might like to try.

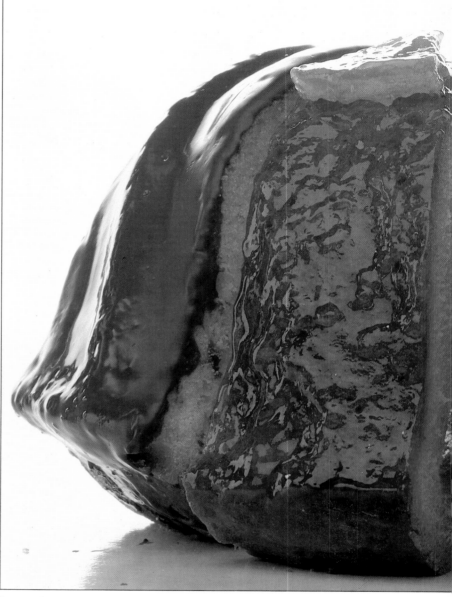

1. Plain chocolate

For a sponge you will need about 300 g/11 oz plain chocolate (see pages 246–7). To get a nice shiny surface, rather than a flat, greyish finish, follow these instructions: melt two-thirds of the chocolate in a heatproof bowl over a pan of simmering water. Then add the remaining chocolate in small pieces and stir in, off the heat, until this too has melted. At this point the chocolate should be no more than hand-warm and easily brushed on to the sponge. For a smoother finish, just pour the chocolate over the sponge. Place the cake on a wire rack over a bowl to catch excess drips that can be used again.

If you want to, you can scatter other decorations on to the chocolate before it sets. Try using crystallised sugar, whole or chopped almonds, pistachios or walnuts, silver balls or chocolate vermicelli.

2. Apricot glaze

Put 450 g/1 lb apricot jam in a saucepan with 3 tablespoons water and 1 tablespoon sugar and bring to the boil over a moderate heat. Cook for a few minutes, remove from heat and brush on to the sponge. Once the glaze has set you can ice on top of it if you like and decorate it with candied orange slices.

6. Marzipan

Sponges made in a round or loaf tin can be covered in marzipan. First cover the sponge with a fruit glaze (see pages 248–9) to the marzipan to stick firmly. Then mix 350 g/ 12 oz raw marzipan with 225 g/8 oz icing sugar to give a firm mixture. Roll out to a 5-mm/$\frac{1}{4}$-in thickness on a board sprinkled with icing sugar and wrap around the sponge.

Trim the edges and decorate the top with sugar flowers, buttercream or nuts.

3. Icing sugar

For a simple finish just dust the cool sponge evenly with 3 tablespoons icing sugar.

4. Icing

Beat 225 g/8 oz icing sugar with 1 egg white in a bowl. Brush the icing on to the sponge and add decorations like glacé cherries, nuts, crystallised violets, for example, before the icing has set.
Variations:
Replace the egg white with lemon juice, water, rum or other aromatic forms of alcohol. You can colour the white icing by adding dissolved saffron powder or a food colouring.

5. Milk chocolate

Take 350 g/12oz milk chocolate and proceed as for the Plain chocolate method. Finally, sprinkle with praline – bought or home-made (see pages 272–3).

Sponges with a difference

There is scarcely any other type of sponge mixture which can make so many different cakes just by adding something extra to it – cocoa powder, nuts, dried fruit, chocolate to name but a few. The basic mixture remains the same, but, with a few extra ingredients, you can turn it each time into a completely different cake.

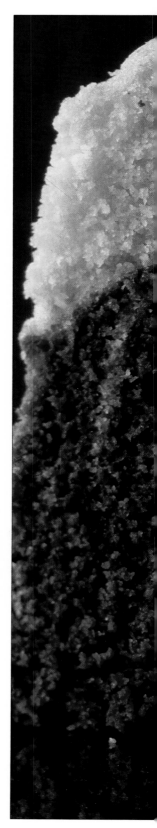

Marble cake

5 eggs
300 g/ 11 oz butter
300 g/ 11 oz caster sugar
300 g/ 11 oz self-raising flour
3 tablespoons cocoa powder

1. Make a sponge from the basic recipe (see page 87).
2. Stir the cocoa powder into half the cake mixture.
3. First pour the plain mixture into a greased and floured fluted ring mould.
4. Then cover this layer with the chocolate mixture. Stir in lightly with a fork to create a marbled effect.
5. Bake as in the basic recipe (see page 87).

Raisin cake

5 eggs
300 g/ 11 oz butter
300 g/ 11 oz caster sugar
300 g/ 11 oz self-raising flour
150 g/ 5 oz raisins
1 tablespoon flour

1. Make a sponge as described in the basic recipe (see page 87).
2. Wash and thoroughly drain the raisins. When they are moist rather than wet, mix with the flour and shake off excess in a sieve. Fold into the mixture. The flour prevents the raisins from sinking to the bottom of the tin.
3. Bake in a greased and floured fluted ring mould as in the basic recipe (see page 87).

Macaroon sponge

5 eggs
300 g/ 11 oz butter
300 g/ 11 oz caster sugar
300 g/ 11 oz self-raising flour
1 egg white
2 tablespoons sugar
100 g/ 4 oz ground almonds

1. Make a sponge from the basic recipe (see page 87).
2. Whisk the egg white until stiff, adding in the sugar. Finally, stir in the almonds.
3. Pour the sponge mixture into a greased and floured fluted ring mould. Pour the almond mixture on top and fold in carefully using a fork.
4. Bake as in the basic recipe (see page 87).

Hazelnut sponge

5 eggs
300 g/ 11 oz butter
300 g/ 11 oz caster sugar
300 g/ 11 oz self-raising flour
150 g/ 5 oz ground hazelnuts

1. Make a sponge as in the basic recipe (see page 87).
2. Heat the hazelnuts in a dry pan without fat over a moderate heat until they seem nicely roasted.
3. Cool, and fold into the sponge.
4. Bake in a greased and floured fluted ring mould as in the basic recipe (see page 87).

Sunken fruit to make the sponge moist

Unlike a fruit flan where fresh or stewed fruit goes into a pre-baked flan case, a fruit sponge has the fruit cooked inside it. As the fruit inevitably produces juice, you have to make the sponge mixture more solid by adding extra flour, but to keep it light, baking powder is added with the flour. The method is straightforward and easy to follow. The sponge mixture is spread in the tin and then thickly covered with the prepared fruit.

Basic recipe for Morello cherry sponge

(illustrated, springform tin)

250 g/9 oz butter

250 g/9 oz caster sugar

4 eggs

400 g/14 oz self-raising flour

1 teaspoon baking powder

1 kg/2¼ lb Morello cherries, washed and stoned

To decorate:

2 tablespoons sugar

1 teaspoon ground cinnamon

1. Brush a 25-cm/10-in springform tin with butter and dust with flour.
2. Cream the butter, which should be at room temperature, with the sugar until light and fluffy, then gradually beat in the eggs.
3. Finally fold in the flour with the baking powder.
4. Pour the mixture into the prepared tin and cover thickly with the cherries.
5. Sprinkle the top with sugar and cinnamon.
6. Bake the cake in a moderately hot oven (190C, 375F, gas 5) for about 1 hour, or until cooked through.

Peach sponge

(illustrated top left)

250 g/9 oz butter

250 g/9 oz caster sugar

4 eggs

400 g/14 oz self-raising flour

1 teaspoon baking powder

800 g/1¾ lb peaches, peeled and sliced

To decorate:

2 tablespoons chopped almonds

3 tablespoons raisins

1. Make the sponge and pour into the prepared tin as in the basic Morello sponge recipe.
2. Cover the top thickly with the peach slices and scatter with chopped almonds and raisins.
3. Bake as in the basic recipe.

Pear sponge

(illustrated top right)

250 g/9 oz butter

250 g/9 oz caster sugar

4 eggs

400 g/14 oz self-raising flour

1 teaspoon baking powder

800 g/1¾ lb pears, peeled, halved and cored

To decorate:

2 tablespoons crystallised sugar

1 tablespoon chopped pistachio nuts

1. Make the sponge and pour into the prepared tin as in the basic Morello cherry recipe.
2. Place the pear halves, rounded side uppermost on the sponge mixture.
3. Scatter with the crystallised sugar and pistachios.
4. Bake as in the basic recipe.

Plum sponge

(illustrated bottom left)

250 g/9 oz butter

250 g/9 oz caster sugar

4 eggs

400 g/14 oz self-raising flour

1 teaspoon baking powder

800 g/1¾ lb plums, halved and stoned

1 tablespoon icing sugar to decorate

1. Make the sponge and pour into the prepared tin as in the basic Morello cherry recipe (left).
2. Cover thickly with the plums and bake as given in the basic recipe (left).
3. When cool decorate with icing sugar.

Apricot sponge

(illustrated bottom right)

250 g/9 oz butter

250 g/9 oz caster sugar

4 eggs

400 g/14 oz self-raising flour

1 teaspoon baking powder

800 g/1¾ lb fresh apricots, halved and stoned

3 tablespoons flaked almonds

3 tablespoons apricot jam to decorate

1. Make the sponge and pour into the prepared tin as in the basic Morello cherry recipe (left).
2. Arrange the apricots over the sponge and scatter with almonds.
3. Bake as given in the basic recipe.
4. Warm the apricot jam and brush evenly over the sponge before the cake cools completely.

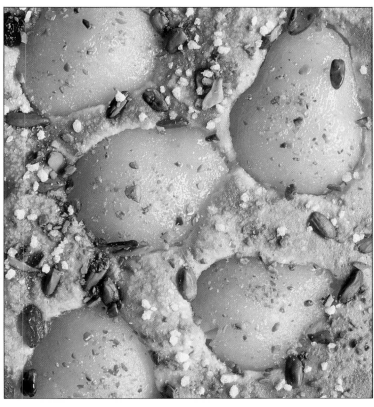
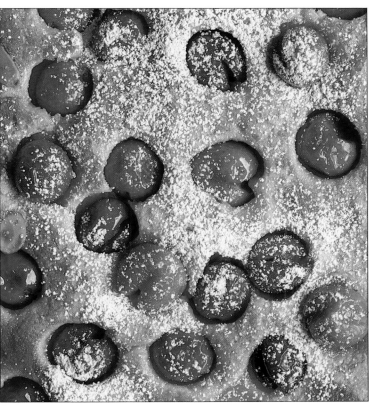

Rich sponges for special occasions

Rich cakes like wedding, birthday or Christmas cakes should be made at least one to three days before you need them, and in most cases much earlier. Wrap them in several layers of aluminium foil to prevent them becoming dry and the various flavours of the separate ingredients will have time to blend with one another. The easy-to-follow chart below shows you how much of each ingredient you need for each cake. The mixture is then quite simply made up and baked as in the basic recipe on pages 86–7. All the cakes given here can be used to make an impressive cake of several tiers, for they are all quite solid and you need have no fear that the bottom tier will collapse under the weight.

Ingredients/ Method	Rich fruit cake (photograph pages 58–9) 23-cm/9-in spring tin 1¼ hours 180C, 350F, gas 4	Dundee cake (photograph pages 60–1) 20-cm/8-in spring tin 1 hour 180C, 350F, gas 4	Light fruit cake (photograph pages 84–5) 900-g/2-lb loaf tin 1 hour 180C, 300F, gas 4	Fruit cake (photograph pages 60–1) 900-g/2-lb loaf tin 1 hour 10 minutes 180C, 300F, gas 4	Spice cake (photograph pages 60–1) 900-g/2-lb loaf tin 1 hour 180C, 350F, gas 4
1. Cream butter	300 g/11 oz	200 g/7 oz	300 g/11 oz	300 g/11 oz	300 g/11 oz
2. Add sugar	300 g/11 oz (brown sugar)	200 g/7 oz	200 g/7 oz	200 g/7 oz	200 g/7 oz
3. Add egg yolks	6	4	5	6	6
4. Add self-raising flour	300 g/11 oz	300 g/11 oz and 1 teaspoon baking powder	300 g/11 oz	300 g/11 oz	300 g/11 oz
5. Whisk egg white	6	4	5	6	6
6. Sprinkle in sugar	—	—	100 g/4 oz	100 g/4 oz	100 g/4 oz
7. Add other ingredients 8. Pour into tin 9. Bake 10. Test if cooked 11. Take out of oven, turn out and cool	175 g/6 oz candied orange and lemon peel 175 g/6 oz glacé cherries 400 g/14 oz sultanas and currants 300 g/11 oz raisins 125 g/4½ oz almonds grated rind of 1 lemon and 1 orange 1 tablespoon syrup ½ teaspoon each salt, freshly grated nutmeg, ground cardamom, aniseed and coriander 6 tablespoons rum	65 g/2½ oz ground almonds 100 g/4 oz currants 100 g/4 oz sultanas 100 g/4 oz raisins 65 g/2½ oz candied orange and lemon peel	125 g/4½ oz currants 125 g/4½ oz raisins 100 g/4 oz candied lemon peel 50 g/2 oz red glacé cherries 50 g/2 oz yellow glacé cherries	200 g/7 oz dried, chopped figs 100 g/4 oz each dried apricots, apple rings, raisins, candied lemon peel ½ teaspoon ground cinnamon ½ teaspoon ground cloves ½ teaspoon freshly grated nutmeg 100 g/4 oz flaked almonds	½ teaspoon ground coriander ½ teaspoon allspice ½ teaspoon freshly grated nutmeg ½ teaspoon ground cinnamon

The most famous cake in the world

A really delicious sponge which originated in Vienna is the Sachertorte. The original recipe is one of the world's best-kept secrets at the Sacher Company in Vienna. The Viennese court baker, Franz Sacher, invented the cake in 1832 for Prince Metternich. The recipe given here is therefore 'only' an attempt to get close to the original, but it is a really delicious version. Unlike the original version, the top of the cake is covered here with a thin layer of marzipan which makes it easier to put the chocolate on smoothly, and in no way detracts from the flavour. Serve the sponge with cups of strong coffee and a vanilla flavoured whipped cream.

Sachertorte

Ingredients for the sponge

200 g/7 oz butter

6 eggs, separated

75 g/3 oz plain chocolate, melted

200 g/7 oz caster sugar

1½ tablespoons cocoa powder

200 g/7 oz self-raising flour

40 g/1½ oz biscuit crumbs

For the filling and topping:

100 g/4 oz apricot jam

175 g/6 oz plain chocolate

40 g/1½ oz icing sugar

40 g/1½ oz marzipan

1. Butter and flour a 23-cm/9-in springform tin.
2. Cream the butter until fluffy. Add the egg yolks, chocolate and 150 g/5 oz sugar and beat to give a thick cream.
3. Stir in the cocoa powder, flour and crumbs and beat the mixture.
4. Whisk the egg whites until stiff, adding the remaining sugar.
5. Stir one-third of the whites into the sponge mixture and then gently fold in the rest.
6. Pour the mixture into the prepared tin and carefully smooth the top.
7. Bake in a moderate oven (180 C, 350 F, gas 4) for 1 hour 10 minutes, or until cooked.

8. Cut round the side of the cake with a sharp knife and turn out on to a wire rack. Leave to cool for about 1 hour.
9. Meanwhile whisk the apricot jam until smooth.
10. Melt half the chocolate in a heatproof bowl over a pan of simmering water.
11. Work the icing sugar into the marzipan and roll out thinly on a board dusted with icing sugar. Use the edge of the springform tin to cut into a circle.

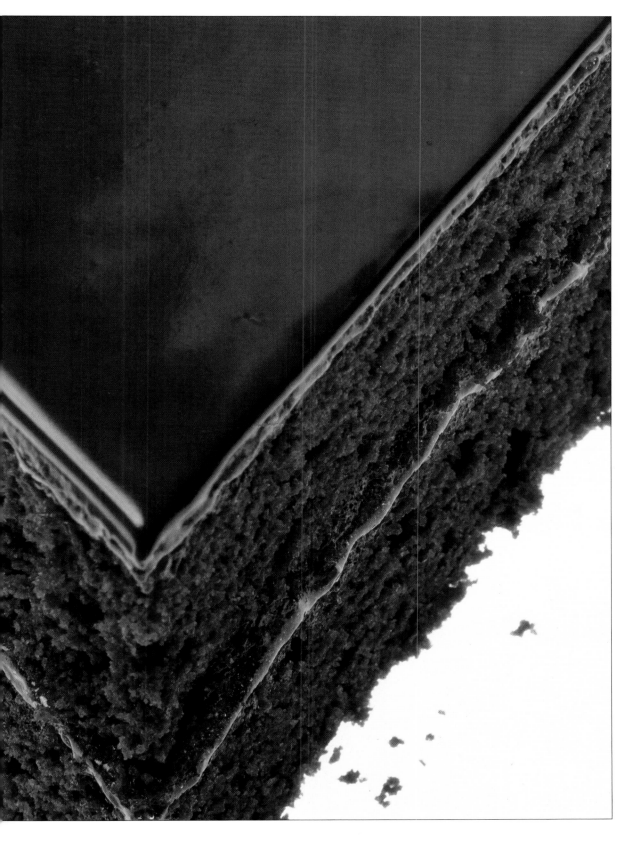

12. Cut the top of the cake flat and then cut in half across.

13. Spread both sponges with apricot jam and sandwich together. Cover the top with the marzipan round.

14. Chop the remaining chocolate and stir into the melted chocolate off the heat until it too has melted. By the time it is smooth it should be the right temperature.

15. Pour about half the chocolate on to the top of the cake, spreading it evenly with a long knife as you slowly turn the cake.

16. Cover the sides with the remaining chocolate.

17. Before the chocolate is completely set, warm a long knife on the top of the oven or in hot water, dry and cut the chocolate on the top to mark portions. This will prevent it breaking when the cake is cold and you cut it.

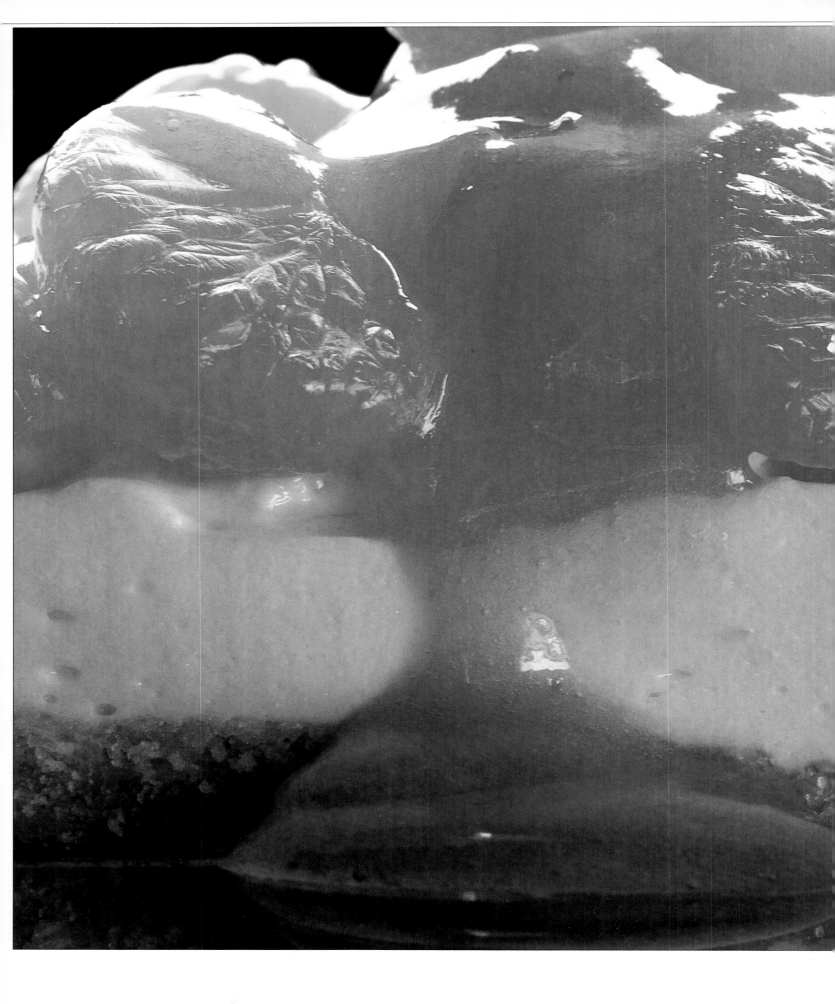

Shortcrust – the best
base for imaginative baking

Shortcrust pastry is one of the most versatile to use, it is crisp in texture yet delicious to eat. You need shortcrust for a wide variety of baking, from tasty mince pies which melt in the mouth to firm pies and flan cases, strong enough to take a heavy filling as in a cheesecake for instance.

Tips on pastry making

☐ Ingredients, hands and the work surface should be nice and cool. A marble slab is ideal to work on, as it is always cool.

☐ Use a fine sugar: a coarse-grained sugar makes brown specks in the pastry. Icing or caster sugar gives a really short, tender pastry.

☐ Don't worry too much if you can still see lumps of butter in the pastry. It is better to knead too little than too long!

☐ Always allow the pastry to rest before baking, preferably in the refrigerator. This makes it much easier to work with.

☐ The more sugar, the crisper the pastry, which is what you need for flans and tarts, but eat the pastry up quickly for the sugar absorbs moisture from the air or filling and makes the pastry soft.

☐ Omit sugar for savoury shortcrust.

☐ Before resting make the pastry into a ball to reduce the surface area and wrap in cling film or aluminium foil to prevent it drying out.

The delicious, tender pastry

Shortcrust is a kneaded mixture for, unlike sponge mixtures which are beaten, shortcrust is made using the hands. It is important that you should cool your hands before you start, preferably under cold running water. For heat can spoil shortcrust making it sticky and soft, and if you try to rescue the situation by adding extra flour, the pastry will then just be rock hard. Professional chefs tend to use their hands only in the final stages, first chopping the ingredients thoroughly with a large knife on the worktop. When the mixture has the consistency of coarse breadcrumbs it is quickly kneaded together with the hands. The best way to make shortcrust is by a combination of chopping and kneading.

Shortcrust is quick to make

Before baking it is essential to leave the pastry to rest for 30 minutes (in the refrigerator) to give it time to firm up and the gluten in the flour time to work.

Baking tips

☐ Shortcrust pastry is baked in a hot oven, (around 200–220C, 400–450F, gas 6–7) so that the sugar caramelises and makes the pastry brown and crisp.

☐ For tarts with moist fillings (fruit, custards, etc.) it is a good idea to bake the pastry case blind in advance (see pages 24–5). This makes it nice and crisp and prevents the moist filling making it soggy.

Preparation

1. Weigh the ingredients and chill before using.

2. Sift the flour into a pile on the work surface.

3. Use the tablespoon to make a well in the centre.

Basic recipe for shortcrust biscuits

Equipment
Sieve
Tablespoon
Large knife
Baking tray
Pastry brush
Rolling pin
Pastry cutter
Wire rack

Ingredients:

Makes 35

300 g/11 oz plain flour
100 g/4 oz caster sugar
1 egg
200 g/7 oz butter

Cooking time:

Preparation time:
45 minutes
Baking time:
10 minutes
Oven temperature
220 C, 425 F, gas 7

Storing

Shortcrust will keep in the refrigerator for up to a week. To freeze (it is excellent for this) wrap in an extra layer of aluminium foil. Defrost in the refrigerator to prevent it from becoming too soft.

4. Sprinkle the sugar into the well.

5. Break the egg into the mixture.

6. Cut the thoroughly chilled butter into small pieces.

7. Arrange the pieces of butter on the flour around the well.

8. Chop all the ingredients thoroughly with a large knife.

9. Using cool hands, work the small pieces quickly together.

10. Make the pastry into a ball, wrap in cling film and then chill for 30 minutes.

11. Meanwhile brush the baking tray with butter.

12. Sprinkle the baking tray evenly with flour.

13. Dust the ball of pastry and work surface with flour.

14. Roll the pastry out very thinly to about 3 mm/$\frac{1}{8}$ in thick.

15. Dip the pastry cutter in flour to prevent the pastry sticking.

16. Cut the rolled pastry into rounds.

17. Arrange the rounds of pastry side by side on the baking tray.

18. Bake in a hot oven (220 C, 425 F, gas 7) for 10 minutes, or until cooked.

Basic recipe for fruit flan case

Halve the ingredients given in the basic recipe for shortcrust biscuits and instead of a whole egg use only the yolk.

1. Make the pastry as shown in the step-by-step photographs and roll out very thinly to about 3–5 mm/$\frac{1}{8}$–$\frac{1}{4}$ in thick. Place the base of the flan tin on the pastry and cut round it.

2. Grease and flour the flan tin and place the round of pastry in it. Prick with a fork to prevent air bubbles forming as it bakes.

3. Shape the pastry offcuts into a roll and press around the sides of the tin.

4. Bake as detailed opposite, then leave to cool.

Note: A flat round of pastry can be used as the base of a fancy gâteau. It will make the cake less fragile and in addition this crisp base contrasts well with the light layers of cream and sponge.

The sun, moon and stars

Shortcrust is ideal for making biscuits. The process is quite easy and always follows the same method. Just roll the pastry out thinly, cut into the chosen shapes and cover or decorate either before or after baking depending on the type of biscuit. You can turn shortcrust into many different biscuits which are suitable for any occasion. Red hearts for a quiet romantic tea for two, stars for Christmas, little rabbits for Easter. You can make them in muted colours and delicate with a pastel coloured icing or, if you prefer, brightly coloured and striking. You can scatter them with chocolate chips, crystallised sugar, nuts, praline or candied fruit – the list is endless and the choice is yours.

Cherry crumble biscuits

Basic shortcrust recipe (page 103)
Crumble ingredients
100 g/4 oz plain flour
50 g/2 oz caster sugar
50 g/2 oz butter
To decorate:
1 egg yolk, beaten
20 glacé cherries, halved

1. Make the pastry and crumble from the basic recipes (see page 103 and page 107).
2. Roll out the pastry very thinly and cut into rounds.
3. Arrange on a greased baking tray, brush with egg yolk and scatter with the crumble. Place a glacé cherry half in the middle.
4. Bake in a hot oven (220C, 425F, gas 7) for 10 minutes, or until cooked.

Red hearts

Basic shortcrust recipe (page 103)
6 tablespoons cherry or beetroot juice
225 g/8 oz icing sugar

1. Make the pastry from the basic recipe (see page 103) and roll out very thinly to about 3 mm/⅛ in thick. Cut hearts of suitable size, or assorted sizes.
2. Bake the hearts in a hot oven (220C, 425F, gas 7) for about 10 minutes, or until cooked.
3. To make the icing reduce the juice (you need not worry about the icing tasting of beetroot!) to 3 to 4 tablespoons to increase the colour.
4. Stir in the icing sugar, mix well together and spread over the hearts.

Sugar and chocolate pretzels

Basic shortcrust recipe (page 103)
1 egg yolk, beaten
100 g/4 oz crystallised sugar
100 g/4 oz plain chocolate, melted

1. Make the pastry from the basic recipe (see page 103), roll out very thinly to about 3 mm/⅛ in thick and cut into pretzels.
2. Brush half the biscuits with egg yolk and then scatter with crystallised sugar.
3. Bake all the biscuits in a hot oven (220C, 425F, gas 7) for 10 minutes, or until cooked.
4. Brush the unsugared biscuits with the melted chocolate.

Jam rings

Basic shortcrust recipe
(page 103)

5 tablespoons

red currant or

blackcurrant jelly

3 tablespoons icing sugar

1. Make the shortcrust
from the basic recipe (see
page 103), and roll out
very thinly to about
3 mm/$\frac{1}{8}$ in thick and cut
into rounds with a zig-zag
edge.
2. Using a smaller round
fluted cutter cut a circle
from the centre of half
the rounds.
3. Bake rounds and rings
in a hot oven (220C,
425F, gas 7) for 10
minutes, or until cooked.
4. Spread the rounds with
blackcurrant jelly. Dust
the rings with icing sugar
and sandwich together.

Iced stars

Basic shortcrust recipe
(page 103)

1 egg yolk, beaten

3 tablespoons flaked

almonds

225 g/8 oz icing sugar

1 tablespoon water

sugar balls

$\frac{1}{2}$ teaspoon ground

cinnamon

1. Make the pastry from
the basic recipe (see page
103), and roll out thinly.
2. Brush one-third of the
stars with egg yolk and
scatter with the almonds.
3. Bake all the biscuits in
a hot oven (220C, 425F,
gas 7) for 10 minutes.
4. Coat half the remaining
biscuits with half the icing
made from the icing sugar
and water and scatter
with sugar balls.
5. Flavour the remaining
icing with the cinnamon
and spread on the
remaining biscuits.

Almond diamonds

Basic shortcrust recipe
(page 103)

2 egg yolks, beaten

225 g/8 oz blanched

almonds, split

1. Make the pastry from
the basic recipe (see page
103) and roll out very
thinly to about 3 mm/$\frac{1}{8}$ in
thick and cut into long
diamond shapes
(2.5 × 5 cm/1 × 2 in) using a
pastry wheel.
2. Brush with beaten egg
yolk and place a split
almond in the centre of
each.
3. Bake in a hot oven
(220C, 425F, gas 7) for 10
minutes, or until cooked.

Cocoa moons

Basic shortcrust recipe
(page 103)

3 tablespoons icing sugar

1 tablespoon cocoa

powder

1. Make the pastry from
the basic recipe (see page
103) and roll out very
thinly to about 3 mm/$\frac{1}{8}$ in
thick and cut into
crescent moons.
2. Bake in a hot oven
(220C, 425F, gas 7) for 10
minutes, or until cooked.
3. Mix the icing sugar
with the cocoa powder
and sprinkle on the
biscuits.

Pistachio trees and shooting stars

Basic shortcrust recipe
(page 103)

3 tablespoons water

225 g/8 oz icing sugar

a little extra icing sugar

red and green colouring

100 g/4 oz pistachio nuts,

chopped

1. Make the pastry from
the basic recipe (see page
103) and roll out very
thinly to about 3 mm/$\frac{1}{8}$ in
thick. Cut into fir tree
and shooting star shapes.
2. Bake in a hot oven
(220C, 425F, gas 7) for 10
minutes, or until cooked.
3. Stir the water into the
icing sugar until smooth,
spread on trees and stars.
4. Thicken remaining
icing with icing sugar.
Colour half red and half
green and use to pipe
round edges of biscuits.
5. Sprinkle with nuts.

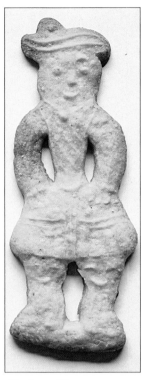

Other members of the shortcrust family

All variations of shortcrust pastry are impressive to use. The simplest among them are flavoured with nutmeg, cloves, cinnamon, cardamom, allspice, coriander or vanilla. Others not only vary in flavour but, by the addition of cocoa powder or finely chopped candied peel or finely grated lemon rind, take on a different colour too. Other types have added egg yolk or butter to make them more rich, extra sugar to make them crisper or are made with ground almonds or other nuts instead of flour to give them a nutty flavour. Although you might not think it, crumble is also a member of this family.

Spicy figures

500 g/18 oz plain flour

200 g/7 oz brown sugar

generous pinch of ground cloves

generous pinch of ground cardamom

1 teaspoon ground cinnamon

2 eggs

200 g/7 oz butter

100 g/4 oz ground hazelnuts

1. Make a shortcrust as in the basic recipe (see page 103).
2. Dip the gingerbread mould in flour and shake off excess.
3. Press the pastry into the mould and trim the edges.
4. Knock the mould to remove the spicy figures and arrange on a greased and floured baking tray.
5. Bake in a moderately hot oven (200 C, 400 F, gas 6) for 15 minutes, or until cooked.

Oatflake biscuits

Makes 50

250 g/9 oz butter

300 g/11 oz caster sugar

2 eggs

300 g/11 oz porridge oats

150 g/5 oz wholemeal flour

2 teaspoons baking powder

100 g/4 oz raisins

1. Work all the ingredients together until a soft dough is formed.
2. Using a teaspoon, spoon the mixture in small piles on to a greased and floured baking tray.
3. Bake in a moderately hot oven (200 C, 400 F, gas 6) for 15 minutes, or until cooked.

Vanilla moon biscuits

125 g/4½ oz caster sugar
200 g/7 oz butter
250 g/9 oz plain flour
200 g/7 oz ground almonds
2 egg yolks
pith of 1 vanilla pod or 1 sachet vanilla sugar
3 tablespoons icing sugar

1. Make up a shortcrust as in the basic recipe (see page 103), adding ground almonds.
2. Shape into rolls 2.5 cm/1 in thick and cut into 1-cm/½-in lengths.
3. Shape the lengths into crescents. Bake in a hot oven (220C, 425F, gas 7) for about 10 minutes until just beginning to colour.
4. Mix the pith of the vanilla pod with the icing sugar on a plate.
5. Coat the warm biscuits in the sugar mixture.

Butter biscuits

250 g/9 oz butter
200 g/7 oz caster sugar
pinch of salt
2 tablespoons milk
400 g/14 oz plain flour
100 g/4 oz caster sugar

1. Heat the butter in a saucepan on medium heat until light brown in colour. Pour into a mixing bowl and leave to cool. When it has set beat until light and fluffy, adding the sugar, salt and the milk.
2. Finally work in the flour until a dough is formed and chill.
3. Take out of the refrigerator and shape into a roll 2.5 cm/1 in thick, coat in the caster sugar and chill for a further 20 minutes.
4. Cut into slices and then bake in a moderately hot oven (200C, 400F, gas 6) for 10 minutes.

Crumble

300 g/11 oz plain flour
150 g/5 oz caster sugar
1 egg yolk
generous pinch of ground cinnamon
150 g/5 oz butter

1. Work all the ingredients together with your fingers to make a coarse breadcrumb mixture. Sprinkle on to cakes or biscuits as a topping.

Checkered biscuits

150 g/5 oz caster sugar
150 g/5 oz butter
300 g/11 oz plain flour
1 egg
1 teaspoon cocoa powder
1 egg white

1. Make a shortcrust from the basic recipe (see page 103). Keep a small amount to one side.
2. Work the cocoa powder into half the remaining dough.
3. Roll the pastry out thinly to about 5 mm/¼ in thick and cut both the doughs into rectangles.
4. Brush the light-coloured dough with egg white and cover with the dark dough.
5. Cut exactly into 5-mm/2¼-in strips.
6. Thinly roll the dough kept to one side and on it arrange the dark and light strips in a checkered pattern, sticking them in place with egg white.
7. Wrap the rolled dough around the strips. Chill.
8. Cut into 5-mm/¼-in slices and bake in a moderately hot oven (200C, 400F, gas 6) for 10 minutes.

Almond biscuits

100 g/4 oz caster sugar
225 g/8 oz butter
350 g/12 oz plain flour
1 egg
For the topping:
100 g/4 oz caster sugar
2 tablespoons butter
6 tablespoons single cream
100 g/4 oz flaked almonds
2 tablespoons chopped glacé cherries

1. Make a shortcrust from the basic recipe (see page 103) and roll out very thinly. Use to cover a greased and floured baking tray and prick with a fork.
2. Slowly brown the sugar in a pan, remove from the heat and stir in the butter, cream, almonds and cherries and spread over the pastry.
3. Bake in a moderately hot oven (200C, 400F, gas 6) for 15 minutes.
4. Cut into diamond shapes while still warm.

Tree biscuits

200 g/7 oz icing sugar
2 eggs
250 g/9 oz plain flour
generous pinch of baking powder
1–2 tablespoons aniseed

1. Make the shortcrust pastry as the basic recipe (see page 103) and work the ingredients into a firm dough.
2. Roll the pastry out to 1 cm/½ in thick.
3. Dip a tree mould in flour, shake off any excess and then press on to the pastry. Cut round the mould.
4. Sprinkle the aniseed on to a buttered and floured baking tray and arrange the shapes on the sheet.
5. Leave to dry in a warm room for 48 hours.
6. Place in a very cool oven (120C, 250F, gas ½) for 2 hours to dry out the biscuits, turning them over after 1½ hours. On no account allow them to get any colour.

Delicious pastry cases for creams and fruits

Tartlets are delicious with tea or coffee and are really quick and easy to make. Crisp pastry cases, either round or boat-shaped, can be frozen until required for baking. They will also keep for several weeks in a tin with a close-fitting lid. Fill with whipped cream or make a vanilla or chocolate custard and top with fresh or canned fruit covered with apricot jam or a flan glaze to give an attractive shine and you will have a delicious treat to offer visitors.

Tartlets

Makes 8 to 10:

100 g / 4 oz caster sugar
225 g / 8 oz butter
350 g / 12 oz plain flour
1 egg
butter for greasing
flour for sprinkling
pulses for baking blind
(see pages 24–5)

1. Make up the pastry using the ingredients as the basic recipe (see page 103).
2. Grease and flour tartlet tins.
3. Roll the pastry out very thinly to about 3 mm / $\frac{1}{8}$ in thick and use to line the tins (see pages 24–5).
4. Line with non-stick baking parchment or aluminium foil and weigh down with pulses.
5. Bake in a moderately hot oven (200 C, 400 F, gas 6) for 15 minutes. Tip out the pulses and remove the paper. Remove the cases from the tins and cool on a wire rack.

Illustrated
An assortment of different tarts to tempt you (clockwise from the left): *Kiwi tarts* with vanilla custard. *Mandarin tarts* with Canache cream (see page 236) and praline. *Mango and papaya boats* with cream. *Strawberry boats* with vanilla custard. *Orange tarts* with vanilla custard and maraschino cherries.

French apple flan

300 g/11 oz plain flour
1 tablespoon caster sugar
1 teaspoon salt
200 g/7 oz butter
1 egg
1 kg/2¼ lb cooking apples,
peeled, halved and cored
2 tablespoons icing sugar,
for dusting

1. Make the pastry as in the basic recipe (see page 103).
2. Line a pie, flan or shallow cake tin with pastry and prick several times with a fork.
3. Cut the apples into thin wedges.
4. Arrange slightly over-lapping in the flan case to give an attractive pattern.
5. Sprinkle with the icing sugar and bake in a very hot oven (240 C, 475 F, gas 9) for 15 to 20 minutes.
6. Serve hot dusted with icing sugar.

Fruit flans, just as the French make them

These world-famous flans are really delicious – a thin, crisp, buttery pastry topped with sliced fruit and baked in a hot oven. Don't worry if the pastry becomes dark in colour or the edges of the fruit almost black – this is just as it should be. The flan is finally dusted with icing sugar before eating hot from the oven. The French love to eat it as a dessert after a light meal. (See also Puff-pastry flans pages 176–7).

Tarte Tatin

For an unusual and striking dessert try an upside-down flan, an idea invented by the Tatin sisters in northern France, from whom the flan takes its name: Tarte Tatin.

If you haven't got a flan tin you can cook it in a frying pan. A springform tin is no good since the juice would escape at the joins.

First caramelise 4 tablespoons caster sugar in an equal amount of butter and pour into flan tins. Arrange peeled and cored apple quarters in a single layer in the tin, standing on the rounded side. Cook on the hob for a while to start the apples off, then cover with a thin sheet of shortcrust pastry. Bake in a moderately hot oven (190C, 375F, gas 5) for 30 to 35 minutes. Turn out of the tin immediately and eat hot. You can make upside-down flans with other fruit such as pears, peaches and apricots in just the same way.

Variations:
You can use any fruit suitable for baking. You can replace the apples with pears, peaches, apricots, plums or damsons, for instance.

Tastes good and looks nice: Before baking sprinkle the fruit with flaked or chopped almonds or glaze after baking with some warmed apricot jam.
For a more filling flan arrange the fruit on a layer of vanilla custard.

The delicious cheesecake

If you can make a good cheesecake you will be loved – there is no doubt about that. No other cake has quite as many fans as this one! Admittedly it's not that simple to make a perfect cheesecake. Usually they rise beautifully in the oven, but can fall again once you have turned your back. So here is a tip which guarantees your cheesecake won't collapse: exactly half way through the baking time, take the cake out of the oven, run a pointed knife between the edge and the filling, leave to stand for 5 minutes and then put it back in the oven to finish baking. That's all you need do, except to accept the compliments of your guests!

Cheesecake

100 g/4 oz caster sugar

225 g/8 oz butter

350 g/12 oz plain flour

1 egg

butter and flour for the tin

pulses for baking blind

For the filling:

450 g/1 lb curd cheese

175 g/6 oz caster sugar

3 teaspoons vanilla sugar

200 g/7 oz sugar

grated rind of 1 lemon

1 tablespoon each plain flour and cornflour

6 eggs, separated

50 g/2 oz butter, melted

1. Make the pastry using the basic recipe (see page 103).
2. Use to line a greased and floured 23-cm/9-in springform tin.
3. Bake the pastry case blind (see pages 24–5) in a moderately hot oven (190C, 375F, gas 5) for 15 minutes. Then remove the beans and greaseproof paper and bake for a further 10 minutes. This keeps it crisp despite the moist filling.
4. To make the filling, beat together the curd cheese, 150 g/5 oz of the sugar, vanilla sugar, lemon rind, flour, cornflour and egg yolks.
5. Whisk the egg whites with the remaining sugar until stiff and fold gently into the filling with the melted butter.
6. Pour into the pre-baked pastry case. Bake in a moderate oven (180C, 350F, gas 4) for about 50 to 60 minutes.
7. Leave the cake in the tin to cool on a wire rack.

Cherry cheesecake

Boil Morello cherries to make a compôte (see page 77), thicken with cornflour and spread in the pre-baked pastry case. Cover with the cheesecake filling above and bake as detailed.

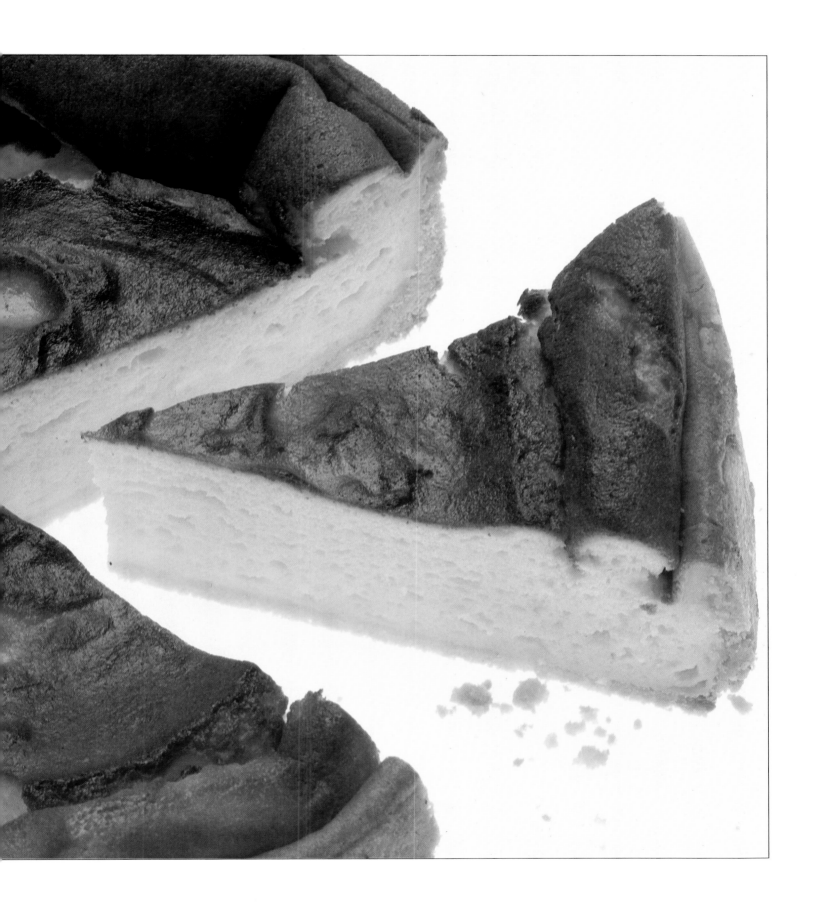

A shortcrust that needs no kneading

Piped cakes

200 g/7 oz soft butter
100 g/4 oz caster sugar
1 egg
6 tablespoons milk
200 g/7 oz plain flour
100 g/4 oz cornflour
butter and flour to grease and dust

1. Whisk the butter, sugar, egg and milk until light and fluffy.
2. Stir in the flour and cornflour, but do not stir too long or the mixture will become tacky.
3. Spoon the mixture into a piping bag (or mincer with piping attachment or a piping tube). Pipe through a fluted nozzle directly on to a greased and floured baking tray.
4. Bake in a moderately hot oven at (190C, 375F, gas 5) for 10 minutes.

This is a different shortcrust mixture that needs no kneading. It contains so much milk that it is easier to mix with a hand whisk. And instead of being rolled out, it is piped. A fluted nozzle gives the strips of mixture an attractive zig-zag effect and you can pipe it into rings, S-shapes, whirls or straight lines.

Tips on decorating:

Piped cakes are more attractive if you decorate them before or after baking, sandwich them together or ice them.
Before baking:
☐ Decorate with pieces of glacé cherry, almond or pistachio halves or scatter with crystallised sugar.
After baking:
☐ Coat one or both ends or all over in chocolate, hazelnut or nougat icing. Before the icing dries scatter with sugar balls, coloured sugar crystals or chopped nuts.
☐ Sandwich together with melted nougat or jam and then coat with more icing, if liked.

Yeast cakes – memories of summer and childhood

The dough that should only go up

Yeast

It must be fresh. You can recognise this by its silky sheen and fresh, sourish smell and the fact that it breaks to give a flat surface. Yeast is usually bought compressed into small cubes (40 g/1½ oz) or as small cakes. Any that you don't need immediately can be frozen for up to three months. Dried yeast in sachets is also very successful and is practical as it keeps for up to a year.

How yeast works

Yeast cells are tiny, living organisms, which need air, warmth, moisture and food if they are to increase. This produces fermentation in which carbonic acid and alcohol are released causing many small bubbles which make the dough rise and more than double its volume. Cold and too much heat are death to the yeast bacteria, so the milk into which you stir it must be exactly hand-hot (35 C/ 95 F). Salt, sugar and butter should not be added directly to yeast as this would halt its effectiveness.

Most people have a healthy respect for yeast dough. It is generally thought to be difficult or tricky to prepare. In fact it is child's play to make providing you have the three essentials – plenty of time, a nice warm kitchen and a little knowledge about that living organism – yeast. The first two are easy and the third will be provided for you here.

Yeast dough variations

For the various types of yeast dough you will need varying amounts of yeast, butter, eggs and flour. Here you can see at a glance what you need.

	Plait	Stollen	Brioche	Sweet yeast dough	Savarin
Flour	500 g/18 oz	375 g/13 oz	500 g/18 oz	475 g/17 oz	500 g/18 oz
Yeast	40 g/1½ oz	40 g/1½ oz	20 g/¾ oz	30 g/1¼ oz	40 g/1½ oz
Sugar	50 g/2 oz	75 g/3 oz	60 g/2¼ oz	90 g/3½ oz	60 g/2¼ oz
Eggs	2	1	6	2	5
Milk	250 ml/18 fl oz	6 tablespoons	4 tablespoons	8 tablespoons	250 ml/18 fl oz
Butter	–	150 g/5 oz	400 g/14 oz	90 g/3½ oz	150 g/5 oz

Tips before you start

☐ Have even heating and keep the doors and windows closed! An even room temperature of 21 C/70 F is ideal.
☐ Take all the ingredients out of the refrigerator in good time to allow them to come to room temperature.
☐ Work on a pastry board rather than a marble slab. The cold stone would prevent the yeast working properly.

Second method

The classic method of making yeast dough is shown in the step-by-step photographs on the opposite page, but there is a second method which is easier but more time-consuming. Here all the ingredients are mixed at the same time in a food processor. The dough is made into a ball and placed in a floured bowl, covered with a cloth and left in the refrigerator to rise. After 4 hours the dough is given a vigorous kneading to give the yeast cells air. After a further 4 hours the dough is ready to be used.

Preparation

Equipment
Sieve
Pan
Tablespoon
Rolling pin
Baking tray

Ingredients:

500 g / 18 oz plain flour	
40 g / 1½ oz fresh yeast	
60 g / 2¼ oz sugar	
pinch of salt	
2 eggs	
250 ml / 8 fl oz milk	
50 g / 2 oz butter, cut into	
flakes	
for a sweet dough:	
50 g / 2 oz butter	
40 g / 1½ oz sugar	

Cooking time:

Preparation: 20 minutes	
Resting: 3–4 hours	
Baking: 20 minutes	
Oven temperature: 180–	
200 C, 350–400 F, gas 4–6	
Cooling: 10–20 minutes	

Storing

Yeast dough keeps for a day in the refrigerator and will freeze for 2 to 5 months depending on fat content. *After baking.* Always eat fresh. To store, freeze while still lukewarm. Then thaw at room temperature and quickly reheat in a hot oven.

Note: If using dried yeast, sprinkle the yeast over the milk in step 4. Leave in a warm place until dissolved and frothy.

1. Measure the ingredients and bring to room temperature.

2. Sift the flour into a large mixing bowl.

3. In a saucepan warm the milk over a low heat.

4. Crumble the yeast into the lukewarm milk or if using dried yeast see note.

5. Add 4 tablespoons flour and stir to a thick paste.

6. Add a pinch of sugar.

7. Cover the pan and leave the yeast starter to rise for 30 minutes.

8. Mix the flour with the sugar and salt and make a well in the centre.

9. Break the eggs into the well.

10. Add the butter flakes to the flour.

11. Pour on the yeast starter from the pan.

12. Work all the ingredients together to give a smooth dough.

13. Cover and leave to rise for 30 minutes or until doubled in size.

14. Knead through once more vigorously.

15. Roll the dough out thinly on a floured work surface.

16. Carefully transfer to a greased and floured baking tray.

17. For a sweet dough, dot with butter, leave for a further 15 minutes.

18. Sprinkle the top evenly with sugar.

19. Place the tray in the moderately hot oven (200 C, 400 F, gas 6).

20. After 20 minutes remove from the oven and allow to cool.

Tray yeast cakes

These will bring back childhood memories of delicious-smelling yeast cakes from the baking tray, scattered with sweet crumble or caramelised almonds.
You'll be reminded of hectic birthday parties with musical chairs and blind man's buff. For baking-tray cakes are ideal when there are a lot of hungry mouths to feed. But of course that doesn't mean that these delicious cakes are only for the children . . .

Butter cake

(illustrated top)

1 basic yeast dough recipe (page 119)
250 g / 9 oz butter, cut into flakes
5 tablespoons sugar
3 tablespoons flaked almonds

1. Make up a yeast dough from the basic recipe (see pages 118–9). Roll out and cover a greased and floured baking tray.
2. Spread the butter flakes evenly over the dough. Leave to rise for 10 minutes.
3. Scatter with sugar and flaked almonds.
4. Bake in a moderately hot oven (200 C, 400 F, gas 6) for 30 minutes.

Crumble cake

(illustrated bottom)

1 basic yeast dough recipe (page 119)
300 g / 11 oz plain flour
150 g / 5 oz butter
150 g / 5 oz sugar
1 egg yolk
generous pinch of ground cinnamon

1. Make a yeast dough using the basic recipe (see pages 118–9). Roll out and cover a greased and floured baking tray.
2. Mix all the other ingredients together to make a crumble.
3. Spread evenly over the dough and leave to rise for 10 minutes.
4. Bake in a moderately hot oven (200 C, 400 F, gas 6) for 25 minutes.

Almond cake

*1 basic yeast dough recipe
(page 119)*
150 g/5 oz butter
100 g/4 oz sugar
250 ml/8 fl oz single cream
*300 g/11 oz chopped or
flaked almonds*

1. Make the dough from
the basic recipe (see pages
118–9), and roll out and
place on a greased and
floured baking tray.
2. Melt the butter in a
saucepan over a low heat.
3. Dissolve the sugar in
the butter but do not
brown.
4. Add the cream and
bring to the boil.
5. Add the almonds, leave
to cool slightly and spread
over the dough.
6. Bake in a moderate
oven (180 C, 350 F, gas 4)
for 30 minutes.

Variation:
Almond cake is delicious
with a filling of butter
cream (see page 231) or
vanilla custard (see page
237). Cut the cake into
individual pieces and cut
through each piece.
Sandwich the two halves
together with the cream
mixture.

Yeast dough snails

(illustrated page 45)
*1 basic yeast dough recipe
(page 119)*
250 g/9 oz marzipan
250 ml/8 fl oz milk
100 g/4 oz raisins
*50 g/2 oz chopped mixed
peel*
1 egg yolk for glazing

1. Make the yeast dough
as in the basic recipe.
2. Mix the marzipan with
the milk and stir to give a
smooth paste.
3. Roll the dough to
about 1 cm/$\frac{1}{2}$ in thick and
spread with the creamy
marzipan.
4. Scatter over the raisins
and peel.
5. Roll up the dough.
6. Cut the roll into 1-cm/
$\frac{1}{2}$-in slices and place side
by side on a greased and
floured baking tray.
7. Brush the yeast dough
snails with the egg yolk
and bake in a moderate
oven (180 C, 350 F, gas 4)
for 15 to 20 minutes.

The toast of the summer

The summer is a glorious time for an abundance of fruit – of all types. Fruit flans are therefore ideal to make in the summer months and can be a tantalising addition to a summer dinner or buffet party. Choose whatever fruit there is plenty of and get ready for the admiration that is going to come your way!

Tips on the dough

☐ If you prefer a thin, crispy base rather than a soft, crumbly one, halve the ingredients given in the basic yeast dough recipe (see page 119).
☐ To prevent the base being made too soft because of the juicy fruit, it should be sprinkled with breadcrumbs or ground nuts before you add the fruit.
☐ Vanilla custard, spread on the base under the fruit, also serves the same purpose.

Plum flan

1 basic yeast dough recipe (page 119)
4 tablespoons breadcrumbs
2 kg/4½ lb plums, halved and stoned
6 tablespoons sugar
½ teaspoon ground cinnamon

1. Make the dough from the basic recipe (see page 119), and roll out and place on a greased and floured baking tray.
2. Sprinkle all over with breadcrumbs and leave the dough to rise for 10 minutes.
3. Lay the plums skin-side down, close together on the dough.
4. Mix the sugar and cinnamon together and sprinkle on the plums.
5. Bake in a moderate oven (180 C, 350 F, gas 4) for 45 minutes, or until cooked.

Decorating a fruit flan

There are a few simple ways of making a fresh-baked fruit flan look even more appetising. Ring the changes by sprinkling the cooked flan with crystallised sugar (photograph 1), ground cinnamon or icing sugar, or cover with a flan glaze (photograph 7) or icing (photograph 5). Stir together 250 g/9 oz icing sugar and 4 tablespoons water. Add extra flavour by covering with a jam glaze. To make this boil up 400 g/14 oz red currant jelly (photograph 2) or apricot jam (photograph 9) with 2 tablespoons sugar and 3 tablespoons water for 4 minutes. Pour hot on to the baked flan.

Extra touches before baking

Before baking sprinkle fruit with:
— raisins soaked in rum (photograph 3)
— flaked almonds (photograph 8)
— grated coconut (photograph 6)
— crumble (see page 107, photograph 4)
— meringue (see pages 224–5)
— peanuts
— pistachio nuts
— pine nuts
— oatflakes cooked in butter and sugar

Apple flan

1 basic yeast dough recipe (page 119)
2.5 kg/5½ lb cooking apples, peeled, cored and quartered
lemon juice
2 tablespoons sugar
½ teaspoon ground cinnamon
4 tablespoons rum
100 g/4 oz raisins
50 g/2 oz flaked almonds

1. Make the dough as in the basic recipe (see page 119), roll out thinly and place on a greased and floured baking tray and leave to rise for 10 minutes.
2. Cut the apple quarters into thin segments and dip in lemon juice to stop them discolouring.
3. Arrange the apples on the dough and sprinkle with sugar and cinnamon.
4. Finally scatter with rum-soaked raisins and flaked almonds.
5. Leave the flan to rise for a further 30 minutes and then bake in a moderate oven (180 C, 350 F, gas 4) for 30 minutes or until cooked.

A firmly established favourite from Switzerland

Cherry flan

(First photograph)

$\frac{1}{2}$ basic yeast dough recipe (see page 119)

butter to grease tin

400 g/14 oz Morello cherries, stoned

2 eggs

6 tablespoons single cream

2 tablespoons sugar

$\frac{1}{4}$ teaspoon ground cinnamon

50 g/2 oz icing sugar for dusting

1. Make the dough as in the basic recipe (see page 119) and roll out to about 1 cm/$\frac{1}{2}$ in thick.
2. Grease a shallow 25–cm/10–in tin (pizza tin or pie plate) with butter and cover with the dough.
3. Spread the cherries over the dough.

4. Beat together the eggs, cream, sugar and cinnamon and pour over the cherries.
5. Bake in a moderate oven (180 C, 350 F, gas 4) for 40 minutes. Dust with icing sugar and eat straightaway.

The Swiss have their own recipe for fruit flans which would satisfy
even the heartiest appetites. Why not try making one for a change
and see how your family and friends ask for it again and again.

Cranberry flan

(Second photograph)
Use 400 g/14 oz fresh
cranberries (not bottled).
Wash and sort them and
dry well. Spread over the
basic dough mixture (see
page 119) and pour on the
egg and cream mixture.
For a sweeter flan
sprinkle with extra sugar
before adding the egg
mixture.

Pear flan

(Third photograph)
Peel and halve 400 g/14 oz
pears and remove the
cores using a potato
peeler. Place the pears,
rounded side uppermost
on the basic dough
mixture (see page 119).
For extra colour you can
place a few bilberries or
red currants at the
centre. Pour on the egg
and cream mixture and
bake as in the basic
recipe.

Bilberry flan

(Fourth photograph)
Sort 400 g/14 oz bilberries
carefully and pull off any
stalks and leaves. Wash
and drain the fruit and pat
dry with kitchen paper.
Then spread on the basic
dough mixture (see page
119), cover with the egg
mixture and bake as in
the basic recipe.

The cake with the funny name

The Guglhupf is the famous German yeast cake which is baked in a special tin, round and deep with fluted sides and a chimney in the middle. The effect is to distribute the heat evenly even at the centre.

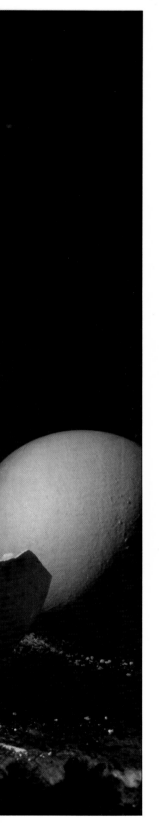

Where the cake comes from

The Guglhupf originates somewhere in southern Germany or Austria. It did not, however, reach France by this route but, as the *Larousse gastronomique* tells us, from the friendship between Carême and the personal chef to the then Austrian ambassador Schwarzenberg.

The name itself seems to come from the shape of the cake which is round and tall like a cone ('Kegel' in German) – in southern Germany a hill of similar shape is called a 'Kogel'. The -hopf or -hupf part derives from 'Hüpfen' (to jump) and probably refers to the way the yeast rises.

Guglhupf

500 g/18 oz plain flour	
40 g/1½ oz fresh yeast or	
20 g/¾ oz dried yeast	
60 g/2¼ oz sugar	
pinch of salt	
3 eggs	
250 ml/8 fl oz milk	
For the filling:	
200 g/7 oz raisins	
6 tablespoons rum	
100 g/4 oz blanched	
almonds	
50 g/2 oz icing sugar	

1. From the first set of ingredients make a yeast dough as in the basic recipe (see page 119).
2. Soak the raisins in the rum.
3. Coarsely chop the almonds.
4. On a floured worktop roll the dough into a rectangle about 2 cm/¾ in thick. Scatter with the raisins and almonds. Gently roll up from the long side.
5. Place the roll of dough in a ring in the greased and floured tin. Cover with a cloth and leave to rise for 1 hour.

6. Bake in a moderate oven (180 C, 350 F, gas 4) for 50 to 60 minutes.
7. Turn the cake out hot on to a plate and dust with icing sugar. For the best results eat while still hot.

Guglhupf variations

The Guglhupf in our basic recipe is neutral in flavour. It can be eaten for tea or even breakfast with butter and a little jam, or just as it comes with a glass of wine.

If you prefer a sweet Guglhupf you can vary the filling mixtures, replacing the raisins and almonds in the basic recipe with:

1. *Candied peel*
100 g/4 oz raisins
50 g/2 oz each chopped candied orange and lemon peel.

2. *Marzipan*
200 g/7 oz marzipan, diluted with 250 ml/8 fl oz milk and an extra 100 g/4 oz coarsely chopped almonds.

3. *Nuts*
200 g/7 oz chopped walnuts with 2 teaspoons ground ginger, 5 tablespoons rum and 4 tablespoons sugar.

Stollen – the ideal cake for winter

Stollen is the popular German fruit cake which is traditionally served at Christmas. Like the British Christmas cake it should be made a few weeks before Christmas to let the flavours really develop. Wrap the cake in foil and the cake will keep nice and moist.

Christmas stollen

Makes 2:

1 kg/2¼ lb plain flour
90 g/3½ oz fresh yeast or
45 g/1¾ oz dried yeast
100 g/4 oz sugar
pinch of salt
2 eggs
375 ml/13 fl oz milk
500 g/18 oz butter
½ teaspoon ground cinnamon
½ teaspoon ground cardamom

For the filling:
300 g/11 oz raisins
6 tablespoons rum
200 g/7 oz almonds, chopped
100 g/4 oz candied lemon peel
100 g/4 oz candied orange peel
100 g/4 oz melted butter for coating
100 g/4 oz icing sugar for dusting

1. Make a yeast dough following the basic recipe (see page 119) and knead in the cinnamon and cardamom.
2. Soak the raisins in the rum.
3. Roll the dough out to about 2 cm/¾ in thick and scatter with the drained raisins, almonds and candied peel. Roll up and then knead lightly to distribute the ingredients evenly but prevent the dough being discoloured by the raisins. Divide into two halves. Shape each half into a loaf shape, cover and leave to rise for 20 minutes.
4. Then give each loaf the typical stollen shape by running a wooden skewer along the centre and rolling one side flat. Fold the flat side over the other side and press down.
5. Place the two stollen on a greased and floured baking tray, cover once more and leave to rise until doubled in size.
6. Bake in a moderate oven (180C, 350F, gas 4) for 1¼ to 1½ hours.
7. While still hot brush the stollen with melted butter and then dust thickly with icing sugar.

Wrap tightly in aluminium foil and keep for two to four weeks before eating.
8. Before cutting to serve dust once again with icing sugar.

The brioche shape

A typical brioche is relatively narrow in diameter but rises high above the sides of the tin with a small ball on top. The tin in which it is baked gives it the attractive fluted sides. The brioche tins are available in a variety of sizes, but all have sides that slope steeply outwards.

If you don't have a brioche tin you can bake the dough in a loaf tin, without the ball on top, of course! Instead of this make a deep slit along the top of the dough to allow the brioche to rise fully.

Tips on the dough

☐ Always use absolutely fresh butter, preferably unsalted for this gives the best flavour.

☐ The brioche will have the best consistency if you let it rise slowly, ideally overnight in the refrigerator.

☐ The dough is excellent for freezing but, because of the high butter content, it should not be kept for longer than 1 month. Defrost slowly in the refrigerator for 24 hours before using. Then knead through and bake as given.

☐ Baked brioches should be lukewarm when frozen. Thaw slowly and quickly crisp up in the oven.

One of the best yeast cakes

Made from a yeast dough that is rich in butter and eggs, a brioche can be a superb cake, tender, crumbly and with an incomparable flavour. The brioche is neither sweet nor savoury. It can be eaten with just a knob of butter or a spoonful of jam for breakfast. For tea it goes well with fresh or stewed fruit. Serve it plain with pâté, an elegant salad or a fine ragoût instead of the normal toast.

Brioche

Makes 12 individual brioches or 1 large one:

350 g / 12 oz plain flour	
15 g / ½ oz fresh yeast or	
7 g / ¼ oz dried yeast	
25 g / 1 oz sugar	
3 tablespoons milk	
3 eggs	
pinch of salt	
175 g / 6 oz butter	
1 beaten egg yolk for glazing	

1. Make a yeast dough using the flour, yeast, sugar, milk, eggs and salt, as in the basic recipe (see page 119).
2. Knead the butter with the ball of your hand on the work surface (remember to take it out of the refrigerator in good time!).
3. Work the butter a little at a time into the dough, kneading it vigorously to incorporate air.
4. Shape the dough into a ball, place in a floured bowl, cover with a tea-towel and leave to rise for about 1 hour.
5. Sprinkle the work top thickly with flour and knead the dough once more. Cut off a quarter of the dough.
6. To make the large brioche, shape both pieces of dough into a ball. For individual brioches make each piece into 12 small balls.
7. Place the large ball in the buttered and floured tin and, using your fingers, make a hollow in the centre.
8. Make the small ball into a pear-shape and place in the hollow. This gives the brioche its typical shape.
9. Leave to rise for a further hour under a tea-towel and then brush with beaten egg yolk.
10. Bake in a moderate oven (180C, 350F, gas 4) for 45 to 50 minutes until golden brown. Bake individual brioches for just 20 minutes.
11. Turn the brioches out of the tin and serve lukewarm.

Spicy sausage in brioche

(large photograph)
Served hot in slices, this makes an unusual starter or snack with aperitifs. Wrap a spicy continental sausage in brioche dough (see opposite). Bake in a loaf tin in a moderate oven (180C, 350F, gas 4) for 50 minutes.

The most refined of desserts

Savarin

Baked in a large, round, smooth-sided savarin tin.

500 g / 18 oz plain flour
40 g / 1½ oz fresh yeast or
20 g / ¾ oz dried yeast
60 g / 2¼ oz sugar
250 ml / 8 fl oz milk
pinch of salt
5 eggs
150 g / 5 oz butter
For the filling:
100 g / 4 oz sugar
250 ml / 8 fl oz water
250 ml / 8 fl oz cherry brandy or rum
100 g / 4 oz apricot jam
6 tablespoons water
1 tablespoon sugar
450 g / 1 lb strawberries
1 tablespoon icing sugar

1. Make the dough from the ingredients as in the basic recipe (see page 119) and bake in the greased and floured tin in a moderately hot oven (200 C, 400 F, gas 6) for 40 minutes.

2. Meanwhile make a syrup with the sugar and water and add the alcohol.

3. Soak the hot savarin with the syrup. Bring the apricot jam to the boil in a saucepan with the water and sugar and spread over the savarin.

4. Before serving fill the centre with the fruit and dust with icing sugar.

When you are entertaining, time is often at a premium and you can often best save time with the dessert, providing you bear two things in mind. It must be suitable for preparing in advance, and it must be so attractive as to bring cries of admiration from your guests when you carry it in. Why not try it with these recipes:

Babas

(illustrated pages 48–9)
These are made like the savarin, but are baked in plain, individual, cylindrical tins (known as timbales).

Makes 10:
Make up the dough as for the Savarin recipe (opposite)

150 g/5 oz raisins

6 tablespoons rum

1. Soak the raisins in the rum and then work into the dough. Bake in the buttered and floured tins in a moderate oven (180C, 350F, gas 4) for 30 minutes.
2. Soak in the babas in cherry brandy syrup and cover with jam as for the savarin (see opposite).
3. Serve with strawberries or other fruit of your choice and cream.

Variations:
— When the babas are freshly glazed with jam sprinkle with icing sugar, flaked almonds, coarsely chopped pistachios or walnuts.
— Try filling the savarin with other fruit: raspberries, bilberries, blackberries, red currants, stewed rhubarb, pineapple, peaches or apricots will all be suitable.

Yeast plait

500 g / 18 oz plain flour

40 g / 1½ oz fresh yeast or

20 g / ¾ oz dried yeast

50 g / 2 oz sugar

pinch of salt

2 eggs

250 ml / 8 fl oz milk

For the filling:

50 g / 2 oz candied lemon

peel, chopped

50 g / 2 oz candied orange

peel, chopped

1 beaten egg yolk for

glazing

I. Make a yeast dough as in the basic recipe (see page 119), working in the candied peel.
2. Divide the dough into three pieces and make each into a roll, 20 cm / 8 in long.
3. Plait the strands and then leave to rise on a greased and floured baking tray, covered by a tea-towel, for 1½ hours.
4. Brush the top of the dough with the beaten egg and bake in a moderate oven (180 C, 350 F, gas 4) for 40 minutes.

Poppy seed twist

1 quantity yeast dough, as

for Yeast plait (see left)

For the filling:

750 ml / 1¼ pints milk

100 g / 4 oz caster sugar

175 g / 6 oz ground poppy

seeds

3 tablespoons raisins

3 egg yolks

50 g / 2 oz icing sugar

I. Make the yeast dough as in the basic recipe (see page 119).
2. Bring the milk to the boil with the sugar and sprinkle in the poppy seeds. Boil up once to thicken. Add the raisins and egg yolks, take off the heat and cool.
3. Roll the dough out to a 25 × 35 cm / 10 × 14 in rectangle and cut in half lengthways.
4. Spread both pieces with the poppy seed mixture and roll in from the sides.
5. Twist together into a spiral. Cover and leave to rise for 1 hour.
6. Place on a greased baking tray and bake in a moderate oven (180 C, 350 F, gas 4) for 45 minutes. Dust with icing sugar.

Nut plait

1 quantity yeast dough, as

for Yeast plait (see left)

For the filling:

300 g / 11 oz hazelnuts,

coarsely chopped

50 g / 2 oz walnuts,

chopped

50 g / 2 oz breadcrumbs

100 g / 4 oz caster sugar

6 tablespoons rum

2 tablespoons water

100 g / 4 oz icing sugar

I. Make a yeast dough as in the basic recipe (see page 119).
2. Mix the other ingredients together for the filling.
3. Roll the dough out to a 25 × 30 cm / 10 × 12 in rectangle.
4. Spread with the filling mixture, roll up and place on a greased and floured baking tray. Cut a zig-zag line along the top using scissors.
5. Cover and leave to rise for 1 hour. Then bake in a moderate oven (180 C, 350 F, gas 4) for 45 minutes.
6. Stir the water into the icing sugar until smooth to make the icing and spread on the plait.

Plaited, rolled and woven breads for tea

These are the classic breads for afternoon tea that you can eat every day. You can cut yourself a slice whenever you fancy as the rich fillings keep them nice and moist.

A plait must be plaited correctly

This is quite easy to do even though plaited hair might have gone out of fashion! The most important thing to remember is to make the three dough strands of equal thickness and to dust them lightly with flour to prevent them sticking.

Onion flan

(illustrated left)

500 g/18 oz plain flour
250 ml/8 fl oz milk
40 g/1½ oz fresh yeast or
20 g/¾ oz dried yeast
pinch of sugar
pinch of salt
2 eggs
5 tablespoons oil
For the filling:
1 kg/2¼ lb onions
4 tablespoons oil
500 ml/17 fl oz soured cream
250 ml/8 fl oz milk
4 eggs
1 teaspoon ground caraway seeds
salt and pepper

1. Make the dough as in the basic recipe (see page 119) and roll out to about 5 mm/¼ in thick. Place on a greased and floured baking tray and prick a few times with a fork. Make a shallow rim around the edge. Cover and leave to rise for 1 hour.
2. Meanwhile cut the onions into thin rings and gently fry in the oil without browning. When cool spread over the dough.
3. Beat the remaining ingredients together and pour over the onions.
4. Bake in a moderately hot oven (190C, 375F, gas 5) for 45 minutes.

A useful stand-by . . .

As soon as the first baking tray comes out of the oven, hot and smelling wonderful, the next one should go in. Just make sure that you have made plenty and never underestimate how much your guests will eat! You can never make too much, especially if the evening is to be a long one, so be sure to borrow plenty of baking trays from your friends.

Variations:
You can make other savoury flans using different vegetables and seasonings. Here are three suggestions:

Leek flan

(illustrated right)
Spread 1 kg/2¼ lb leeks, cut into rings, and 100 g/4 oz bacon cut in thin strips, over the dough. Cover in egg and milk mixture, as given for Onion flan and bake in the same way (see opposite).

Spinach flan

Spread 675 g/1½ lb spinach, which has been blanched and pressed out, over the dough. Add 5 finely chopped onions and 100 g/4 oz cubed bacon to the dough. Sprinkle with 100 g/4 oz grated cheese and season with salt, pepper and freshly grated nutmeg. Bake as for Onion flan (see opposite).

Bacon flan

Over a high heat fry 400 g/14 oz thinly sliced bacon in a frying pan without fat. Drain and spread over the dough mixture. Beat 2 egg yolks with 250 ml/8 fl oz single cream and 100 g/4 oz grated cheese and pour over the bacon. Bake as for Onion flan (see opposite).

. . . when you expect a lot of guests

Onion flan is an ideal appetiser when you have got people round. It is best served with a dry, light and crisp white wine but is also good with red wines. Try with Beaujolais nouveau when it has just come in.

Quiche Lorraine

Once a simple meal for hard-working miners this flan is nowadays an elegant nibble with aperitifs in the best restaurants. Bake a large flan as part of a main course or – for a starter – bake individual flans in small tins.

1. Make a dough as in the basic recipe (see page 119) and roll out thinly. Use to line a 25-cm/10-in spring-form tin. Prick the base several times with a fork. Cover with a cloth and leave to rise for 30 minutes.
2. Meanwhile blanch the bacon in boiling water in a saucepan for 2 minutes and then drain.
3. Fry the onions lightly in the butter for a few minutes until golden.
4. Beat the milk with the eggs, nutmeg and salt.
5. Arrange half the bacon rashers in the flan case. Sprinkle with the onion and pour on the egg and milk mixture. Arrange the remaining bacon over the top.
6. Bake in a moderately hot oven (190C, 375F, gas 5) for 50 minutes until firm.

Variations:
— Stir chopped herbs and about 100 g/4 oz grated cheese into the egg and milk mixture.
— Instead of yeast dough make the case with a shortcrust (see page 110 but omit sugar) or puff pastry (see page 166–7).

Quiche Lorraine

250 g/9 oz flour	
20 g/¾ oz fresh yeast or	
15 g/½ oz dried yeast	
6 tablespoons milk	
pinch of sugar	
2 eggs	
2 tablespoons oil	

pinch of salt

For the topping:
200 g/7 oz thin rashers streaky bacon	
6 onions, finely chopped	
1 tablespoon butter	
175 ml/6 fl oz milk	
3 eggs	
freshly grated nutmeg	
salt	

Hard to believe, but the Italians did not invent it!

Not in their own country at least, because for centuries in Italy there was only Pizza Napoletana, a thick cake of dough about the size of a tea-plate, topped with a little dab of the famous tomato sauce known as Pizzaiola. When in the late 1950s Italians began to open restaurants throughout Europe, a thinner pizza with richer, more varied toppings became popular, and has remained so – even in Italy.

Pizza base

500 g/ 18 oz plain flour
40 g/ 1½ oz fresh yeast or
20 g/¾ oz dried yeast
pinch of sugar
pinch of salt
250 ml/8 fl oz water
5 tablespoons olive oil

1. Make the ingredients into a yeast dough as in the basic recipe (see page 119). Roll the dough out and use to cover a greased or floured baking tray or four 20-cm/8-in pizza tins. Prick with a fork.

Pizzaiola

2 onions, finely chopped
2 cloves garlic, chopped
3 tablespoons olive oil
1 (397-g/14-oz) can
chopped tomatoes
1 teaspoon oregano
1 bay leaf
salt
pepper

1. Fry the onion and garlic lightly in the oil in a saucepan. Add the tomatoes and seasonings.
2. Simmer gently in the open pan over a low heat to make a thick, highly flavoured sauce.

Note:
The pizza topping will stay nice and moist if sprinkled with a little olive oil before baking. This also prevents it becoming too brown.

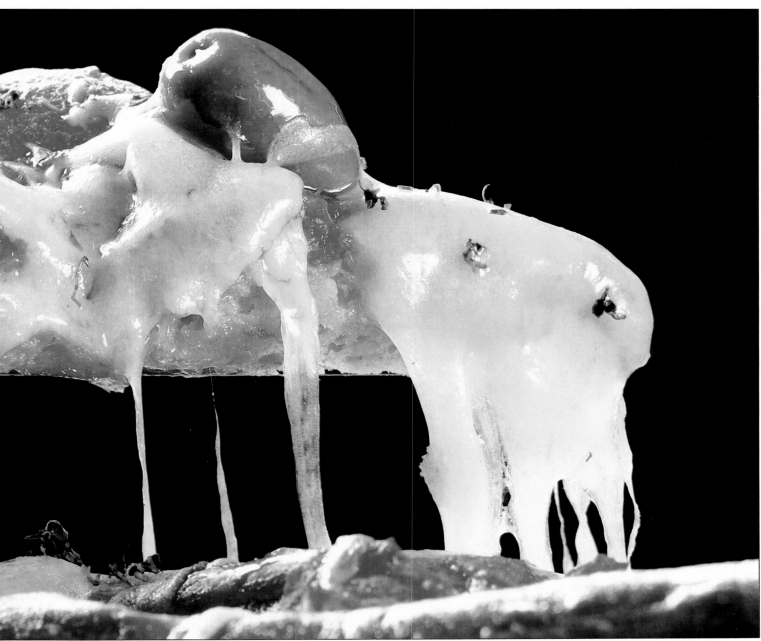

Pizza Margherita

Spread the pizza base with Pizzaiola (see opposite). Cover with slices of Mozzarella or milk Tilsit cheese. Sprinkle all over with oregano, salt, pepper and, if you like, finely chopped basil. Sprinkle with olive oil. Bake in a moderately hot oven (200C, 400F, gas 6) for 10 to 15 minutes.

Pizza funghi

Make this pizza in the same way as Pizza Margherita using the basic dough base and Pizzaiola (see opposite). Add about 100 g/4 oz thinly sliced mushrooms.

Pizza salami

Make this pizza in the same way as Pizza Margherita using the basic dough base and Pizzaiola (see opposite). Top with about 100 g/4 oz very thin slices salami.

Pizza Siciliana

Make this pizza in the same way as Pizza Margherita using the basic dough base and Pizzaiola (see opposite). Add a sprinkling of anchovies (first soaked in water) and halved black olives. Use Pecorino instead of Mozzarella cheese and parsley instead of basil.

Pizza Milano

Make this pizza in the same way as Pizza Margherita using the basic dough base and Pizzaiola (see opposite). Top generously with about 100 g/4 oz thin-cut boiled ham and, if you like, slices of boiled egg.

Pizza quattro stagioni

Make this pizza in the same way as Pizza Milano using the basic dough base and Pizzaiola (see opposite). Add about 100 g/4 oz quartered artichoke hearts and 50 g/2 oz sliced mushrooms.

Pizza frutti di mare

Make this pizza in the same way as Pizza Margherita using the basic dough and Pizzaiola (see opposite). Add any seafood: prawns, shrimps, squid or mussels – either fresh and cooked briefly in white wine, or alternatively canned. Use parsley instead of basil.

Doughnuts – the cakes that everybody wants to eat

The best doughnuts should be deep-fried in the best fat you can use to give the most flavour. A doughnut is one of those most tempting cakes, crisp and sugary on the outside with that delightful surprise of the jam inside when you bite into it.

Tips on doughnuts

☐ For light, crumbly doughnuts, use only the yolk of the egg in the dough, for egg white dries them out.
☐ The white line round the middle of the doughnut shows that they have been cooked properly, and at the right temperature (see page 189), in pure fat (impurities can make the fat bubble too much so that the white line can't form), with enough air in the dough to make them rise.
☐ The pan should be covered initially as this traps the steam which makes the doughnuts rise. After turning the doughnuts finish frying them in the open pan.

Doughnuts

Makes 16:

500 g/18 oz plain flour
250 ml/8 fl oz milk
40 g/1½ oz fresh yeast or
20 g/¾ oz dried yeast
60 g/2¼ oz sugar
pinch of salt
4 egg yolks
50 g/2 oz butter
For the filling:
5 tablespoons jam
1 egg white (for sealing)
3 tablespoons sugar

1. Make a yeast dough as described in the basic recipe (see page 119).
2. On a floured work top roll the dough out to 2 cm/¾ in thick. Using a glass or small mould, cut into 5-cm/2-in rounds.
3. Place ½ teaspoon jam on half the rounds and brush the edges with egg white.
4. Cover with a plain round and press the edges firmly together. Cover with a tea-towel and leave to rise for 1 hour.
5. Deep-fry the doughnuts for 10 minutes in batches in hot fat, turning them half way through.
6. Drain and coat in sugar while still hot.

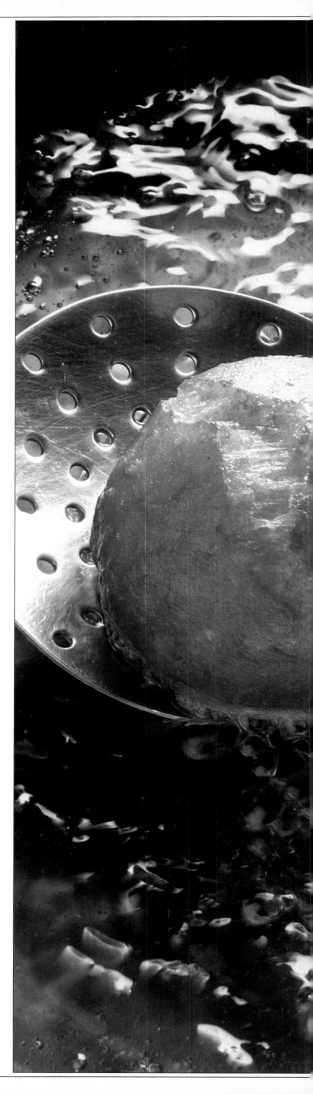

Apple doughnuts

Use fairly tart cooking apples, which should be peeled and cored and then cut horizontally into thin slices. Roll and cut out the dough as for doughnuts. Place slices of apple between two rounds of dough. Press together well, leave to rise and deep-fry (see opposite).

Raisin doughnuts

Work 225 g/8 oz raisins into the dough and on a floured work top shape it into a roll 2.5 cm/1 in thick. Cut into 1-cm/$\frac{1}{2}$-in slices and roll each into a ball. Leave to rise on a floured baking sheet. Deep-fry in hot fat. Drain well and coat in sugar and ground cinnamon while still hot (see opposite).

Our daily bread – by no
means an ordinary food

Basic recipe for toasting bread

500 g/18 oz plain flour
20 g/¾ oz fresh yeast or
15 g/½ oz dried yeast
pinch of sugar
175 ml/6 fl oz lukewarm water
½ teaspoon salt

1. In a mixing bowl, stir 5 tablespoons flour with the crumbled yeast, sugar and water. Leave to rise in a warm place for 30 minutes.
2. Mix the remaining flour with the salt and sift into the bowl. Knead all the ingredients together to make a firm dough.
3. Shape into a ball, cover with a tea-towel and leave to rise for a further 30 minutes.
4. Knead the dough once more. Shape into a long loaf and place in a buttered 450-g/1-lb loaf tin.
5. Cover again and leave to rise for 1 hour.
6. Using a sharp knife, cut along the top to allow the loaf to break open.
7. Bake in a moderately hot oven (200C, 400F, gas 6) for 50 minutes, or until cooked.

Tips on the dough

☐ If the ingredients listed above give a dough which is too solid or too soft, simply add a little more liquid or flour. It is impossible to give absolutely exact measurements as every flour is different.
☐ For a more crumbly, softer bread add a little butter (50 g/2 oz) to the dough or replace the water with milk (which contains fat).

The finest of breads and highly versatile

Sadly, although it must be said, the sliced bread normally bought for toasting has come down in the world, for it seems to have little in common with the delicious bread that it once was. Is this an exaggeration? You can easily find out by trying out the following recipe . . .

☐ Always bake a soft dough in a tin for it would spread on a baking tray.
☐ Firm doughs can be shaped into a loaf and baked without a tin.
☐ To cut down on the time needed for the dough to rise, place the bowl of dough in a barely warmed oven (50C, 120F, gas low).

Baking tips

To give the bread a nice shiny surface, brush with water before and immediately after baking. Steam in the oven will prevent the bread becoming too dry, so place a small ovenproof bowl of water on the bottom of the oven. Turn the baked loaf out of the tin immediately and cool on a wire rack. This will prevent it sweating and keep it crisp.

Hot buttered bread

(illustrated top left)
Cut a freshly cooked loaf while still warm into fairly thick slices. Butter generously.

Toast

(illustrated top right)
Toast is one of the favourite breakfast foods and is a good way to use up bread left from the previous day. It will taste (almost) like fresh bread. Slice the bread and toast.

Aniseed toast

(illustrated bottom left)
This toast is made in the oven. Spread the slices of bread with melted butter, scatter with aniseed and granulated sugar, then bake on a baking tray in a moderately hot oven (200C, 400F, gas 6) for 15 minutes. Eat this toast with jam.

Bread pancakes

(illustrated bottom right)
Dip slices of bread in beaten egg and fry both sides in butter. Serve with cinnamon sugar and stewed fruit.

What you can make with toasting bread . . .

. . . when it is no longer fresh enough just to eat.

Zuppa pavese
(See pages 46–7) This is a clear soup with an egg yolk added and topped with a slice of white bread thickly sprinkled with grated Parmesan cheese which is browned under the grill.

Butter cakes
(See page 53) These are made from slices of white bread placed on a baking tray and thickly coated in flaked almonds, sugar and melted butter. Bake for 15 minutes in a moderately hot oven (200C, 400F, gas 6) and sprinkle with rum.

Bread and currant pudding
(See pages 46–7) Arrange layers of white bread and red currants in a buttered baking dish. Pour on a beaten mixture of egg and milk. Bake in a moderately hot oven (200C, 400F, gas 6) for 30 minutes.

Sandwich
(See pages 46–7) Butter half slices of white bread and top with salad, roast pork, pickles and sweet-corn.

Apple Charlotte
(See pages 48–9) Cook 1.5 kg/3¼ lb cooking apples with 150 g/5 oz sugar and 250 ml/8 fl oz water until soft. Cut slices of white bread into fingers and fry one side in 50 g/2 oz butter. Use the bread to line the sides of a greased and floured Charlotte mould, fill with the apple and bake in a moderately hot oven (200C, 400F, gas 6) for 30 minutes. Leave to cool and turn out.

Hawaiian toast
(See pages 46–7) Cover a slice of toast with boiled ham, pineapple and cheese and brown in a very hot oven (240C, 475F, gas 9) for 10 minutes.

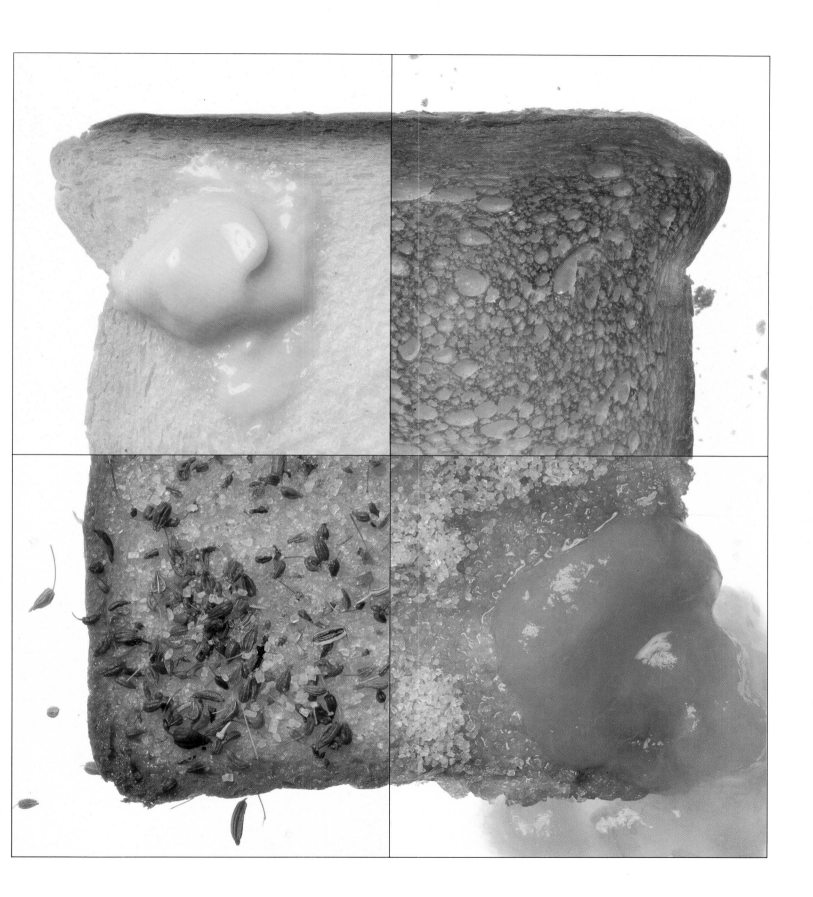

Turning bread into snails

Making snail shapes with bread is supposed to bring good luck and a long life! Bread has always been more than a mere food, it is reputed to have symbolic values. A gift of bread and salt when you move into a new house, for example, is supposed to mean that you will never be hungry.

Basic recipe for white yeast bread

Make the dough as for toasting bread (see page 146). Twist or roll into the required shape. Leave the shaped loaf to rise on a greased and floured baking tray for about 30 minutes. Brush with water and bake in a moderately hot oven (200C, 400F, gas 6) for between 20 and 40 minutes (depending on size). Make sure you produce enough steam in the oven (see page 146).

Spiral loaf

Arrange dough rolls 1 cm/½ in thick in a spiral on the baking tray and press a small ball of dough on to the centre.

Pretzel

Shape the dough into thin rolls and twist into pretzels. Scatter with a little rock or sea salt before baking.

Horns

Make rolls of dough which become thicker at both ends and bend into horns.

Double horns

Join two small horns at their thickest point using a thin strip of dough.

Triangular rolls

Make the dough into a roll 2 cm/¾ in thick. Cut into slices and pinch the edges to form triangles.

Round loaf

Shape the dough into a ball, flatten slightly and cut across the top.

Baguette rolls

Shape the dough into rolls 10 cm/4 in long and round off the ends.

Baguette

A long roll of dough about 5 cm/2 in thick. Make several slanting cuts across the top.

Clover-leaf rolls

For each roll place three small balls of dough close together on the baking tray. Cut a cross into the top of each ball with scissors.

Grissini

Make very thin, long strips of dough and place on the baking tray.

Ears of corn

Like a baguette, but cut left and right sides with scissors, rather than across the top.

Baps

Shape dough into flat rounds or ovals and roll with rolling pin.

Breakfast rolls

Twist two thin strips of dough together into a rope.

Snails

Roll thin lengths of dough into snail shapes, pressing slightly flat.

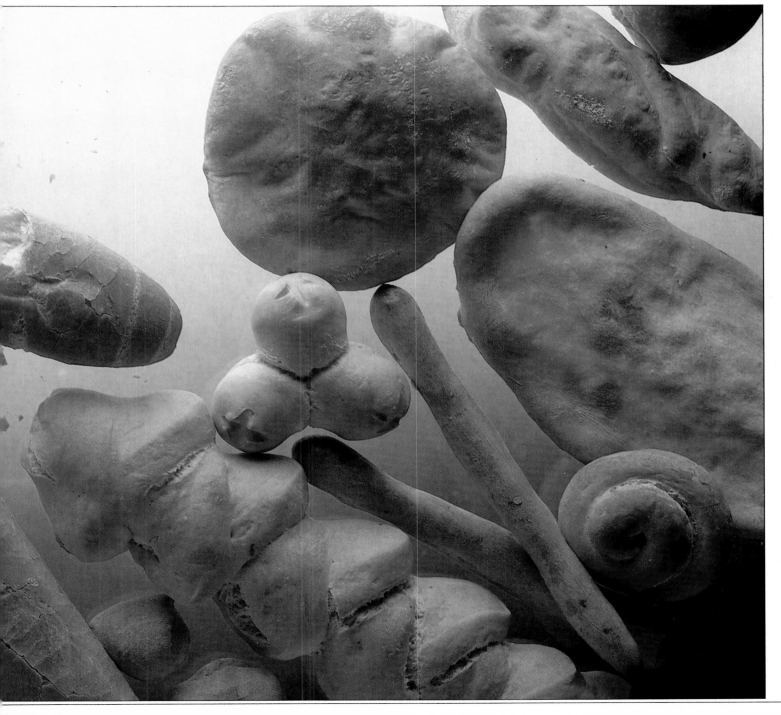

Simple but attractive bread using sesame seeds, rock salt, caraway seeds and pistachios

Ring rolls

Makes a ring of 7–8 rolls:

500 g/18 oz plain flour

20 g/¾ oz fresh yeast

pinch of sugar

375 ml/13 fl oz lukewarm water

½ teaspoon salt

For decoration:

1 tablespoon grated cheese

1 teaspoon linseed

1 teaspoon wheatbran

1 teaspoon rock or sea salt

1 teaspoon caraway seeds

1 teaspoon sesame seeds

1 teaspoon chopped pistachio nuts

1. Make a yeast dough using the basic recipe (see page 146).
2. Shape into a roll 3–5 cm/1½–2 in thick and cut into 3-cm/1½-in lengths.
3. Shape the slices into balls, pressing them slightly inside out so that the smooth cut edge forms a perfect surface.
4. Arrange six or seven balls in a ring on a floured baking tray. Place the last ball in the centre.
5. Brush with water and scatter with flavouring.
6. Leave to rise for about 45 minutes.
7. Bake in a hot oven (220C, 425F, gas 7) for 35 minutes.

Flavourings *on* rather than *in* rolls serve several purposes — they add bite, make it obvious what type of roll it is and add attractive decoration. If, as is more usual, they are included in the dough they can merely add flavour. So put your flavourings on the top of rolls to add colour and variety and to turn a simple loaf into a crunchy feast.

Variations
By varying the ingredients used for decoration you can create a different effect every time you make this recipe. The rolls will both look and taste different. Here are a few suggestions:

Poppy seeds, use whole seeds. You will have to press them well into the dough with the flat of your hand to prevent them rolling off the flat surface.
Walnuts, coarsely chopped or simply broken into pieces. Crack the shells, remove all the brown skin and you will find that walnuts have never tasted so good.
Hazelnuts. Best roasted in the shell on a baking tray in a hot oven. Then shell them and the skin will rub off easily between two cloths. Crush coarsely in a mortar or with a rolling pin.
Cashew nuts, again use chopped.
Almonds. These can be used as flakes or just chopped.
Grains of cereal or simply *flour* can also be used to decorate the dough.

Adding to the basic loaf

Bread can be made in so many different forms, for example, a plain yeast dough, seasoned and coloured with various ingredients, becomes scarcely recognisable as an ordinary loaf. These extra ingredients are worth their weight in gold, especially if they consist of fresh foods which will keep the bread nice and moist.

Raisin bread

(illustrated top left)

500 g/18 oz plain flour

20 g/¾ oz fresh yeast or

15 g/½ oz dried yeast

pinch of sugar

375 ml/13 fl oz lukewarm water

½ teaspoon salt

For the filling:

100 g/4 oz raisins, washed and dried

1. Make a yeast dough as described in the basic recipe (see page 146). Work in the raisins.
2. Cover the dough and leave to rise for 1 hour. Knead thoroughly and shape into a loaf.
3. Place in a buttered 900 g/2 lb loaf tin. Cover with a cloth and leave to rise for just under 1 hour.
4. Brush with water and bake in a moderately hot oven (200 C, 400 F, gas 6) for 50 to 60 minutes, or until cooked.
5. Turn out of the tin and cool slightly on a wire rack before slicing.

Tomato bread

(illustrated top right)
Make a basic yeast dough as described previously (see page 119), but colour the water with 2 tablespoons concentrated tomato purée and season to taste.

Herb bread

(illustrated left of 2nd row)
Mix 4 tablespoons freshly chopped mixed herbs into the basic dough mixture as described previously (see page 119). Try using parsley, chives, dill, basil, thyme, tarragon.

Prune bread

(illustrated right of 2nd row)
Work 225 g/8 oz stoned, chopped prunes into the basic dough mixture (see page 119).

Poppy bread

(illustrated left of 3rd row)
Mix 175 g/6 oz ground poppy seeds with the flour and make a dough as in the basic Raisin bread recipe (see left).

Carrot bread

(illustrated right of 3rd row)
Work 100 g/4 oz grated carrots into the basic dough mixture (see page 119).

Onion bread

(illustrated bottom left)
Finely chop 150 g/5 oz onions, fry for a few minutes in butter and then work into the basic dough mixture (see page 119).

Pepper bread

(illustrated bottom right)
Finely dice ½ red, green and yellow pepper and work into the basic dough mixture (see page 119).

Tips on the dough

You can vary the dough in many other different ways, but always make sure that the ratio of dry to liquid ingredients does not alter substantially or you will not get the right crumbly texture.
☐ Add an extra teaspoon of salt to savoury doughs.
☐ Knead the dough well to make sure the ingredients are evenly distributed. If they stay together in a clump the yeast won't be able to work properly and the dough won't rise.
☐ For variety, make double the quantity of dough, divide it up and make several different loaves.

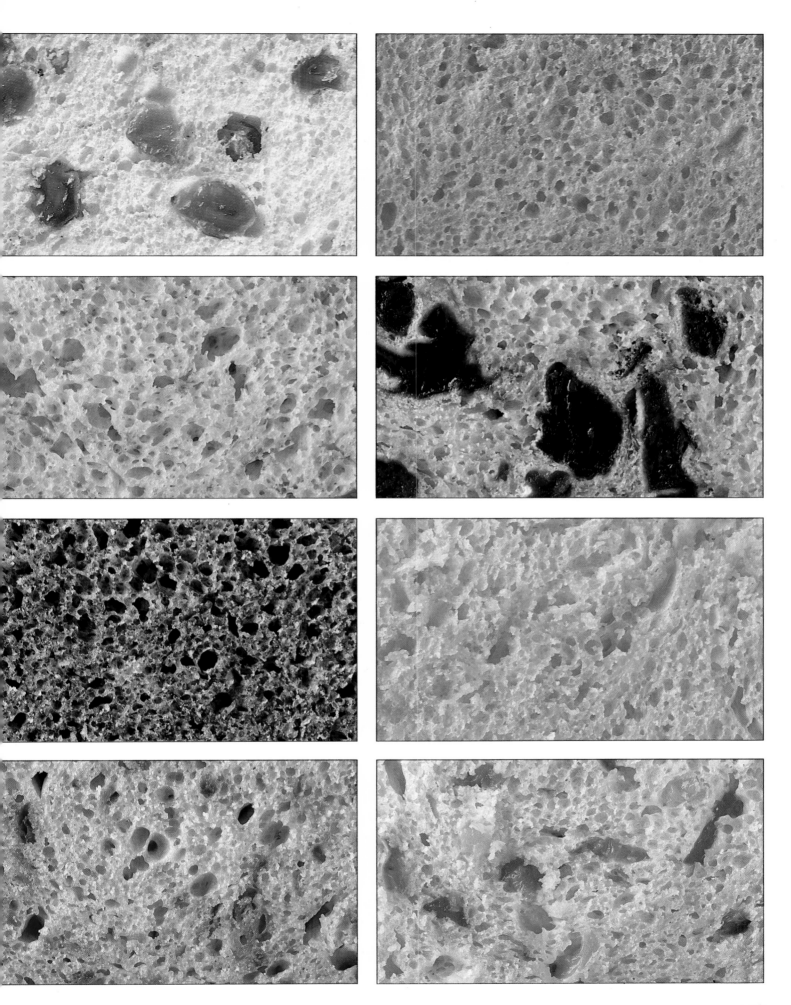

Making use of grains and seeds

Note:
You can use the following recipe as a basis for your own mixtures. If you plan to include whole or coarse-chopped grain, you will have to first soak it overnight to prevent it absorbing moisture from the dough. Otherwise the dough becomes too dry and fragile and will crack open during baking.

I. **Wheatflake bread**

300 g/11 oz wholewheat flour

20 g/¾ oz fresh yeast or 15 g/½ oz dried yeast

pinch of sugar

375 ml/13 fl oz lukewarm water

½ teaspoon salt

200 g/7 oz wheat flakes

I. Make a yeast dough as described in the basic recipe (see page 146), working in the wheat flakes.
2. Shape into a loaf. Place in a greased 450-g/1-lb loaf tin, cover and leave to rise for 1 hour.
3. Brush the top with water. Bake in a hot oven (220 C, 425 F, gas 7) for 50 to 60 minutes. Brush again with water after baking.

This bread will be acceptable even to wholefood addicts who are normally horrified at the thought of eating white bread. Even someone with eagle eyes would find it hard to detect that these chunky loaves are variations on the white bread that many consider to be without character.

2. Maize bread

Instead of the wheat flakes work 200 g/7 oz maize flour into the basic bread recipe (see opposite page). This gives the bread an attractive yellow colour.

3. Bran bread

Instead of the wheat flakes add 200 g/7 oz of wheat bran to the basic bread recipe (see opposite page). This gives a firm, coarse-grained wheat loaf.

4. Oat bread

Replace the wheat flakes in the basic bread recipe (see opposite page) with 200 g/7 oz coarse oatmeal.

5. Buckwheat bread

Replace the wheat flakes in the basic bread recipe (see opposite page) with 200 g/7 oz buckwheat, previously soaked overnight. This gives a solid, coarse-grained loaf of bread.

Prague ham bread

Serves 6 to 8:

2–3 litres/ 3½–5¼ pints water
about 3 kg/ 6½ lb cured ham
3 bay leaves
2 onions
2 tablespoons black peppercorns
For the dough:
40 g/ 1½ oz fresh or
20 g/ ¾ oz dried yeast
500 ml/ 17 fl oz lukewarm water
800 g/ 1¾ lb wholewheat flour
150 g/ 5 oz wholewheat semolina
1 teaspoon sugar
2 teaspoons salt

1. Bring the water to the boil in a large saucepan and over a low heat and put the ham in it and gently simmer with the bay leaves, onions and peppercorns for about 1½ hours.

2. To make the dough, dissolve the fresh yeast in the water or sprinkle the dried yeast on the water and leave in a warm place until dissolved and frothy.
3. Mix the flour and semolina with the salt and sugar in a mixing bowl.
4. Add the dissolved yeast and work together to give a firm dough.
5. Cover the dough with a cloth and leave to rise until the meat is cooked.
6. Take the ham out of the pan and dry on absorbent kitchen paper.
7. Knead the dough once more and roll out to 1 cm/½ in thick.
8. Place the ham in the centre and fold the dough over it. Brush the edges with water and press firmly together. Cover again with the cloth and leave to rise for 10 minutes.
9. Bake on a greased and floured baking tray in a moderate oven (180C, 350F, gas 4) for 1 hour or until cooked.
10. About 10 minutes before the end of the baking time brush the top of the bread with cold water.

International bread recipes for parties and special occasions

Every country in the world has its own bread and there are numerous different recipes which use bread dough as their basis. Here are a few recipes from around the world that you might like to try. The idea of wrapping a juicy piece of ham in bread dough comes from Prague. In Italy a light, crumbly loaf with candied peel and raisins is popular at Christmas time. An old British recipe for little muffins is included and also the famous Turkish pitta bread which is now so popular everywhere.

Other lands, other customs

Where we use butter in baking, Mediterranean countries tend to use the readily available olive oil. And since it is used as much as a flavouring as a fat, it must be top quality olive oil. Look for a first pressing note on the label. This oil is greenish-yellow in colour and full of flavour.

Panettone

*250 ml/8 fl oz lukewarm
milk*
*25 g/1 oz fresh yeast or
15 g/½ oz dried yeast*
1 egg
2 egg yolks
*500 g/18 oz strong plain
flour*
100 g/4 oz sugar
pinch of salt
*100 g/4 oz butter, at room
temperature*
*40 g/1½ oz chopped mixed
peel*
90 g/3½ oz raisins
*3 tablespoons butter for
greasing the dish and
spreading on the loaf*

1. Stir the fresh yeast into
the milk or sprinkle the
dried yeast over the milk
and leave in a warm place
until dissolved and frothy,
and then add the egg and
egg yolks.
2. Mix the flour with the
sugar and salt. Work in
the yeast mixture and all
the other ingredients to
give a firm dough. Leave
to rise for 1 hour.

3. Meanwhile grease and
flour a 15-cm/6-in soufflé
dish and line the sides
with greaseproof paper or
non-stick baking
parchment to come
5 cm/2 in above the rim of
the dish.
4. Knead the dough once
more, shape into a ball
and place in the prepared
dish. Cut a cross in the
top using a sharp knife.
5. Before baking leave to
rise for a further hour.
6. Melt the remaining
butter, allow to cool
slightly and brush on the
loaf. Bake in a moderately
hot oven (190C, 375F,
gas 5) for 40 minutes, or
until cooked.

Muffins

Makes 24:
*15 g/½ oz fresh yeast or
7 g/¼ oz dried yeast*
*500 ml/17 fl oz lukewarm
milk*
500 g/18 oz plain flour
½ teaspoon salt
1 tablespoon oil

1. Dissolve the fresh yeast
in the milk or sprinkle the
dried yeast over the milk
and leave in a warm place
until dissolved and frothy.
2. In a mixing bowl, mix
the flour with the salt.
Add the milk and yeast
and work into a soft
dough. Cover with a tea-
towel and leave to rise in
a warm place for 1 hour.
3. Grease muffin or bun
tins with the oil.
4. Using two tablespoons,
make the dough into balls
and place in the bun tins.
5. Place the tins in a
warm place and leave the
dough to rise once more.
6. Bake the muffins in a
moderate oven (180C,
350F, gas 4) for 20
minutes, or until cooked.

Note: Serve the muffins
for tea straight from the
oven. Break them open,
spread with fresh butter
and sandwich them back
together before eating.

Pitta bread

Makes 18:
*15 g/½ oz fresh or
7 g/¼ oz dried yeast*
*375 ml/13 fl oz lukewarm
milk*
575 g/1¼ lb plain flour
1 teaspoon salt
*3 tablespoons first
pressing olive oil*

1. Dissolve the fresh yeast
in the milk or sprinkle the
dried yeast over the milk
and leave in a warm place
until dissolved and frothy.
Then add the remaining
ingredients and work to a
firm dough. Cover with a
tea-towel and leave to rise
for 1 hour.
2. Shape the dough into a
roll 2.5 cm/1 in thick and
cut into 1-cm/½-in slices.
Shape each slice into a
small ball. Cover and
leave to rise for a further
10 minutes.
3. With the rolling pin
roll each ball into a flat
oval. Bake on a greased
and floured baking tray in
a very hot oven (240C,
475F, gas 9) for 8 to 10
minutes until the pitta
bread inflates.

Note: Serve as has
become so popular with
taramasalata or pâtés.
They can also be served
filled with grilled meat,
salad and dressing to eat
with the fingers.

The dough that keeps bread fresh

To make some brown breads you need 'sour dough'. Rye dough will not rise with yeast, as it contains a lot of protein which makes the dough so elastic and glutinous that the bacteria in yeast cannot work properly. Sour dough on the other hand breaks down the protein and also makes bread keep better.

Tips on the dough

☐ When you have made the sour dough it is a good idea to keep a small quantity of it in the refrigerator. If you add this the next time you make dough, it will speed up the rising process.

☐ Never leave the finished dough longer than 3 to 4 hours before baking or it will fall.

Sour dough

20 g/¾ oz fresh yeast or

15 g/½ oz dried yeast

(sprinkle over water and

leave in a warm place

until dissolved and frothy)

500 ml/17 fl oz hand-warm

water

300 g/11 oz plain flour

Top six step-by-step photographs:
1. Crumble the yeast into a bowl.
2. Add the water.
3. Whisk together until the yeast has dissolved.
4. Gradually add the flour.
5. Whisk thoroughly together.
6. Leave to stand for 3 days at room temperature.

Basic recipe for rye bread

600 g/1 lb 6 oz rye flour

300 g/11 oz plain white

flour

1 teaspoon salt

1 quantity sour dough

(see left)

400–450 ml/14–15 fl oz

warm water

Cooking time:

Preparation time: 20 to 30

minutes

Resting time: 9 hours

Oven temperature: 190C,

375F, gas 5

Baking time:

1 hour 20 minutes

Cooling time: 15 to 30

minutes

Preparation

Bottom six step-by-step photographs:
1. In a mixing bowl mix the two types of flour with the salt.
2. Add the sour dough and warm water.
3. Knead all the ingredients together well.
4. Cover with a tea-towel and leave the dough to rise for 45 to 60 minutes or until doubled in size.
5. When the dough is fully risen, knead once more and shape into a loaf.
6. Cut a cross in the top with a knife. Place on a greased and floured baking tray. Leave to rise for 30 to 45 minutes before baking.

Two more tips:
☐ You will be able to tell when the bread is cooked. It will make a dull, hollow sound when you knock on the bottom.
☐ If you put an ovenproof bowl of water on to the bottom of the oven, the steam will help to keep the bread moist.

Solid, filling and healthy: wholemeal bread

Farmhouse bread

(Far left)

575 g/1¼ lb wholewheat flour

300 g/11 oz rye flour

1 teaspoon salt

100 g/4 oz sour dough (⅓ recipe, see page 158)

20 g/¾ oz fresh yeast or 15 g/½ oz dried yeast (sprinkle over the water and leave in a warm place until dissolved and frothy)

375 ml/13 fl oz warm water

1. Mix the two flours with the salt.
2. Stir together the sour dough, yeast and water.
3. Work into a firm dough as in the basic recipe (see page 158) and leave to rise.
4. Shape into a loaf and make slanting cuts on the top with a knife. Bake as in the basic recipe (see page 158).

Black bread

(Round loaf, centre)

600 g/1 lb 6 oz rye flour

300 g/11 oz wholewheat bran

1 teaspoon salt

300 g/11 oz sour dough (1 quantity, see page 158)

20 g/¾ oz fresh yeast or 15 g/½ oz dried yeast

375 ml/13 fl oz warm water

To decorate:

2 tablespoons wholewheat bran

1. Work the ingredients together to make a dough as in the basic recipe (see page 158).
2. Shape into a roll and dip in wheat bran.
3. Shape into a long loaf or place in a 900-g/2-lb greased and floured loaf tin. If preferred make a round loaf on a baking tray as illustrated.
4. Leave to rise again and bake as in the basic recipe.

Three-grain loaf

(Square loaf, centre)

300 g/11 oz wholewheat flour

300 g/11 oz oat flakes

300 g/11 oz rye flour

1 teaspoon salt

300 g/11 oz sour dough (1 quantity, see page 158)

25 g/1 oz fresh yeast or 15 g/½ oz dried yeast

375 ml/13 fl oz warm water

wholewheat flour for sprinkling

Coarse meal and whole grain, dark flour and bran, these make loaves which are full of flavour. They do give you something to chew and bite on. Bread like this is really delicious just as it comes, but thickly buttered and maybe with a sprinkling of salt, it is particularly moreish.

1. Make a dough as in the basic recipe (see page 158).
2. Place the dough in two 900-g/2-lb loaf tins which you have greased and sprinkled with flour. Sprinkle the top with flour.
3. Leave the dough to rise once more and bake as in the basic recipe.

Mixed bread

(Round loaf, top right)

20 g/¾ oz fresh yeast or	
15 g/½ oz dried yeast	
375 ml/13 fl oz warm water	
800 g/1¾ lb wholewheat flour	
150 g/5 oz rye flour	
1 teaspoon salt	
100 g/4 oz sour dough (⅓ recipe, see page 158)	

1. Dissolve the yeast in the water and leave to stand until it begins to froth.
2. Then mix with the other ingredients to make a dough as in the basic recipe (see page 158).
3. Shape into a round loaf, leave to rise and bake as given (see page 158).

Wholemeal barley loaf

(Round loaf, right)

20 g/¾ oz fresh yeast	
375 ml/13 fl oz warm water	
300 g/11 oz barley meal	
300 g/11 oz rye flour	
300 g/11 oz wholewheat flour	
150 g/5 oz sour dough (generous ⅓ recipe, see page 158)	

1. Dissolve the yeast in the water and leave to stand until it begins to froth.
2. Then mix with the other ingredients to a firm dough as in the basic recipe (see page 158).
3. Shape into a loaf and cut along the top with a knife. Leave to rise once more and bake as in the basic recipe (see page 158).

Salami sandwich

Try making an open sandwich with slices of salami, tomato and cucumber, garnished with whole, mild chillies.

Pear and Roquefort sandwich

Slice a pear half and arrange on the bread. Top with crumbled Roquefort cheese and walnuts.

Ham sandwich

Take some thin slices of smoked or air-dried ham. Arrange on bread and garnish with gherkins.

Cold spam sandwich

Place cones of spam or luncheon meat, filled with waldorf salad and carrot fingers, on the bread. Garnish with egg and parsley.

Roast beef sandwich

Take some thin slices of roast beef and place on the bread. Garnish with mixed pickles.

Prawn sandwich

Cover the bread with scrambled egg. Top with peeled, cooked prawns. Garnish with chives.

Liver pâté sandwich

Take some thin slices of liver pâté and place on the bread. Garnish with mushrooms and thyme.

Tartare sandwich

Spread bread with minced steak and garnish with onion and capers.

Savoury open sandwiches

Open sandwiches as a snack. These are no longer as popular as they once were. Yet they are a really practical idea if you just want a snack with a glass of beer or wine. We hope that the ideas included here will give open sandwiches a revival – and encourage you to think up your own ideas.

Banana sandwich

Spread bread with a chocolate nut spread. Top with sliced banana and coconut.

Colourful fruit sandwich

Top the buttered bread with fresh kiwi slices and strawberry halves.

Sweet curd sandwich

Spread the bread with whipped, sweetened curd cheese. Top with orange segments and decorate with mint.

Apple sandwich

Cook apple slices in a little water with a few raisins and a little sugar. Drain and spread on the buttered bread.

Jelly sandwich

Just spread some red currant jelly on top of the buttered bread.

Peanut butter sandwich

Spread thickly with peanut butter and decorate with chopped peanuts.

Plum purée sandwich

Spoon the plum purée on to the buttered bread.

Honey sandwich

Butter bread thickly before spreading with some honey.

. . . or sweet open sandwiches

For lunch, for a children's snack, for afternoon tea or as a supper snack, for those with a sweet tooth, why not try a sweet topping on your sandwich. Use white bread or brown bread, the choice is up to you.

Puff pastry — noble and refined, the most sophisticated of pastries

Incomparably crisp and light: the pastry with a thousand layers

This pastry is aptly named in French, mille feuille – a thousand leaves. This is something of an exaggeration, although a good puff pastry can easily have at least a hundred layers. This makes puff pastry light as air, providing it is eaten fresh and preferably while it is still warm.

What gives the pastry its layers?

The basic puff pastry is wrapped round a block of butter and the main point in the procedures that follow is always to roll the pastry into a perfect rectangle. Folding the pastry exactly into three from left to right, you roll again and the more times you repeat this step, the better the pastry will turn out. Experts refer to this as 'making a turn'. This gives a thin layer of butter between each layer of pastry and prevents the layers sticking together. During baking the water in the butter turns to steam and makes the pastry rise in layers.

The versatility of puff pastry

Puff pastry is extremely versatile and can be used for both sweet and savoury dishes. Try using it as the basis of a splendid gâteau with cream, custard and fruit or for a savoury steak and kidney pie. Alternatively, serve it almost as it comes as savoury cheese nibbles with wine or as cream puffs for tea.

Equipment
Large mixing bowl
Hand sieve
Measuring jug
Rolling pin
Cake ring
Small knife
Pastry brush
Fork
Cling film

Ingredients:

500 g / 18 oz plain flour
50 g / 2 oz butter, at room temperature
1 teaspoon salt
375 ml / 13 fl oz water
2 tablespoons vinegar
450 g / 1 lb butter, chilled

Cooking time:

Preparation time:
30 minutes
Baking time:
15–20 minutes
Oven temperature:
220–230C, 425–450F, gas 7–8

Tips on preparation

☐ The pastry must be of the right consistency – soft, smooth and malleable, so that it will roll properly.

☐ Chill the butter thoroughly before using. It must not melt during rolling. If necessary put the pastry in the refrigerator between turns.

☐ It is a good idea to roll the pastry on a marble slab as this helps to keep it nice and cool.

Preparation

1. Measure the ingredients ready for use.

2. Sift the flour into a large mixing bowl.

3. Add 50 g/2 oz butter. It must be at room temperature.

4. Rub in using your fingertips to make coarse crumbs.

5. Sprinkle the salt on to the flour and butter mixture.

6. Add the vinegar.

7. Add the water slowly, not all at once.

8. Mix all the ingredients thoroughly together by hand.

9. Knead together to make a firm dough.

10. Shape into a ball, wrap in cling film and chill.

11. Place the chilled butter between two layers of cling film.

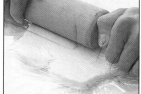
12. Using the rolling pin, roll it into a perfect rectangle.

13. Roll the pastry into a rectangle and place the butter on it.

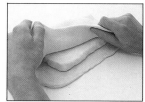
14. Fold the pastry over the butter.

15. Press the edges securely together.

16. Roll the pastry into a narrow rectangle.

17. Fold over exactly to make three layers.

18. Roll once more into a narrow rectangle.

19. Fold into three again and chill for 10 minutes.

20. Sprinkle the pastry with flour and roll again.

21. Fold into three once more.

22. Sprinkle with flour and roll out to 3–5 mm/$\frac{1}{8}$–$\frac{1}{2}$ in thick.

23. Lift the corners to relax the pastry.

24. Place the cake ring on the pastry and cut round it.

25. Brush a baking tray generously with water.

26. Place the round of pastry on the baking tray.

27. Prick several times with a fork.

28. Place the baking tray in a hot oven (220C, 425F, gas 7).

29. Bake for about 15 minutes until the pastry is golden brown.

30. Take the pastry out of the oven and leave to cool.

Fruit delight – the strawberry flan

Your guests will look on this as a feat of magic. When unexpected guests arrive you can have this magnificent, delicious-looking flan on the table in a quarter of an hour. Let's hope your coffee maker can be as quick!

Strawberry flan

200 g / 7 oz puff pastry from
basic recipe (page 167)

450 g / 1 lb fresh, whole
strawberries

350 g / 12 oz red currant jelly

1 tablespoon sugar

1. Roll the puff pastry out thinly. Cut round a cake ring and bake on a wet baking tray as in the basic recipe (see page 167).

2. Wash and hull the strawberries and dry separately on absorbent kitchen paper. When the pastry is almost cold arrange the strawberries on the top.

3. In a small pan, simmer the red currant jelly with the sugar over a low heat for 1 minute. Allow to cool slightly.

4. Brush the glaze generously over the strawberries.

Fruit flan variations

You can make flans using other fruit in exactly the same way as the Strawberry flan, depending on the season or what you have handy. You can use any sort of soft fruit or a mixture of several types, fresh or stewed apricots or peaches, exotic fruits such as mangoes or kiwis – in fact just about anything that tastes good and looks attractive. For an extra touch place the fruit on a layer of custard and sprinkle with chopped or flaked nuts. If preferred, replace the red currant jelly with apricot jam. Always eat the flan immediately as the juice from the fruit will make the base moist and then it becomes heavy.

Delicious for breakfast or with an aperitif

In the course of the day there are always many other opportunities to enjoy tasty pastries, either savoury or sweet. Bake in bulk and freeze some and then you will only need to warm the pastries through in the oven and they are ready to eat.

Cheese straws

(illustrated top row)

300 g/11 oz puff pastry from basic recipe (page 167)

200 g/7 oz freshly-grated cheese (e.g. Gruyère)

1 teaspoon sweet paprika

1. Roll the pastry out into a rectangle 20 × 25 cm/ 8 × 10 in and 3 mm/$\frac{1}{8}$ in thick. Sprinkle one half with the cheese and paprika.
2. Fold over the uncovered half, run the rolling pin lightly over it and then press firmly together.
3. Cut into strips about 1 cm/$\frac{1}{2}$ in wide and twist. Place on a wet baking tray, pressing the ends down gently.
4. Bake in a hot oven (230 C, 450 F, gas 8) for 10 to 15 minutes or until golden.

Apricot windmills

(illustrated centre row)

300 g/11 oz puff pastry from basic recipe (page 167)

1 (450-g/1-lb) can apricot halves

5 tablespoons apricot jam

1 tablespoon sugar

1. Roll the pastry into a 30-cm/12-in square and cut into nine 10-cm/4-in squares. Cut in from the corners as shown in the first photograph.
2. Fold each corner into the centre.
3. Drain the fruit thoroughly. Place an apricot half in the centre of each square and place on a wet baking tray.
4. Bake in a hot oven (220 C, 450 F, gas 8) for 15 to 20 minutes. Bring the apricot jam to the boil with the sugar and brush the glaze over the windmills.

Variations:
You can make the windmills with other fruit, like Morello cherries, cranberries or peaches.

Pigs' ears

(illustrated bottom row)

300 g/11 oz puff pastry from basic recipe (page 167)

75 g/3 oz sugar or vanilla sugar

1. Roll the pastry into a rectangle 15 × 30 cm/ 6 × 12 in and 3 mm/$\frac{1}{8}$ in thick. Brush with water and sprinkle evenly with sugar.
2. Roll the edges into the centre to make a flat roll.
3. Chill for 30 minutes. Then cut the roll into 5-mm/$\frac{1}{4}$-in slices
4. Place the slices separately on a wet baking tray. Bake in a hot oven (230 C, 450 F, gas 8) for 20 minutes or until cooked.

Crisp cases . . .

A plain pastry case like this has so many advantages. It keeps the filling moist and compact, seals in all the flavour and conceals the filling that perhaps would not be very attractive served on its own. It can turn something like a simple sausage into a tempting snack.

You will find different sorts of pasties in cook-books from every part of the world, for the idea of turning leftovers into something good and appetising is international. Here are a few suggestions from European and Far Eastern cooking. The fillings range from mild to fiery hot flavours.

Shapes

Rectangular like an envelope, square, folded into a triangle, rolled into a horn, round or half-moon-shaped; pasties come in a variety of shapes. And the same rule applies in every case. Roll the pastry (made from basic recipe pages 166–7) out to a 3 mm/$\frac{1}{8}$ in thickness, cut out the shape and place a little of the filling in the centre of each and brush the edges with egg white. This sticks the edges firmly together. Brush the top with egg yolk for a glazed finish when baked. Decorate with chopped nuts, poppy, sesame or caraway seeds.

Bake in a hot oven (230 C, 450 F, gas 8) for 15 to 30 minutes depending on size, until the pasties are fully risen and golden brown in colour. Then eat them as soon as possible, preferably while still hot.

Turkey filling

(illustrated right, centre top)

1 tablespoon butter
100 g/4 oz turkey breast, finely diced
75 g/3 oz luncheon meat, finely diced
75 g/3 oz uncooked ham, in fine strips
1 egg
100 g/4 oz Parmesan cheese, freshly grated
freshly grated nutmeg
salt and freshly ground black pepper

1. Dissolve the butter in a frying pan and quickly fry the turkey over a high heat for a few minutes, stirring continuously.
2. Place in a bowl and mix well with the remaining ingredients.

Sausage meat filling

(illustrated right, top right)

450 g/1 lb sausagemeat
1 onion, finely chopped
1 teaspoon salt
1 bread roll, softened in water
1 egg yolk
1 tablespoon finely chopped parsley

1. Work all the ingredients together in a mixing bowl to make a smooth, pliable filling.

Curry filling

(illustrated right, top left)

450 g/1 lb fresh apricots
100 g/4 oz walnuts, chopped
50 g/2 oz raisins
1 tablespoon curry powder
3 tablespoons grated coconut

1. Scald the apricots in boiling water and remove the skins. Cut in half and take out the stones. Cut the halves into wedges.
2. Mix the fruit with the remaining ingredients.

Spinach and ricotta filling

(illustrated left of centre row)

450 g/1 lb fresh spinach

225 g/8 oz ricotta (Italian cream cheese)

2 eggs

100 g/4 oz Parmesan cheese, freshly grated

salt and freshly ground black pepper

olive oil

1. Sort and wash the spinach and cook quickly for a few minutes in a pan of boiling, salted water. Rinse in cold water. Using your hands squeeze out excess water, then coarsely chop the spinach.
2. Crumble the ricotta into a bowl and mix well with the spinach, eggs and Parmesan.
3. Season with salt and pepper and a few drops of olive oil.

Tomato and red pepper filling

(illustrated middle of centre row)

4 large beefsteak tomatoes

2 red peppers, deseeded

1 tablespoon paprika

2 tablespoons chopped fresh basil

salt and freshly ground black pepper

2 egg yolks

1. Scald and peel the tomatoes, remove the seeds and finely chop. Leave to drain in a sieve.
2. Finely dice the peppers.
3. Mix all the ingredients together binding with the egg yolk and use immediately.

Bacon and spring onion filling

(illustrated right of centre row)

225 g/8 oz rindless streaky bacon finely diced

275 g/10 oz spring onions, cut into thin rings

salt and freshly ground black pepper

1. Fry the bacon in a dry pan over a high heat. Drain and mix with the onions.
2. Season sparingly with salt and generously with pepper.

Chinese filling

(illustrated bottom left)

350 g/12 oz pork, minced or finely chopped

50 g/2 oz mushrooms, finely chopped

½ teaspoon cornflour

2 teaspoons soy sauce

2 teaspoons sherry

1 teaspoon sesame oil

225 g/8 oz peeled, cooked prawns, coarsely chopped

100 g/4 oz spring onions, cut into fine rings

salt and freshly ground black pepper

½ teaspoon sugar

1. Thoroughly mix together the meat, mushrooms and cornflour.
2. Then mix in the remaining ingredients, blending well together.

Mushroom filling

(illustrated centre bottom)

3 slices white bread

350 g/12 oz mushrooms, chopped

3 onions, diced

3 tablespoons olive oil

salt and freshly ground black pepper

1. Remove the crusts from the bread and crumble into breadcrumbs.
2. Fry the mushrooms and onions in the oil in a frying pan over a high heat for a few minutes. Cool slightly and then mix with the breadcrumbs. Season to taste.

Meat and raisin filling

(illustrated bottom right)

2 onions, chopped

1 tablespoon olive oil

225 g/8 oz minced beef

2 tablespoons raisins, soaked in water

1 teaspoon dried chillies, deseeded and crumbled

¼ teaspoon ground caraway seeds

salt and freshly ground black pepper

1. Fry the onions in the oil in a frying pan over a high heat. Remove and cool.
2. Mix the onions thoroughly with the rest of the ingredients.

Upside-down flans, where the base becomes the lid

This sounds stranger than it is. The basic idea is really a very good one. Since juicy fruit soon makes the crispest flan case soggy, the whole thing has simply been turned on its head so that the filling becomes the base and the base becomes a lid.

First the right equipment

Pie dishes are traditionally oval in shape, but an ovenproof ceramic or stoneware flan dish with a fluted edge makes a pretty substitute.
Pies are served straight from the oven in the baking dish, so it is a good idea to choose a plain white one as this goes with anything. To serve, cut an opening in the top with a sharp knife to allow you to spoon out the filling.

Decoration

To reroll leftover pastry, don't press it into a ball, as this destroys the fine layers, but lay the pieces flat on top of one another. Using a pastry wheel or small cutters cut out hearts, circles, leaves, moons, stars or strips. Strips of pastry twisted together and placed around the rim look very attractive.

Rhubarb pie

Ingredients for a 23-cm/9-in dish:

675 g/ 1½ lb young rhubarb
100 g/ 4 oz sugar
½ teaspoon cinnamon
350 g/ 12 oz puff pastry
from basic recipe
page 167
1 egg yolk for coating

1. Trim the rhubarb and cut into 5-cm/2-in lengths. Mix with the sugar and cinnamon.
2. On a floured worktop roll the pastry to 5 mm/ ¼ in thick. Cut a circle 2.5–5 cm/ 1–2 in larger in diameter than the dish.
3. Place the fruit in the dish. Wet the outside rim of the dish with water. Place the pastry lid on the dish and press firmly to the rim.
4. Brush the pastry with egg yolk.
5. Cut the remaining pastry into decorative shapes, arrange on the lid and brush with egg yolk.
6. Bake in a hot oven (220C, 425F, gas 7) for about 40 minutes.

Variations:
Instead of rhubarb try ripe plums, peaches or apricots. Since the puff pastry is neutral in flavour it can also be used to make savoury meat pies.

Hot apple tarts for dessert

These tarts are something really special. As is so often the case, they were invented by the food-loving French, who always know a good thing when they see one. On a crisp and light pastry base, sliced apple is arranged decoratively and dusted with icing sugar. These flans should be eaten hot straight from the oven.

Dessert ideas

A dessert like this is the ideal thing for a dinner party. You can make up the tarts and keep them in the refrigerator all ready to go into the oven when you need them. Another advantage is that you can freeze them in the same way, and cook them from frozen. They will only need a few minutes' extra baking. The photograph contains a few suggestions on how to serve these apple tarts. Accompany them with a raspberry sorbet, for example, a chocolate mousse, nut ice cream or strawberry purée, garnished with fresh strawberries. Any other sort of fruit sauce is also delicious or a spoonful of vanilla or coconut ice slowly melting on the tart . . . the possibilities are almost endless.

Apple tarts

Makes 4 to 6:

250 g / 9 oz puff pastry from basic recipe (page 167)

4–6 small dessert apples

100 g / 4 oz icing sugar

1. On a floured worktop roll the pastry out very thinly to 3 mm/$\frac{1}{8}$ in thick. Cut four or six circles of about 10-cm/4-in diameter.
2. Place on a wet baking tray and prick several times with a fork.
3. Peel, halve, core and thinly slice the apples.
4. Arrange them neatly around the pastry, slightly overlapping to give an attractive pattern, leaving a narrow border of about 1 cm/$\frac{1}{2}$ in.
5. Sprinkle the apples with icing sugar.
6. Bake in a very hot oven (240 C, 475 F, gas 9) for 10 to 15 minutes.

Variation:
Instead of puff pastry you can use shortcrust pastry (see Apple flan, page 110–1).

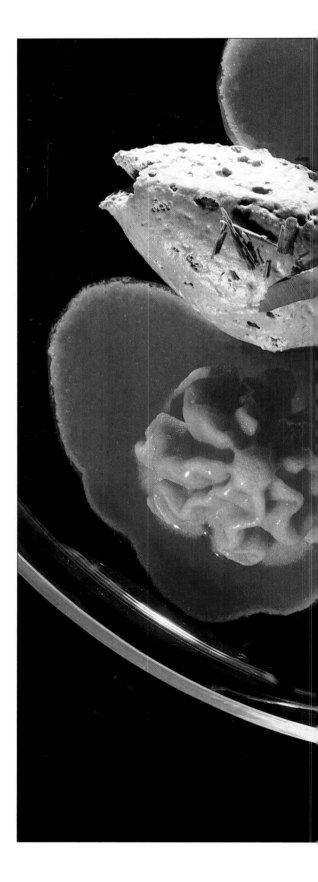

Cream slices

puff pastry from basic
recipe (page 167)

1 litre/1¾ pints milk

1 vanilla pod

8 egg yolks

200 g/7 oz sugar

40 g/1½ oz plain flour

50 g/2 oz icing sugar (for dusting)

1. Roll the pastry out very thinly to 3 mm/⅛ in thick and cut three rectangles the same size as the baking tray. Place each on a wet baking tray and prick with a fork.

2. Bake in a hot oven (230C, 450F, gas 8) for 15 minutes or until cooked.

3. Bring the milk to the boil in a saucepan with the vanilla pod.

4. Beat the egg yolks with the sugar and flour to give a thick paste, continuing until the sugar has dissolved. Add to the boiling milk. Return to the boil and then remove from the heat.

5. Strain the hot custard.

6. Trim the edges of the pastry with a knife.

7. Spread half the warm custard on to one sheet of pastry.

8. Cover with a second sheet of pastry and add the rest of the custard.

9. Top with the last sheet of pastry and dust with the icing sugar.

10. Using a sharp, saw-toothed knife, cut the cake into rectangles or squares.

Dutch cherry gâteau

300 g/11 oz puff pastry
from basic recipe (page 167)
500 g/18 oz fresh Morello
cherries
40 g/1½ oz sugar
generous pinch of ground
cinnamon
1 tablespoon cornflour
2 tablespoons water
600 ml/1 pint double
cream
2 tablespoons sugar
250 g/9 oz icing sugar

1. On a floured worktop roll the pastry out very thinly to 3 mm/⅛ in thick. Use a cake ring to cut into three rounds.
2. Place on a wet baking tray and prick with a fork.
3. Bake in a hot oven (220 C, 450 F, gas 8) for 15 minutes or until cooked.
4. Meanwhile gently cook the cherries with the 40 g/1½ oz sugar and cinnamon in a covered pan to produce some juice and then bring to the boil. Keep 8 cherries on one side for decoration and reserve 2 tablespoons juice to go in the icing.
5. Dissolve the cornflour in the water and add to the boiling cherries. Return to the boil and then remove the pan from the heat.

A dream of a cream cake

6. Arrange the hot cherries on one of the rounds of pastry and leave to cool.
7. Whip the cream until stiff, gradually adding the 2 tablespoons sugar. Spoon the cream into a piping bag with a fluted nozzle.
8. Pipe half the cream around the cherries.
9. Cover exactly with a second round of pastry and cover with the remaining cream, keeping a little back to decorate.
10. Stir the reserved cherry juice with the icing sugar to make a thick icing. Spread on the third round of pastry and place on top of the gâteau.
11. Decorate the top with whirls of cream and the reserved cherries.

The trick we mentioned: To avoid squashing the layers more than necessary when you cut the cake, cut the top into portions before you place it on the gâteau.

Who could resist it? A wonderful gâteau whose charm lies in the contrast between the crisp layers of puff pastry and the smooth fruit cream. It is extremely easy to make, although cutting it may prove more of a problem. But there is a trick to help here . . .

The delicious strudel, Danish pastry and all those other specialities

Tips on the dough

First you make a yeast dough exactly as in the basic recipe (see page 119), then you leave it to rise before working in the butter by rolling and folding as for puff pastry. There are several points to watch:

☐ The yeast dough must be quite firm. If it is too soft the butter will be absorbed into it and no layers will be formed. It is a good idea to leave the dough to rise overnight in the refrigerator and by the following morning it will be just the right consistency.

☐ The butter should not be used straight from the refrigerator or the dough will prove difficult to roll.

☐ As a basic rule both dough and butter should be of similar consistency.

☐ To prevent the dough sticking to the worktop as you roll it, sprinkle it repeatedly with flour.

☐ Use the dough immediately or it will dry out, break and be almost impossible to roll.

The results of a happy partnership

If you prepare yeast dough in the same way as puff pastry, you get a really excellent pastry which combines the qualities of both. It has the lightness and body of yeast pastry while being as crisp and tender as freshly baked puff pastry. Like puff pastry it has hundreds of separate layers and a delicious buttery flavour. The best-known example of this type of pastry are croissants, the delicious crescents which the French love for breakfast.

What makes croissant dough so good?

There are two ingredients which make croissant dough what it is. First the yeast which gives it volume and a crumbly texture, then the layers of butter which make it light. The basic dough contains very little butter, for most of the butter is incorporated in a block by repeated rolling and folding.

Tips on baking

☐ Leave plenty of space between the croissants on the baking tray which should be greased or covered with non-stick baking parchment. They rise during baking and need plenty of space if they are not to stick together and be difficult to separate.

☐ Before baking, leave the croissants to rise for 30 to 60 minutes. If you cover them with a damp cloth they will not dry out.

☐ Keep an eye on the croissants as they bake. They won't necessarily all brown at the same time as the heat in the oven is not always evenly distributed. Take the croissants out of the oven as soon as they are golden brown, leaving any paler ones for a few minutes longer.

☐ For a nice shiny finish, brush the croissants with warm water or cream before they go into the oven.

☐ For that famous shiny, crusty finish brush the croissants with a little beaten egg yolk.

☐ Cool the cooked croissants quickly on a wire rack, but always serve them while still warm for this is when they are at their best and they just melt in the mouth.

Equipment
Mixing bowl
Sieve
Saucepan
Tea-towel
Rolling pin
Ruler
Pastry wheel

Ingredients:
12 croissants

500 g/18 oz plain flour	
250 ml/8 fl oz milk	
40 g/1½ oz fresh yeast or	
20 g/¾ oz dried yeast	
25 g/1 oz sugar	
pinch of salt	
2 eggs	
250 g/9 oz butter	

Cooking time:
Preparation time:	
20 minutes	
Resting time:	
about 3 hours	
Oven temperature:	
200 C, 400 F, gas 6	
Baking time:	
15 minutes	
Cooling time:	
about 10 minutes	

Storing

Croissant dough freezes well. If you freeze the dough in a block it will take a very long time to thaw, so the best way is to freeze the ready-baked croissants. To do this place the cold croissants on a flat dish and freeze in the fast freeze compartment before transferring them to plastic bags.

Thawing

Reheat the croissants from frozen on a greased and floured baking tray in a moderately hot oven (200 C, 400 F, gas 6). It takes only 5 minutes for them to thaw and warm through. Take them out of the oven and leave them on the baking tray for 10 minutes. They will taste just as delicious as freshly baked croissants!

Preparation of yeast dough Step-by-step photographs page 119

1. Measure the ingredients and bring to room temperature.

2. Sift the flour into a large mixing bowl.

3. Warm the milk slightly in a saucepan over a low heat.

4. Crumble the yeast into the lukewarm milk.

5. Add a little flour and stir to give a thick paste.

6. Sprinkle the mixture with a pinch of sugar.

7. Cover the paste with a cloth and leave to stand for 30 minutes.

8. Mix remaining sugar and salt into the flour; make a well in the centre.

9. Break the eggs into the well.

10. Cut 50 g/2 oz butter into flakes and scatter over the flour.

11. Pour on the yeast paste from the pan.

12. Work all the ingredients together to make a smooth dough.

Preparation of croissant dough

13. Cover the bowl and leave the dough to rise for 2 to 3 hours.

14. When the dough has doubled in volume, knead it through.

15. Roll the dough out into a square.

16. Make the butter into a block and dust with flour.

17. Place the block of butter across the centre of the dough.

18. Fold the corners of the dough over the butter.

19. Roll the block of dough out very precisely into a rectangle.

20. Fold the dough over into three.

21. Roll out again, fold over and repeat the whole process.

22. Cover the dough with a tea-towel and leave to rise for 15 minutes.

23. Roll the dough out to 50 × 30 cm/20 × 12 in. Cut into 15-cm/6-in strips.

24. Using a ruler and pastry wheel, cut into triangles.

25. Roll up the triangles starting at the base and curve slightly.

26. Place on a greased and floured baking tray leaving room for expansion.

27. Again cover with a tea-towel and leave to rise for about 30 minutes.

28. Bake in the preheated oven for 20 minutes until golden brown.

Sweet or savoury: versatile croissants

Croissant dough is neutral in flavour. The small amount of sugar in the basic dough serves only to stimulate the yeast, not to sweeten the dough. So you can use croissant dough for any type of filling. With sweet fillings they are delicious for breakfast or tea time. Filled with ham and cheese they make an appetising savoury snack served with an aperitif or a glass of wine.

Cheese croissants

(illustrated top left)
Allow about 50 g/2 oz cheese per croissant. Use a cheese with plenty of flavour which will stand out above the buttery flavour of the dough. Emmental, Gruyère or a mature Gouda are all very good. Cut the cheese into thin fingers and place across the base of the triangle. Sprinkle with paprika, roll up the croissant from the base of the triangle and bend into a croissant shape.

Ham croissants

(illustrated top right)
Use a good flavoured uncooked ham (such as Parma), or alternatively a smoked ham. The ham should be cut as thin as possible allowing one slice per croissant. To make the croissant more moist use strips of boiled ham mixed with chopped fresh herbs and lightly fried chopped onion and roll in the croissant dough.

Filled nut croissants

(illustrated bottom left)
For the filling allow 1 tablespoon chopped hazelnuts with 1 teaspoon each sugar and rum per croissant. Mix the filling together and spread along the base of the triangle, roll up and curve into a croissant shape. Instead of hazelnuts you can use almonds, walnuts or pistachios. If you would like to include a few raisins, soak them first in rum for extra flavour.

Chocolate croissants

(illustrated centre bottom)
You can use plain or milk chocolate, whichever type you prefer, or try a chocolate flake which melts faster than whole pieces of chocolate during baking and so soaks more into the pastry. If you like you can also add a little grated or chopped nut which gives the croissants a nice bite. When cooked, the croissants can also be iced if you like (see page 248).

Apple croissants

(illustrated bottom right)
You can make this filling in advance. Peel, quarter, core and thinly slice a small cooking apple. Sprinkle with a little white wine and cook in a covered saucepan until soft. Sweeten to taste and add a drop of rum or Calvados if you like. Stir in a few raisins or flaked almonds. Leave the filling to stand for a short time before rolling in the croissant dough.

Danish pastries which in fact come from Vienna!

In Vienna they are known as Copenhagen pastries, in Copenhagen as Viennese pastries. Each country courteously credits the other with the honour of having invented them. Whoever did invent them, one thing is certain: they are delicious pastries with their custard or fruit fillings – eating one is just not enough.

Apple pasties

(illustrated far left and right)
Makes 12:

*basic croissant dough
recipe (page 183)*
800 g / 1¾ lb cooking apples
100 g / 4 oz sugar
1 cinnamon stick
*250 ml / 8 fl oz dry white
wine*
egg white
For coating:
1 beaten egg yolk
100 g / 4 oz apricot jam

1. Make the dough as in
the basic recipe (see page
183) and roll out into a
rectangle 3 mm/⅛ in thick.
Cut into pieces
15 × 13 cm/6 × 5 in.
2. To make the filling,
peel, quarter, core and
slice the apples. Cook
with the sugar, cinnamon
and white wine in a
covered pan over a low
heat for 10 to 15 minutes,
or until cooked.
3. When the filling has
cooled slightly, spread it
over half of each piece of
pastry. Brush the edges
with a little egg white to
seal them well.
4. Fold the plain half over
the filling and press firmly
around the edges.
5. Make a few cuts along
the join on the long side
and brush the top with
the egg yolk. Place on a
greased and floured
baking tray.
6. Bake in a moderately
hot oven (200 C, 400 F, gas
6) for 20 to 30 minutes, or
until cooked.
7. Heat the apricot jam
gently in a small saucepan
and brush over the pasties
while still warm.

Curd Danish pastries

(illustrated front left)
Makes 12 to 15:

*basic croissant dough
recipe (page 183)*
*250 g / 9 oz low-fat curd
cheese*
2 egg yolks
3 tablespoons sugar
2 tablespoons raisins
For coating:
1 beaten egg yolk
100 g / 4 oz apricot jam

1. Make the dough as in
the basic recipe (see page
183) and roll out very
thinly to 3 mm/⅛ in thick.
Cut the pastry into 13-
cm/5-in squares.
2. To make the filling,
mix the curd cheese with
the egg yolks and sugar
either in a blender or
with an electric whisk.
Then fold in the raisins.
3. Place 1 tablespoon
filling on each square of
pastry. Fold the edges in
to make a narrow rim.
4. Brush the rim with
beaten egg yolk. Bake the
pastries on a greased and
floured baking tray in a
moderately hot oven
(200 C, 400 F, gas 6) for 15
to 20 minutes.
5. Heat the apricot jam
gently in a small saucepan
and brush over the
pastries while still warm.

Marzipan rings

(illustrated centre)
Makes 12:

*basic croissant dough
recipe (page 183)*
200 g / 7 oz marzipan
250 ml / 8 fl oz milk
200 g / 7 oz flaked almonds
For coating:
1 egg yolk
100 g / 4 oz apricot jam

1. Make the dough as in
the basic recipe (see page
183) and then roll out
very thinly into a
rectangle 3 mm/⅛ in thick.
2. Using a pastry wheel,
cut into rectangles of
13 × 7.5 cm/5 × 3 in.
3. Dilute the marzipan
with the milk. This is
easiest to do in a small
saucepan over a low heat.
Then blend in a liquidiser
to give a smooth paste of
spreading consistency.
4. Thinly spread the
marzipan over the pastry.
5. Fold the pastry over
lengthways and cut along
the centre, leaving the
ends intact.
6. Twist the ends through
the centre slit, twisting
one over from above, the
other from below.
7. Brush with the beaten
egg and scatter with
flaked almonds. Bake on a
greased and floured
baking tray in a
moderately hot oven
(200 C, 400 F, gas 6) for 15
to 20 minutes until golden
brown.
8. Heat the apricot jam
gently in a small saucepan
and stir until smooth.
Brush over the pastries
while still warm.

Cherry Danish pastries

(illustrated bottom right)
Makes 12 to 15:

*basic croissant dough
recipe (page 183)*
450 g / 1 lb Morello cherries
5 tablespoons sugar
pinch of ground cinnamon
3 tablespoons cornflour
3 tablespoons water
egg white
For coating:
1 beaten egg yolk
100 g / 4 oz apricot jam

1. Make the dough as in
the basic recipe (see page
183) and roll out very
thinly to 3 mm/⅛ in thick.
Cut into 15-cm/6-in
squares.
2. In a covered pan over a
moderate heat, cook the
cherries with the sugar
and cinnamon for about
10–15 minutes. Stir the
cornflour with the water
and stir into the cherries.
Bring to the boil and then
simmer for a few minutes
until the juice has
thickened.
3. Spoon 1 tablespoon of
cherries into the middle
of each square of pastry.
4. Brush one corner with
egg white. Fold the
opposite corner over the
cherries and press down.
5. Brush the pastry with
the egg yolk and decorate
with thin strips of leftover
pastry.
6. Bake on a greased and
floured baking tray in a
moderately hot oven
(200 C, 400 F, gas 6) for up
to 20 minutes, or until
cooked.
7. Heat the apricot jam
gently in a small saucepan
and brush over the
pastries while still warm.

Crispy outside, tender inside and quite irresistible

Nevertheless, there are many who regard fruit fritters, or beignets as they are known in France, with much suspicion, as they do anything that is deep-fried. It is frying in fat that puts people off them, but if they are fried at the right temperature, very little fat is absorbed by the batter. You can always get rid of any excess fat by just blotting the fritters with some absorbent kitchen paper.

Tips on deep-frying

☐ It is entirely a matter of personal taste whether you use oil, lard or vegetable fat. Butter is, however, unsuitable for it is impossible to get it hot enough.

☐ Fat for deep-frying needs to be at a temperature of 180C/350F. With an electric frier you can set the correct temperature, but if you use a chip pan, you will have to test for the correct temperature by placing the handle of a wooden spoon in the fat. If it produces small bubbles, the fat has reached the right temperature.

Note: Never try to fry too much at once as this will cool the fat. By the time the fat has reheated the batter will have absorbed fat and will not crisp up.

Tips on the batter

☐ Instead of using beer you can substitute mineral water in the batter. Always leave the batter to stand for 30 minutes before folding in the egg whites. This gives the flour time to develop its gluten content and makes the batter lighter.

☐ Begin frying as soon as the egg whites are added, otherwise the ingredients will separate and the batter won't cling to the fruit.

Basic pineapple fritters

Makes 30

| 2 egg yolks |
| 250 ml/8 fl oz beer |
| 5 tablespoons flour |
| 2 egg whites |
| 3 tablespoons sugar |
| 8 canned pineapple rings |
| flour for coating |
| oil or lard for frying |
| To decorate: |
| 3 tablespoons sugar |
| 2 teaspoons ground cinnamon |

I. Using an electric whisk, or better still a liquidiser, blend the egg yolks, beer and flour to give a smooth, thin batter. Leave to stand for 30 minutes.

2. Just before you want to use the batter, whisk the egg whites until stiff, slowly adding the sugar. Keep whisking until the whites are again stiff and the sugar dissolved.

3. Fold the egg whites into the batter.

4. Thoroughly dry the pineapple rings on absorbent kitchen paper. Coat in flour and shake off any excess.

5. Dip the rings one at a time in the batter and fry in the hot fat for 2 to 3 minutes until golden.

6. Drain the fritters on absorbent kitchen paper and serve dusted with sugar and cinnamon.

A gingerbread house for Christmas!

The Ancient Greeks regarded gingerbread as symbolic of long life, while in the Middle Ages it was fed to the seriously ill as an elixir of life to make them recover. As recently as the last century midwives were rewarded with gingerbread after helping a new baby into the world. So, as you can see, the symbolism of birth and life is very strong with gingerbread and Christmas is the ideal time to make a gingerbread house.

Basic recipe for gingerbread

350g/12oz clear honey

100g/4oz sugar

100g/4oz butter

1 egg

grated rind of 1 lemon

1 tablespoon cocoa powder

½ teaspoon each ground cinnamon, ground cloves, ground cardamom, freshly grated nutmeg, allspice, ground coriander, ground ginger, baking powder and bicarbonate of soda

1 tablespoon water

500g/18oz plain flour

1. Stirring continuously warm the honey, sugar and butter in a saucepan over a low heat, until the sugar has completely dissolved. Cool until the mixture is hand-hot.
2. Add the egg, lemon rind, cocoa powder and all the spices. Dissolve the baking powder and bicarbonate of soda in the water and add to the honey mixture with the flour. Knead well together to give a firm dough.
3. Wrap the dough in aluminium foil and leave to stand for 24 hours at room temperature.
4. Knead the dough thoroughly and roll out very thinly on a floured worktop to 1.5–3 mm/$\frac{1}{16}$–$\frac{1}{8}$ in thick.
5. Cut the dough into rectangles or other shapes and place on a greased and floured baking tray. Bake in a moderate oven (180C, 350F, gas 4) for 15 to 20 minutes.
6. Remove from the baking tray while still hot and cool on a wire rack. Pack with a few slices of apple in an airtight tin to increase moisture.
7. After three to five days the gingerbread will be soft and ready for coating with icing or chocolate and decorating.

Gingerbread house

Using the diagram below as a guide, cut cardboard patterns from a sheet the same size as your baking tray. Try assembling the cardboard to make sure the pieces fit together properly. Then using the basic gingerbread recipe (see left) but doubling the quantities, make your gingerbread and roll out very thinly to 1.5–3 mm/$\frac{1}{16}$–$\frac{1}{8}$ in thick. Bake on two baking trays. One piece serves as a base. Using the cardboard patterns, cut the other piece into the required sections of the house: 2 gables, 2 side walls, 2 roofs.
Cut the remaining gingerbread to make fencing, doors, shutters, etc. Assemble the house, sticking the sections together with white icing. Use sheets of red fondant for windows. Decorate as illustrated or use your own ideas.

Gingerbread buns

(illustrated page 60)

1 basic gingerbread recipe (see left)

For the filling:

100g/4oz marzipan

6 tablespoons cherry liqueur

125g/4½oz raisins

100g/4oz almonds, chopped

50g/2oz hazelnuts, chopped

4 tablespoons apricot jam

1. Make the gingerbread as in the basic recipe (see left). Roll out into a rectangle 3 mm/$\frac{1}{8}$ in thick.
2. Mix the filling ingredients and spread on the gingerbread.
3. Roll up the gingerbread from the long side.
Cut into slices, about 1 cm/½ in thick, and place cut side uppermost on a greased and floured baking tray. Bake in a moderate oven (180C, 350F, gas 4) for 35 to 40 minutes, or until cooked.

Gingerbread Basle-style

(illustrated page 60)

375g/13oz honey

175g/6oz sugar

250g/9oz almonds, chopped

generous pinch each of ground cardamom, ground cinnamon, ground nutmeg and ground coriander

100g/4oz chopped mixed peel

2 tablespoons cherry liqueur

375g/13oz plain flour

For the icing:

100g/4oz icing sugar

2 tablespoons water

1. Heat the honey and sugar in a saucepan. Work in remaining ingredients.
2. Spread the mixture out to a 1-cm/½-in thickness on a greased baking tray. Bake in a moderate oven (180C, 350F, gas 4) for 20 to 25 minutes.
3. Mix the icing sugar with the water and spread on the hot cake. Cut into small rectangles.

Honey cake

(illustrated page 61)

100g/4oz honey

6 tablespoons sunflower oil

100g/4oz brown sugar

60g/2½oz plain chocolate

90g/3¼oz ground almonds

pinch of salt

½ teaspoon ground cinnamon

½ teaspoon ground cloves

2 eggs

3 tablespoons rum

2 teaspoons baking powder

250g/9oz plain flour

For the topping:

50g/2oz blanched almonds, chopped

60g/2½oz raisins

50g/2oz candied lemon peel, chopped

50g/2oz candied orange peel, chopped

50g/2oz red glacé cherries

50g/2oz walnut halves

100g/4oz whole almonds

50g/2oz crystallised sugar

1. Stirring continuously, heat the honey, oil and sugar in a saucepan over a moderate heat until the sugar completely dissolves.
2. Leave to cool to hand-hot and then melt the chocolate into the mixture. Stir in the ground almonds, salt, cinnamon, cloves, eggs and rum. Transfer to a mixing bowl.
3. Mix the baking powder with the flour. Sift into the mixture and stir in thoroughly.
4. Spread the mixture over a greased and floured, shallow 25-cm/10-in square tin. Spread evenly with the ingredients for the topping.
5. Bake in a moderate oven (180C, 350F, gas 4) for 1 hour.
6. Cool on a wire tray, cut into rectangles and serve.

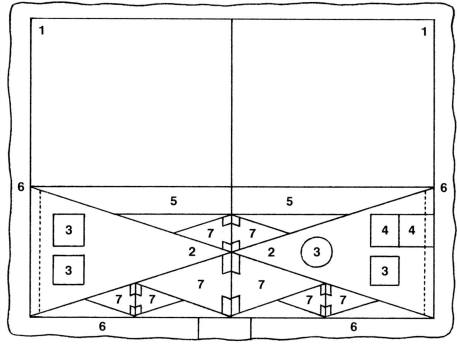

Gingerbread-house patterns

1. Roof   2. Gable   3. Window   4. Door   5. Chimney   6. Fence   7. Fir trees

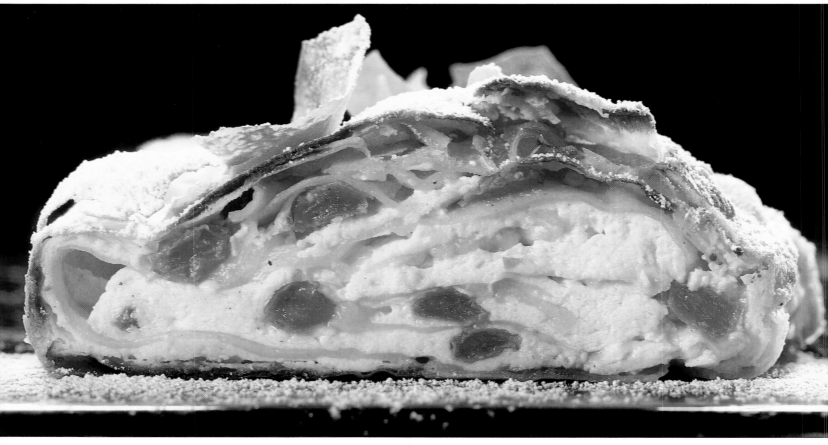

How to make wonderful strudels

The world record holder for making strudels is a Viennese pastry cook Heinrich Wittmann who made only one attempt at the record, the very first time the competition was held. And when his fellow-competitors saw the lightning speed with which he produced five perfect strudels within ten minutes, they could do nothing but concede victory. His secret is not to pull and stretch the pastry over the backs of his hands as the cookbooks recommend, a process that requires time and patience, but to throw it repeatedly into the air until it forms a sheet the size of a tablecloth and as thin as air. Don't try it yourself until you are confident about making strudels!

Basic recipe for strudel

Makes 2:

250 g / 9 oz plain flour
pinch of salt
1–2 tablespoons oil or melted butter
2 egg yolks
up to 9 tablespoons lukewarm water
oil or melted butter for coating

1. Sift the flour with the salt into a mixing bowl.
2. Make a well in the centre and sprinkle in the oil or cooled, melted butter.
3. Add the egg yolks. Work in using the dough hook attachment of an electric mixer, adding sufficient water to give a soft, uniform dough. Continue beating until the dough comes away from the sides of the bowl. Alternatively knead by hand for 10 to 15 minutes.

4. Knead through on a floured worktop, throwing it repeatedly on to the worktop until the dough is soft and elastic.
5. Shape the dough into a flattened ball and brush with oil or melted butter. Leave to stand for at least 30 minutes (preferably overnight), wrapped in aluminium foil or, better still, under a pan rinsed out with boiling water, for the dough must on no account dry out.

Stretching the pastry

This is done on a large cloth. Spread the pastry on the worktop (allowing plenty of space to work) and sprinkle with flour. Halve the pastry and stretch each piece separately. First roll with the rolling pin to about the size of a dinner plate. Brush with oil and butter. Then run the backs of your hands under the pastry, stretching it as you go until it is extremely thin and covers the whole cloth. Cut off any thick portions around the edges. Fill immediately to prevent the pastry from drying out.

Curd cheese strudel

Two strudels to serve 6 to 8:

1 basic strudel recipe (see left)

For the filling:

1 kg/2¼ lb low-fat curd cheese

200 g/7 oz sugar

25 g/1 oz soft butter

2 eggs

2 egg yolks

grated rind of 1 lemon

50 g/2 oz raisins

100 g/4 oz melted butter for coating

100 g/4 oz breadcrumbs for coating

50 g/2 oz icing sugar for dusting

1. Make the pastry as in the basic recipe (see left) and leave to rest.

2. To make the filling drain the curd cheese in a sieve. Beat together the sugar, butter, eggs and egg yolks until thick. Add the lemon rind and the raisins.
3. Strain the curd cheese through the sieve into the filling and stir well.
4. Stretch the pastry until thin. Brush with the butter and sprinkle with breadcrumbs.
5. Spread the curd filling on half the pastry, leaving a narrow border.
6. Lift the long side of the tea-towel where the filling is and the strudel will roll up itself.
7. Fold the ends over. Place the strudel with the join underneath in a greased and floured baking tin. Brush generously with butter. Bake in a hot oven (220 C, 425 F, gas 7) for 45 to 55 minutes.
8. Leave the strudel to stand for 10 minutes before cutting to give the filling time to set. Serve dusted with icing sugar.

Fruit strudel

1 basic strudel recipe (see left)

For the filling:

100 g/4 oz butter, melted

150 g/5 oz gingerbread crumbs

150 g/5 oz dried apricots

200 g/7 oz dried figs

100 g/4 oz candied peel

100 g/4 oz dried pears

50 g/2 oz pistachio nuts

50 g/2 oz icing sugar for dusting

1. Make the pastry as in the basic recipe (see left), leave to rest and then stretch.
2. Brush with butter and scatter with the gingerbread crumbs. Chop and mix the remaining ingredients and spread over half the pastry.
3. Roll the strudel as given in the Curd strudel recipe (see left), bake and serve.

Linzer torte

This is one of the most famous of cakes from Vienna and is also one of the oldest. The recipe was first recorded in 1719 in Conrad Hagger's *Salzburg Cookery Book*. Since then many bakers have added their own variations. One thing, however, is common to all the recipes and that is that the pastry contains the aromatic cinnamon and cloves.

150 g / 5 oz butter, chilled
150 g / 5 oz plain flour
150 g / 5 oz ground,
unpeeled almonds
1 egg yolk
2 hard-boiled egg yolks,
sieved
grated rind and juice of
1 lemon
generous pinch each of
ground cinnamon and
ground cloves
pinch of salt
For the topping:
250 g / 9 oz raspberry jam
1 beaten egg yolk for
coating

1. Mix all the pastry ingredients and work quickly together into a ball. Wrap in aluminium foil and chill for 1 hour.
2. Roll two-thirds of the pastry out very thinly to 3 mm/$\frac{1}{8}$ in thick. Use to line a 25-cm/1-in springform tin, bringing the pastry 1 cm/$\frac{1}{2}$ in up the sides and cutting off the rest.
3. Cover the base with jam.
4. Cut the remaining pastry into strips 5 mm/$\frac{1}{4}$ in wide and arrange in a lattice pattern over the jam.
5. Brush with the egg yolk. Bake in a moderately hot oven (200 C, 400 F, gas 6) for 35 to 40 minutes, or until cooked.
Note: Leave the cake to cool in the tin before turning out to allow it to firm up for the pastry tends to be very crumbly.

Macaroon pastry

For light, crispy macaroons you need what is called an egg-white mixture. This consists of egg whites and plenty of sugar, with almonds or other nuts added instead of flour, or alternatively coconut. For lighter macaroons whisk the egg whites before adding the marzipan.

Almond macaroons

Makes 16:
200 g / 7 oz marzipan
50 g / 2 oz ground almonds
1 egg white
50 g / 2 oz sugar
50 g / 2 oz flaked almonds

1. Work the marzipan with the egg white and sugar until smooth.
2. Spoon the mixture into a piping bag fitted with a plain nozzle. Pipe small balls on to a greased and floured baking tray and sprinkle with extra sugar. Alternatively shape into a roll about 3 cm/$2\frac{1}{2}$ in. in diameter and cut into 2-cm/$\frac{3}{4}$-in slices.
3. Shape each slice into a small roll, coat in flaked almonds and shape into crescents or balls.

4. Place the crescents or balls on a greased and floured baking tray. Bake in a moderately hot oven (190 C, 375 F, gas 5) for 15 minutes until pale gold in colour.
Note: Almond macaroons are best eaten fresh, but they will stay crisp for a few days if stored in an airtight tin immediately on cooling.

Baumkuchen cake

Baumkuchen cake, that slender, towering cake with its thin, delicious layers is one of the very best. The delicate mixture which is rich in eggs but contains only a little flour or cornflour (which makes it extremely light), is not baked in a tin but on a rotating plate in front of a source of heat. At home it can be baked in layers in a springform tin. This makes it truly a gâteau.

200 g / 7 oz butter, softened

pinch of salt

8 egg yolks

3 tablespoons milk

175 g / 6 oz cornflour

10 egg whites

200 g / 7 oz sugar

200 g / 7 oz apricot jam

For the icing:

200 g / 7 oz icing sugar

2 tablespoons lemon juice

1. Line a 25-cm/10-in springform tin with non-stick baking parchment.
2. Using an electric whisk, cream the butter in a mixing bowl until fluffy, adding the salt. Add the egg yolks two at a time, each time with a little milk and a quarter of the cornflour and beat thoroughly. Wait each time until you have a thick, uniform mixture before adding any more.
3. Whisk the egg whites until stiff. Then whisk in the sugar.
4. First fold in a quarter of the egg white with a spatula or whisk.
5. Then fold in the remaining egg white gently, but thoroughly, until you can see no more lumps of white.
6. Use the mixture at once without leaving it to stand.
7. Spread a ladle of mixture over the bottom of the tin to give a layer 5 mm/¼ in thick at the most. Place the tin in a hot oven (220 C, 425 F, gas 7) for 3 to 4 minutes until the top is dull and pale brown in colour. (If it does not brown use the heat at the top of the oven or even the grill.)
8. Spread another ladle of mixture on the cooked base and bake until light brown. Continue in this way until you have used all the mixture.
9. Leave the cooked cake to cool. Do not turn out for 6 to 7 hours to allow the cake to set fully.
10. You can then spread the cake with apricot jam and cover with the icing made from the icing sugar and lemon juice.

Curd dough

This dough is the ideal answer when you want something freshly baked but can't spare a lot of time in the kitchen. The curd mixture is extremely versatile. You can use it instead of yeast dough for a baking tray fruit flan or (leaving out the sugar, vanilla and lemon peel) for a savoury flan. Or just try using it for a sweet nut ring.

Nut ring

100 g / 4 oz butter, softened

175 g / 6 oz curd cheese

6 tablespoons oil

4 tablespoons milk

100 g / 4 oz sugar

2 tablespoons vanilla sugar

grated rind of 1 lemon

450 g / 1 lb plain flour

2 teaspoons baking powder

For the filling:

200 g / 7 oz white marzipan

4 tablespoons milk

2 tablespoons rum

50 g / 2 oz raisins

50 g / 2 oz currants

50 g / 2 oz flaked almonds

100 g / 4 oz ground hazelnuts

65 g / 2½ oz each candied orange and lemon peel

2 tablespoons sugar

For coating:

1 beaten egg yolk

25 g / 1 oz flaked almonds

150 g / 5 oz apricot jam

1. Using an electric whisk beat the butter, curd cheese, oil, milk, sugar, vanilla sugar and lemon rind until smooth.
2. Mix the flour with the baking powder and sift over the mixture. Work together thoroughly to give a smooth dough.
3. Cream the marzipan with the milk and rum.
4. Roll the dough into a rectangle 45 × 23 cm/ 18 × 9 in and spread with the marzipan cream. Scatter evenly with the other ingredients.
5. Lightly roll up the dough. Shape into a ring. Place on a greased floured baking tray. Make slanting cuts in the top, brush with egg yolk and scatter with flaked almonds.
6. Bake in a moderately hot oven (200 C, 400 F, gas 6) for 45 minutes, or until cooked.
7. Brush while still hot with the melted apricot jam, and drizzle with a little glacé icing, if liked.

Choux pastry –
as light as air

Basics

The main thing is never to guess quantities, but always to weigh and measure exactly.
Bring the water to the boil quickly and then remove it immediately from the heat to prevent evaporation which would reduce the necessary quantity.
Add the eggs separately. If the eggs are large you may not need the last one. The mixture should be glossy and form firm peaks.

Tips on the pastry

□ Tip the flour into the simmering water all at one go, otherwise you will get lumps forming.
□ Beat the flour mixture continuously over a moderate heat until it forms a ball and a white film covers the base of the pan.
□ Transfer the hot mixture to a chilled mixing bowl. If added to the hot pan the eggs may separate and will no longer bind the pastry.
□ For sweet pastries you can sweeten the pastry slightly as a last step (add 1 to 2 tablespoons sugar or vanilla sugar at the most). For savoury dishes flavour the pastry with grated cheese, coarsely crushed pepper, ground caraway seeds or paprika.

The pastry that is cooked before it is baked

Making choux pastry is considered a delicate operation. The word 'delicate' aptly describes the cakes that are made from it. They are incomparably tender and crisp – as light as air . . . But to describe the preparation of choux pastry as delicate is quite wrong. For no other type of mixture is so quick and easy to make, providing you follow the quantities and the cooking and baking times exactly.

Why you have to cook choux pastry

The flour is dissolved in a precisely measured quantity of water and fat, and cooked on the stove until the water has been absorbed. This breaks down the starches in the flour to form a firm, tacky mixture and not the usual crumbly texture which cake and pastry mixes usually take on during baking. The eggs which are beaten into this mixture then make the pastry rise so that, instead of a crumbly texture, large air bubbles are formed.

Getting the right shapes

The pastry is very soft, so you can't knead or shape it with your fingers. You can take balls of mixture with two spoons and place them on the baking tray or pipe the pastry through nozzles of various sizes to make balls, whirls or any other shape.
For a light cake base spread choux pastry flat on a baking tray or in the bottom of a springform tin.

Tips on baking

□ Always grease and flour the baking tray well or, better still, cover with non-stick baking parchment.
□ Leave plenty of room between the cakes on the baking tray. They will double or even treble in size during baking and will stick together if they are too close.
□ Always preheat the oven thoroughly. On no account should you open the oven door during the first half of the baking time – the texture of the pastry is extremely delicate and it would be bound to fall.
□ If you are going to fill the pastry, the cakes must be split while still hot. If you wait until they are cool, they will break in the wrong place. You should, of course, wait until they are cool before filling them.

Preparation

Equipment
Saucepan
Wooden spoon
Mixing bowl
Electric hand whisk
Piping bag
Pastry brush
Baking tray

Ingredients:
Makes 12 cream puffs or
35–40 profiterolles:

250 ml/8 fl oz water
½ teaspoon salt
100 g/4 oz butter
150 g/5 oz plain flour
4 eggs

Cooking times:

Preparation time:
20 to 25 minutes
Baking time:
15 to 25 minutes
Oven temperature:
200 C, 400 F, gas 6
Cooling time:
15 to 20 minutes

Storing

Choux pastry should always be used immediately. It becomes grey, crumbly and forms a crust if left to stand for any length of time.
But you can freeze it. Since it contains little fat you can freeze it for up to a year before defrosting and using like a freshly-made pastry.
Since it is quicker to make choux pastry than to wait for it to thaw, it is better to freeze the finished cakes. They will defrost at room temperature in about 30 minutes. You can speed up the process by warming them through in a hot oven for 5 minutes. Always eat choux pastry immediately. Moisture in the air soon makes it go soft, especially if it is filled with custard or cream.

1. Measure the ingredients and have them ready.

2. Bring the water to the boil with the salt in a large pan.

3. Add the butter and dissolve in the hot water.

4. Tip in the flour at one go, stirring continuously.

5. Beat over a moderate heat until the mixture forms a ball.

6. Dry out the ball of pastry for 2 minutes, turning it often.

7. Transfer the ball of pastry to a mixing bowl.

8. Add the eggs one after the other and beat in.

9. Always wait until one egg is completely worked in before adding the next.

10. Brush a baking tray with melted butter.

11. Sprinkle the greased baking tray with flour.

12. Spoon the pastry mixture into a piping bag.

Cream puffs

1. For cream puffs use a large, fluted nozzle.

2. Pipe whirls, about the size of tennis balls on to the baking tray.

3. Bake in a moderately hot oven (200 C, 400 F, gas 6) for 20 to 25 minutes.

4. Cool on a wire rack.

Profiterolles

1. For profiterolles pipe walnut-sized whirls on to a greased baking tray.

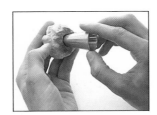

2. Bake in a moderately hot oven (200 C, 400 F, gas 6) for 15 to 20 minutes.

3. Use a piping nozzle to make a hole in the base of the profiterolles.

4. Pipe custard or cream into the profiterolles.

Best when no one is watching

Mandarin cream puffs

1 basic choux pastry recipe (see page 199)
For the filling:
1 (312-g/11-oz) can mandarin segments
600 ml/1 pint double cream
2–3 tablespoons sugar
2 tablespoons icing sugar for dusting

1. Bake, cut and cool the cream puffs as in the basic recipe.
2. Drain the mandarin segments in a sieve and use the juice elsewhere.
3. Spread the mandarins on the bottom of the cream puffs.
4. Whisk the cream until stiff and sweeten with the sugar. Spoon into a piping bag and generously fill the cream puffs.
5. Place the tops in position and dust with icing sugar.

Raspberry cream puffs

1 basic choux pastry recipe (see page 199)
For the filling:
450 g/1 lb fresh raspberries
2–3 tablespoons sugar
600 ml/1 pint double cream
icing sugar for dusting

1. Bake, cut and cool the cream puffs as in the basic recipe.
2. Arrange 400 g/14 oz raspberries on the bases of the cream puffs and sweeten with the sugar.
3. Purée the remaining raspberries in a blender or through a sieve and mix into the stiffly-whipped cream.
4. Use to fill the cream puffs.
5. Add the tops and dust with the icing sugar.

Cream puffs

1 basic choux pastry recipe (see page 199)
For the filling:
600 ml/1 pint double cream
2–3 tablespoons sugar
icing sugar for dusting

Make the cream puffs as in the basic recipe and fill with the stiffly-whipped, sweetened cream. Add the tops and dust with icing sugar.

Naturally sophisticated people will cut up a cream puff delicately
with a pastry fork, as they have been taught. But when no one is
watching, have a go at eating it the way children do, taking the
cream puff in both hands and biting into it. You will have trouble
with crumbs and the cream will run out and down your chin. But
this is the only way to experience what a cream puff should be –
crisp top and bottom and with a filling that melts beautifully
in the mouth . . .

Strawberry cream puffs

1 basic choux pastry recipe (see page 199)

For the filling:

450 g/1 lb fresh strawberries

2–3 tablespoons sugar

600 ml/1 pint double cream

2–3 tablespoons sugar

icing sugar for dusting

1. Make the cream puffs as in the basic recipe. Cover with halved or sliced strawberries and sweeten with half the sugar.
2. Fill with the stiffly-whipped, sweetened cream.
3. Cover with the tops and dust with icing sugar.

Iced cream puffs

Cream puffs look attractive and taste twice as good if you ice them. For example try using:
Sugar icing: stir 150 g/5 oz icing sugar with 1 tablespoon water, rum or lemon juice.
Chocolate icing: Melt 100 g/4 oz plain or milk (or cooking) chocolate in a heatproof bowl over a pan of water. Brush on to the cream puffs.
Apricot glaze: Bring 4 tablespoons apricot jam to the boil in a saucepan

with 1 tablespoon sugar and 1 tablespoon water. Brush hot on to the cream puffs.
Caramel icing: Boil 10 tablespoons sugar in 4 tablespoons water in a saucepan over a moderate heat, stirring continuously to form a golden brown caramel (see pages 208–9). Spoon on to the tops.

Note: Serve and eat filled cream puffs immediately, for the moist filling soon makes them soft. They will stay crisper longer if you put the fruit on a bed of custard (see pages 236–7).

Curls, rings, pretzels – cakes light as air

With the help of a piping bag you can turn the soft choux pastry into the most varied shapes. Depending on the size of the nozzle, you can make dainty bite-sized morsels, decorations or cakes in individual portions for a dessert. With a sweet filling they are delicious with tea or coffee, or try filling with a cheese or herb cream to eat as a savoury.

Almond rings

(illustrated top left)

250 ml / 8 fl oz water
½ teaspoon salt
100 g / 4 oz butter
150 g / 5 oz plain flour
4 eggs
50 g / 2 oz flaked almonds to decorate

1. Make the pastry as in the basic recipe (see page 199).
2. Spoon into a piping bag fitted with a small fluted nozzle. Pipe several small rings (about 8–10-cm/ 3½–4-in. in diameter) on a greased and floured baking tray.
3. Scatter the rings with the flaked almonds. Bake in a moderately hot oven (200 C, 400 F, gas 6) for 25 minutes, or until cooked.

Variation:
Instead of individual rings pipe one large ring on to the baking tray, using a large fluted nozzle. If you like you can pipe over the ring once or twice to make it thicker. Again bake in a moderately hot oven (200 C, 400 F, gas 6) for 40 minutes, or until cooked. If preferred you can replace the flaked almonds with chopped pistachio nuts or crystallised sugar.

Varying the shape

In each case make the pastry as in the basic recipe for Almond rings (see left), but pipe into different shapes. Here are a few ideas:

Pretzels

(illustrated bottom left)
Use a medium-sized fluted nozzle. Pipe into a pretzel shape and scatter with crystallised sugar.

Ornaments

(illustrated centre top)
To decorate gâteaux or desserts. Use the smallest nozzle or twist greaseproof paper into a piping bag (see page 246–7). Bake for only 5 to 10 minutes. (Ideas for further shapes are on pages 254–5).

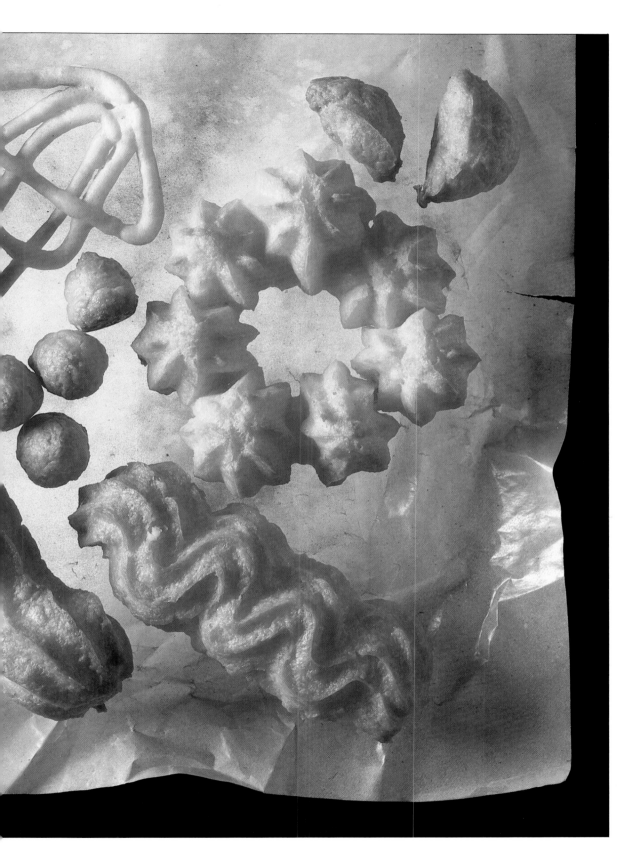

Profiterolles

(illustrated centre and
page 199)
Use a small plain nozzle.
Pipe balls about the size of
a hazelnut on to the
baking tray. Bake for 5
minutes only. You can use
a sweet or savoury filling
or just use plain in soup.

Éclairs

(illustrated centre and
bottom right)
Use a medium-sized fluted
nozzle. Pipe straight or
slightly wavy lines about
10 cm/4 in long. Bake for
about 10 minutes.

Moons

(illustrated top right)
Take teaspoons of pastry
and push on to the baking
tray using your finger.
This produces the moon-
like shape. Bake for 10
minutes. Serve sprinkled
with sugar for tea or dip
in salt to serve with
sparkling wine or
champagne.

Ring of stars

(illustrated centre right)
Using a small fluted
nozzle, pipe a ring of stars
on to the baking tray and
bake for 20 minutes.

Swans' necks

(illustrated pages 208–9)
Using a small fluted
nozzle, pipe swans' necks
in a question mark shape
and bake for 10 minutes.
Use them for decoration.

The best piped cakes of all

These classic piped cakes are cooked in the deep-fryer rather than the oven. They brown more quickly – just as we do in the hot sun! Deep frying makes these cakes really crisp. In Spain where both the browning sun and these browned pastries are available, they tend to prefer the pastries to the sunshine. These hot Churros are most popular of all as an early morning pick-me-up after a night out on the town.

Raisin doughnuts

(illustrated top)

1 basic choux pastry recipe (page 199)

50 g/2 oz raisins

oil or lard for frying

4 tablespoons icing sugar

1. Sift the raisins into the choux pastry.
2. Cut into balls with a tablespoon and deep-fry in the hot oil until golden.
3. Drain and dust with icing sugar.

Churros

(illustrated bottom)

1 basic choux pastry recipe (page 199)

oil or lard for frying

To decorate:

½ teaspoon ground cinnamon

2 tablespoons sugar

1. Spoon the pastry into a piping bag fitted with a medium-fluted nozzle.
2. Pipe lengths about 15 cm/6 in long into hot oil and deep-fry.
3. Mix the cinnamon and sugar together and coat the churros.

Pretty piped cakes

(illustrated centre)

1 basic choux pastry recipe (page 199)

oil or lard for frying

To decorate:

6 tablespoons icing sugar

1 tablespoon water

1. Spoon the pastry into a piping bag fitted with a medium-fluted nozzle.
2. Pipe whirls on to a strip of greased greaseproof paper. Push into the hot oil and deep-fry until golden.
3. Mix the icing sugar with the water to make an icing and brush on to the cakes.

Tips on deep-frying

☐ Use an oil or vegetable fat which can be heated to a high temperature.
☐ Never add too many cakes at once to the hot fat, or it will reduce the temperature too much and they will not cook properly.
☐ Fry when the fat is around 190C/375F. The fat is hot enough when large bubbles rise from the handle of a wooden spoon dipped into the fat. With an electric deep-fryer the thermostat automatically gives the right temperature.
☐ Use a perforated spoon to lift the cakes out of the fat and drain well. Place on a thick layer of absorbent kitchen paper to take up any excess fat.

A toast to St Honorius!

He was the saint who gave his name to a gâteau which is truly one of the masterpieces of pâtisserie. Why this should be so is unknown even to the usually well-informed reference work, the *Larousse Gastronomique*. Nevertheless, this saint (who was Bishop of Amiens around 660 AD) is now the patron saint of bakers. *Larousse* can find no event in his life to explain this but there is no doubt that the Honoré gâteau exists and this should be enough for us.

St Honoré gâteau

1 basic choux pastry recipe (page 199)

200 g/7 oz puff pastry, homemade from basic recipe (page 167) or bought frozen

3 tablespoons sugar

For the filling:

500 ml/17 fl oz milk

1 vanilla pod

100 g/4 oz sugar

pinch of salt

5 egg yolks

30 g/1¼ oz plain flour

3 egg whites

2 tablespoons sugar

For the caramel:

10 tablespoons sugar

4 tablespoons water

1. Roll out the puff pastry thinly, cut a 25-cm/10-in round and prick several times with a fork. Using a large, plain nozzle, pipe on to it a spiral of choux pastry working outwards from the centre (photograph top left).
2. Use the remaining choux pastry to pipe 14 to 16 small balls on to the baking tray. Sprinkle all over with sugar and bake on a greased and floured baking tray in a moderately hot oven (200 C, 400 F, gas 6) for 30 to 40 minutes. Both the base and the balls should be a deep gold colour (photograph top right).

3. To make the filling, bring the milk to the boil in a saucepan. Slit the vanilla pod lengthways, scrape out the pith with a knife and add to the milk. Whisk together the sugar, salt and egg yolks until thick and add the flour. Stir in the hot milk and then tip the mixture back into the pan. Warm over a moderate heat, stirring continuously until the mixture is quite thick. Remove from the heat as soon as it boils and stir until it has cooled slightly.
4. Make a hole in the base of the balls using the piping bag nozzle (see page 199) and fill with the warm custard. If the piping bag is too hot to hold, wrap it in a tea-towel. Reserve some custard.

5. Boil the sugar and water to make a medium-brown caramel, as shown on pages 208–9 (steps 3 and 4). Stick each ball on to a fork and dip in the caramel to half-cover. (Be careful as the caramel is very hot.) Place in a ring round the cooked base (photograph bottom left).
6. Whisk the egg whites until stiff, sprinkle in the sugar and fold into the remaining hot custard. Pour into the centre of the gâteau, fluffing it up with a spatula (photograph bottom right).

Note: The same applies here as to all choux pastry, the cake will be at its best for a limited time only. The custard makes the delicate pastry moist and the caramel soft. So do not assemble the cake until ready to eat it, coat with caramel and fill with cream. And eat as soon as possible.

What swans, éclairs and gâteaux all have in common

They are all made from a light choux pastry. Hardly any other type of pastry or cake mixture can provide such a wide variety of cakes. From decorative swans to grace any cake arrangement to gâteaux which make a focal point for any tea table. Caramel makes choux pastries look even more attractive and delicious to eat, and we show you here how to make them.

Swans

I. Make the cream puffs using the basic recipe (see page 199) and swans' necks as shown on page 203.

2. Cut the cream puffs open while still hot. If you wait until they are cool they will break.

Éclairs

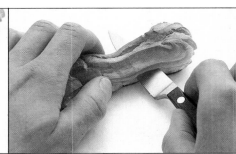

I. It was the French who gave these choux cakes their name.

2. Cut in half with a sharp knife while still hot. Then leave the éclairs to cool.

Gâteau

I. Spread two 2.5-cm/1-in rounds of choux pastry on a greased and floured baking tray. Cook for 15 to 20 minutes.

2. While still hot, cut to shape using a cake ring and leave to cool.

Caramel

I. Stir 10 tablespoons sugar (about 150 g/5 oz) with 4 tablespoons water in a small saucepan over a low heat.

2. Bring to the boil over a high heat, stirring continuously until the water has completely evaporated.

3. Cut the tops in half to make the wings.

4. Fill the bottom half of the cream puff with custard or cream.

5. Place the neck in position and stick the wings in at an angle in the cream.

3. Brush the tops with apricot glaze (see pages 248–9) and leave until cold.

4. Pipe a thick covering of Mocha butter cream (see pages 232–3) into the bottom half.

5. Carefully replace the tops. Serve and eat immediately.

3. Spread the bottom layer with 4 tablespoons plum purée and half of 750 ml/1¼ pints whipped cream.

4. Top with the second round and again cover with plum purée and cream. Cover the sides with cream.

5. Break the off-cuts into small pieces and arrange over the top and dust the top of the cake with icing sugar.

3. Then the caramel will slowly become browner. This is the point where you should reduce the heat.

4. The caramel will go through the various stages of concentration quite quickly.

5. For spun sugar (see pages 210–11) the sugar should be this dark golden-brown colour.

Croquembouche – the formidable pyramid

This impressive pyramid of sweet filled profiterolles is a marvellous feat of baking. The croquembouche's thick web of delicate sugar strands holds the profiterolles in tightly so that it is difficult for anyone to try and eat them!

Where the name originates

The literal translation of croquembouche is 'cracks in the mouth' and this describes it exactly. It is a crispy cake that crackles when you bite into it. Generally, the word describes small nibbles covered with sugar like caramelised sweets. In this particular case we have a beautiful pyramid of profiterolles, filled with cream and covered with caramel in a web of spun sugar. A true masterpiece! For not only is it a delicate process to make the pyramid, but the thin web of sugar strands is difficult to make and requires careful practice.

Don't give up if all you get the first time you try is blistered fingers, you will get it right next time.

Boiling the sugar

You need to use a heavy-based pan. Professional chefs use a copper or stainless steel pan with a reinforced base. The sugar is first dissolved in the water (as shown on pages 208–9) and then boiled until the water has evaporated.

Now things move very quickly with the sugar going through the various stages from clear and transparent to burnt. For spun sugar you need to take the pan off the heat as soon as the sugar is the colour shown in photograph 5 (page 209). Leave the caramel to cool slightly until it is tacky but not quite set. Have the pan right next to the pyramid. Dip a fork into the caramel and lift it out and drape the thread that forms over the pyramid as quickly as you can.
Note: Never touch the hot sugar or you will burn your fingers.

Croquembouche

I basic choux pastry recipe (page 199)	
½ basic shortcrust recipe (page 103)	
600 ml/ I pint double cream	
2 tablespoons real vanilla sugar	
I tablespoon sugar	
For the caramel:	
150 g/ 5 oz sugar	
4 tablespoons water	

I. Using the basic recipe, make walnut-sized profiterolles and bake (see page 199).
2. From the shortcrust make a 23-cm/9-in round and bake (see page 103).
3. Whip the cream until stiff with the vanilla sugar and sugar. Use to fill the profiterolles.
4. Boil the sugar and water to make a light-brown caramel (see page 208). Dip the filled profiterolles into the caramel to half-cover and arrange in a pyramid on the pastry base. (Be careful not to touch the hot caramel.)
5. Reheat the caramel slightly if necessary, draw into threads with a fork and drape carefully over the pyramid to form a spidery web.

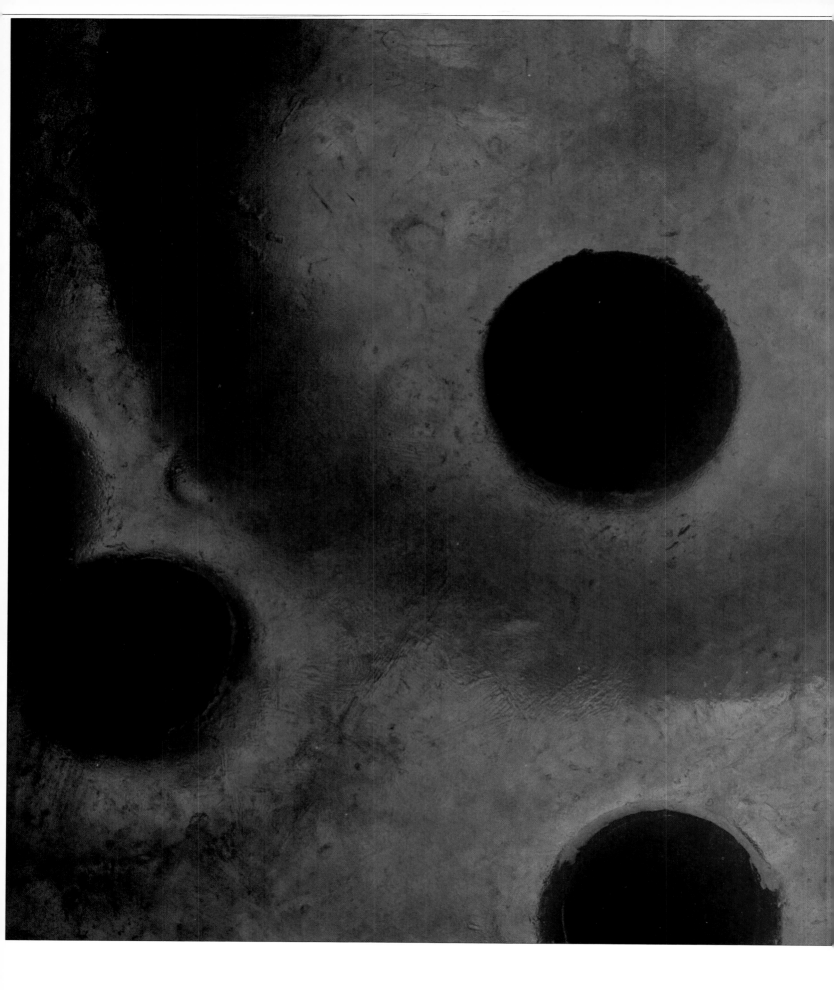

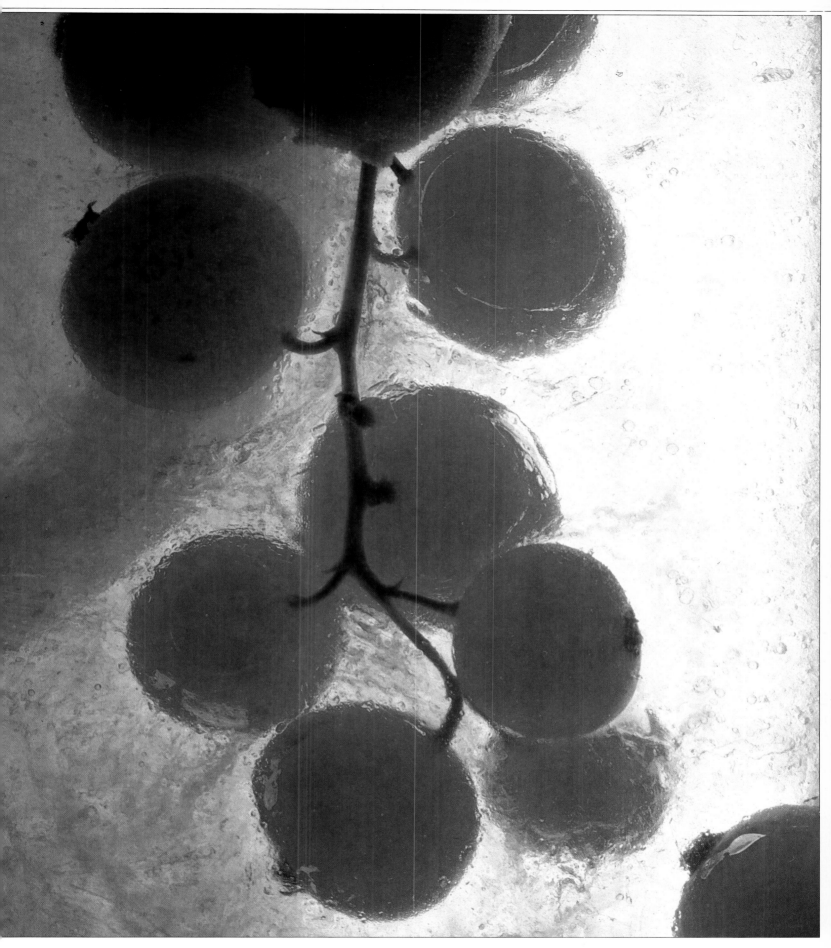

Chilled and iced –
'baking' made easy

Sorbet

(illustrated left)
Light and refreshing, made entirely with fruit juice, fruit purée, wine, herb stock or vegetable stock. The latter two are served before the meat course to refresh the palate in a meal of many courses. Sorbets should ideally be made in an ice-cream-maker. Since they contain a lot of water the crystals that would otherwise form would be unpleasant. If you haven't got an ice-cream-maker, you can make sorbet in the following way. Freeze cleaned fruit; freeze vegetable or herb stock in ice-cube trays. In an electric grinder crush the frozen fruit or ice cubes with a little syrup to give a creamy snow. Serve at once in chilled glasses.

Parfait

(illustrated centre)
In a parfait the egg yolks, together with the cream and alcohol prevent ice crystals forming, so it does not need to be beaten as it freezes. You can freeze the mixture in a bombe mould and turn it out on to a plate to make an impressive dessert. To make the ice cream soufflé shown here, line a soufflé dish with a thick layer of greaseproof paper, bringing it 2.5–5 cm/1–2 in above the rim of the dish. Fill with parfait mixture to come at least 2.5 cm/1 in above the rim of the dish and freeze.

Everyone's favourite: light, melting ice cream

The Chinese were familiar with ice cream as long as five thousand years ago. Hippocrates ate ice cream as a medicine for, as he said, 'It stimulates the humours and produces a feeling of well-being'. And a Roman emperor like Nero would have had his own team of ice cream makers. Ice cream remains extremely popular today – it is a year-round dessert loved by both adults and children.

It comes in various types

Ices are not simply ice. There is fruit ice cream made from a mixture of puréed fruit and whipped cream; fruit ices without cream which are known as sorbets, which can also be made from juice, wine or vegetable stock; and parfaits, very rich ices which contain a lot of egg yolk to make them smooth and creamy. If you simply leave the mixture to freeze, tiny ice crystals form which can prick the tongue as you eat the ice. To avoid this, the mixture must be beaten continuously as it freezes. If this is done by hand it needs a lot of time as the ice cream will take a very long time to freeze. In recent years ice-cream-makers, manual or electric, have become fashionable; these may have their own cooler or go into the freezer.

While parfait is quite expensive to make, it is not difficult and is a good choice if you have no ice-cream-maker. The only thing to remember is that the egg yolks must be whisked hot, but cooled before mixing with the cream and flavourings. You can use parfait mixture to fill an ice-cream gâteau (for basic recipe and step-by-step photographs see right).

Ice cream

(illustrated right)
You can buy ice cream in a choice of qualities and flavours, from expensive ice creams made with real cream to the cheaper varieties made with non-dairy substitutes.

You can make ice cream yourself and it is made easier if you have an ice-cream-maker. Milk and cream are boiled and mixed with egg yolks. As with custard (see pages 236–7) the mixture is beaten over a low heat until thick and creamy. Flavourings, such as chocolate, are added before freezing in an ice-cream-maker. The ice cream is best served in scoops in cornets.

Equipment

Mixing bowls
Saucepan
Electric hand whisk
Fine grater
Spatula
Small knife
Large palette knife
Springform tin (23–25 cm/
9–10 in. in diameter)
Piping bag
Fluted nozzle

Ingredients:

5 egg yolks

200 g/7 oz icing sugar

750 ml/1¼ pints double
cream

7 tablespoons orange
liqueur

rind and juice of 2 oranges

1 sponge base
(see page 71)

300 ml/½ pint double
cream to decorate

1–2 tablespoons sugar

Working time:

Preparation time:

40 minutes

Freezing time:

4–5 hours

Making up:

30 minutes

Ice-cream-maker

There are various models
to suit every pocket, from
manual machines cooled
with a mixture of ice and
salt to electric models to
be used in the freezer
which switch off when the
mixture is the right
consistency. Finally, there
are complete ice-cream-
makers where all you
have to do is to tip in the
ingredients and leave the
machine to do the rest.

Preparation of parfait mixture and ice-cream gâteau

1. Measure the ingredients and place them ready.

2. Place the egg yolks in a mixing bowl (preferably metal).

3. Sprinkle the icing sugar over the yolks.

4. Whisk the egg yolks and sugar in a bowl over hot water until thick.

5. Remove from the water and whisk until cool.

6. Grate the rind of 2 oranges.

7. Using a hand whisk, whip the cream until stiff.

8. Fold in the cream with 3 tablespoons orange liqueur and orange rind.

9. Slice the cake in half using a large palette knife.

10. Place half in a tin and soak with remaining liqueur and juice.

11. Pour the parfait mixture into the tin and smooth the top.

12. Cover with the other sponge and press down gently but firmly.

13. Pour on the remaining juice and liqueur. Freeze for about 4 to 5 hours.

14. Cut round the edge of the gâteau with a knife and transfer to a plate.

15. Whip the cream until stiff and sweeten to taste.

16. Cover the gâteau with cream, decorate with whirls of cream and freeze.

Ice-cold beauties to
make your heart melt!

Orange ice gâteau

Make and freeze the gâteau as shown in the basic recipe (see page 215). Decorate with some zest of orange and very thin slices of lime.

Pineapple ice gâteau

Coarsely chop 150 g/5 oz candied or fresh pineapple and fold into the parfait mixture (see page 215) with 4 tablespoons Arrak. Make up the gâteau as in the basic recipe (see page 215). Decorate with pineapple and cherries.

Strawberry ice gâteau

Purée 250 g/9 oz strawberries and fold into the parfait mixture (see page 215) with 4 tablespoons cherry liqueur. Make up the gâteau as shown (see page 215) and decorate with strawberries.

Cassata gâteau

Coarsely chop 50 g/2 oz walnuts, 50 g/2 oz pistachios and 200 g/7 oz cocktail cherries. Mix into the parfait mixture (see page 215) with 4 tablespoons cognac, 4 tablespoons praline and 3 tablespoons honey. Make up the gâteau as illustrated (see page 215) and decorate with chopped pistachios.

Seven variations on the basic orange ice gâteau on page 215 are detailed here and each one is a masterpiece. The method is quite easy: the parfait mixture (without the oranges) is mixed with other flavourings. To serve: transfer the gâteau from the freezer to the refrigerator one hour before serving. Remove from refrigerator ten minutes before serving.

Kiwi ice gâteau

Peel 4 kiwis, blend in a liquidiser and fold into the parfait mixture (see page 215). Make up the gâteau as in the basic recipe (see page 215). Flavour with white rum and decorate with sliced kiwis.

Chocolate and meringue ice gâteau

Fold 200 g/7 oz coarsely grated chocolate and 100 g/4 oz crumbled meringue (see page 222–3) into the parfait mixture (see page 215). Make up the gâteau as in the basic recipe (see page 215). Flavour with brandy. Decorate the finished gâteau with crumbled meringue and dust with cocoa powder.

Chocolate ice gâteau

Melt 200 g/7 oz plain chocolate in a heatproof bowl over a pan of water (see page 246) and fold into the parfait mixture (see page 215). Flavour with 4 tablespoons rum. Make up the gâteau as illustrated (see page 215) and decorate with grated chocolate.

Black cherry ice gâteau

Fold 175 g/6 oz black cherries and 2 tablespoons juice into the parfait mixture (see page 215). Make up the gâteau as illustrated (see page 215). Decorate with black cherries just before serving.

217

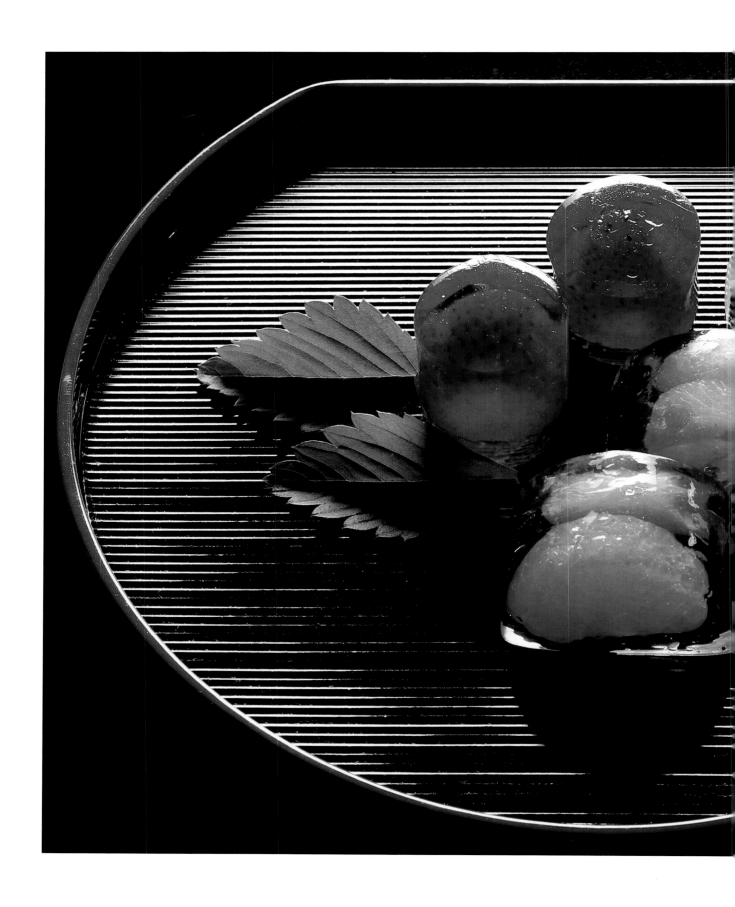

Fruit in jelly: an attractive idea from the Far East

They are pretty as a picture and will remain attractive for some time. They consist of neat pieces of fruit covered in a transparent coat of highly flavoured juice solidified with gelatine. This prevents the fruit becoming dry, gives them a pretty shimmer and holds in the flavour.

Basic recipe for mandarins in jelly

200-g/7-oz can mandarins

25 g/1 oz powdered gelatine

500 ml/17 fl oz fresh mandarin juice (or from can)

juice of 1 lemon

100 g/4 oz sugar

1. Drain the mandarins in a sieve and reserve the juice. (Make up to 500 ml/ 17 fl oz with water if necessary.)
2. Soak the gelatine in cold water for 5 minutes.
3. Warm the mandarin juice, lemon juice and sugar in a saucepan for a few minutes until the sugar has dissolved.
4. Squeeze out the gelatine and stir into the warm juice.
5. Arrange the fruit in small metal, porcelain or plastic moulds and just cover with the jelly.
6. Leave to set in the refrigerator. They should be ready to turn out after 2 to 3 hours. Hold the moulds under hot water for a few seconds to turn out and if necessary run a knife around the edge.

Jelly tips

Using the same recipe you can make other jellies using different fruits or juices (the photograph shows strawberries and mandarins in jelly).
Hard fruits such as apples should first be poached until tender and the juice kept to use in the jelly.
Gelatine not only binds but also neutralises flavour, so always make the juice concentrated, don't worry about over-flavouring.
The larger the mould in which the jelly sets, the longer it has to be chilled. As long as the fruit is not too delicate you can dissolve a jelly that is not strong enough in flavour, add extra flavouring and then reset – it will set just as well each time.
Gelatine comes in powdered form and is colourless. It is also available in leaf form.

Yogurt flan

(illustrated right)

I baked sponge base
(see page 71)
6 tablespoons white rum
40 g/1½ oz powdered
gelatine
I kg/2¼ lb yogurt
75 g/3 oz sugar
I ripe mango
3 kiwis
250 ml/8 fl oz double
cream, whipped
I packet yellow flan glaze

I. Slice the sponge in half (use the top half for another recipe). Place the base in a 23–25 cm/9–10 in springform tin and sprinkle with rum.
2. Soak the gelatine in cold water for 5 minutes.
3. Tip the yogurt and sugar into a large mixing bowl.
4. Heat the gelatine in a metal basin standing in hot water until completely dissolved. Add to the yogurt and quickly whisk in.
5. Pour the yogurt mixture over the sponge in the tin and leave in the refrigerator to set for 2–3 hours.
6. Meanwhile peel the mango and kiwi fruit. Cut the mango off the stone in narrow segments. Slice the kiwis across.
7. Turn the flan out of the tin. Cover the top and sides with whipped cream. Pattern the sides with a zig-zag spatula (see pages 24–5).
8. Arrange the fruit decoratively on the top. Finally cover the top with a yellow flan glaze.

Flans that need no baking

If you live in a bed-sit you may not have the opportunity for baking, for the kitchen area may not have room for an oven. There is no problem with these flans which are 'baked' in the refrigerator. They are just right for summer – cool, light and refreshing – served for tea out on the balcony on a hot, sunny summer afternoon.

Tips on refrigerator flans

☐ Instead of a sponge base you can make one with sponge fingers and butter as in the cream cheese flan recipe (see right). This is very quick to make.
☐ Instead of yogurt you can use curd cheese. This will either increase or reduce the calories depending on whether you use low-fat or cream curd cheese.
☐ The mixture will be lighter (but richer) if you fold in whipped cream.
☐ To add colour and flavour stir in puréed fruit (raspberries or strawberries).

☐ To prevent the sponge base becoming soft if you make the flan in advance, cover it with a layer of toasted breadcrumbs, ground almonds, hazelnuts or walnuts before adding the filling.
☐ Even without the protection of the flan glaze, the whipped cream covering will stay attractive longer if you thicken it with gelatine. To do this stir the hot dissolved gelatine into the liquid cream and chill in the refrigerator until it begins to set. Then using a hand whisk whip as normal until stiff.

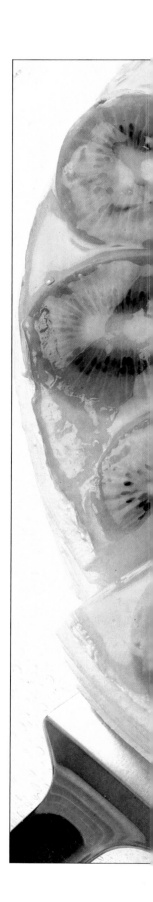

Lemon cheese cake

*150 g | 5 oz sponge fingers
(about 20)*

100 g | 4 oz soft butter

For the filling:

30 g | 1¼ oz geltaine

*500 ml | 17 fl oz double
cream*

250 g | 9 oz cream cheese

*grated rind and juice of 2
lemons*

75 g | 3 oz sugar

lemon slices to decorate

1. Crumble the sponge
fingers and work into the
soft butter. Spread on the
base of a greased
springform tin and flatten
out evenly. Place the tin
in the refrigerator.
2. Soak the gelatine in
cold water for 5 minutes.
3. Whip the double cream
until stiff.
4. Mix the cream cheese
well with the grated
lemon rind, juice and
sugar.
5. Place the gelatine in a
metal bowl in boiling
water until completely
dissolved. Stir into the
cream cheese mixture.
6. Fold in the whipped
cream.
7. Spread the mixture
over the base. Chill for 3
to 4 hours until set.
8. Turn the flan out of the
tin on to a plate and
decorate with slices of
lemon.

'Baisers' – light, melting, crisp – kisses you can eat

Meringue nests

Makes 10:

Basic baiser recipe

4 egg whites

pinch of salt

200g/7oz caster sugar

1 tablespoon vanilla sugar

For the filling:

200g/7oz strawberries, hulled

200g/7oz raspberries, hulled

200g/7oz red currants, topped and tailed

200g/7oz sweet or Morello cherries

1. Cover a baking tray with non-stick baking parchment.
2. In a large mixing bowl, slowly whisk the egg whites and salt until stiff, gradually adding the sugar and vanilla sugar.
3. Spoon the mixture into a piping bag with a fluted nozzle (see also pages 24–5). Pipe directly on to the parchment to make the nests illustrated.
4. Place the baking tray in a cool oven (150C, 300F, gas 2). Reduce the temperature to low (80C, 175F, gas low). If you have an ordinary oven, prop the door slightly open with the handle of a

wooden spoon. In convection ovens this is not necessary.
5. Dry rather than bake the nests for 5 to 6 hours – they should remain snow-white in colour.
6. Leave the meringues to cool and then carefully peel off the paper.
7. Fill with the fruit. If you like you can coat the fruit with currant jelly (quickly boiled) or a glaze. Serve with whipped cream, vanilla ice cream or sorbet.

Chocolate baiser

Make the basic baiser recipe (see left) and stir in 2 tablespoons cocoa powder at the end. Pipe the meringue on to a baking sheet and dry as in the basic recipe.

Nut macaroons

1 basic baiser recipe (see left)

For the filling:

300g/11oz ground hazelnuts

1. Stir the nuts into the stiff baiser mixture.
2. Pipe walnut-sized balls (using either a plain or fluted nozzle) on to a baking sheet. Set the oven at 150C, 300F, gas 2 and reduce to 80C, 175F, gas low when the macaroons go into the oven. Dry for 2 to 3 hours.

Baiser is the French word for kiss. The fact that it is often replaced with the less evocative word meringue is not necessarily due to prudery, for it does in fact describe more precisely what a baiser is: a light, frothy ball. Regardless of whether you use the frivolous term baiser or the more restrained term meringue, both mean a snow-white mixture of whisked egg white and sugar which is dried in the oven rather than baked and which goes so well with many desserts, particularly ice cream or fruit.

Baiser tips

☐ Most important of all are the egg whites. They must whisk to the right consistency or they will just collapse. So the egg white must be completely fresh and pure, without a trace of yolk. The mixing bowl and beaters must also be really clean and completely fat-free.

☐ You will need a large mixing bowl. The tall, narrow bowls that come with the mixer are not suitable – the egg white needs a lot of space.

☐ Whisk on the lowest, or possibly the middle, setting. Egg white needs time to reach the required volume. A food mixer will take the hard work out of this.

☐ A pinch of salt should ensure that the whites whisk up well.

☐ Always use a fine sugar. Icing sugar is best as this dissolves quickly.

☐ The egg white is ready when it has a matt shine and forms soft peaks when you lift out the beaters. Do not beat it until it forms stiff peaks and becomes very shiny, this is too long.

☐ To dry the meringues have the oven temperature too low rather than too high. With a conventional oven you will need to prop the door slightly open to allow for evaporation of moisture.

Coconut macaroons

Make as for the nut macaroons, but use grated coconut instead of hazelnuts.

Cinnamon stars

1 basic baiser recipe (see left)

For the filling:

200 g / 7 oz ground almonds

100 g / 4 oz ground hazelnuts

2 teaspoons ground cinnamon

50 g / 2 oz plain flour

icing sugar for dusting

1. Keep one cup of baiser mixture on one side.
2. Gently fold the other ingredients into the remaining mixture. Do not over-stir or the meringue will fall.
3. Sprinkle the worktop with icing sugar and roll the mixture out to 5 mm/ $\frac{1}{4}$ in thickness. Thinly spread with the plain meringue mixture.
4. Cut to shape with a moistened star-shaped cutter.

5. Place the stars on a greased and floured baking tray.
6. Dry rather than bake the cinnamon stars in a very cool oven (120C, 250F, gas $\frac{1}{2}$) for 1 hour.

223

With coffee or dessert, delicate almond wafers

Quick to make, but guaranteed to impress, for everyone associates these biscuits with the best restaurants where they are served with the dessert or with an after-dinner cup of coffee. Almond wafers should be light and crisp. They contain a lot of sugar and so quickly become soft. If this should happen all you have to do is quickly reheat them to crisp them up.

Almond wafers

200 g/7 oz white marzipan
1 egg
2 tablespoons plain flour
4 tablespoons caster sugar
5 tablespoons milk
butter for greasing
flour for sprinkling

1. Place a baking tray in the freezer.
2. Cream the marzipan with the egg, flour and sugar. Gradually beat in the milk.
3. Brush the baking tray with butter and thinly sprinkle with flour or line tray with baking parchment.
4. To get the exact shapes for the wafers you will need to cut patterns from thick cardboard. Cut circles or leaves of the required size.
5. Place the patterns on the baking tray and draw round them to mark outline in the flour or draw a pencil line on parchment.

6. Place a spoonful of mixture in the centre of each and smooth out with a spatula to fit the pattern exactly.
7. Place the baking tray immediately in a moderate oven (180C, 350F, gas 4) and bake for 15 to 20 minutes until golden brown.
8. Using an oiled, flexible palette knife lift the wafers from the baking tray as quickly as possible while still hot, shape as you wish and leave to cool on a wire rack.

Tulip wafers

(Large photograph right) Bake round wafers 10–13 cm/4–5 in. in diameter. While still hot press into a cup or small bowl making a wavy edge. Finally leave to cool. Serve filled with fruit and cream, custard or ice cream.

Wafer leaves

(illustrated above right) Draw the leaves (the beech leaves shown here are pretty, or try oak or maple leaves) on to cardboard and cut out. Using the cardboard as a pattern, spread the wafer leaves on the baking tray. Colour 2 tablespoons mixture with 1 teaspoon cocoa powder to draw the veins on the leaves (use a paper piping bag, see pages 246–7). Bake the leaves and while hot bend over a rolling pin to curve them slightly.

Wafer horns

(illustrated far left) Bake small round wafers (about 5–7.5 cm/2–3 in. in diameter). Twist into horns while still hot and leave to cool.

Baking tips

☐ Using the patterns is not as easy as it sounds. If you don't need perfectly round circles, it is easier to spread the mixture freehand.
☐ Always spread the mixture evenly or the wafers will not brown evenly.
☐ Always remove them hot from the baking tray or they will stick fast.
☐ You cannot shape the wafers once they have cooled.
☐ They are best eaten fresh. Never leave them standing around uncovered for the moisture in the air will quickly make them soft.

Crumble cake with fruit curds

This cake is made extremely carefully as there is no baking involved. The base is made with butter and crumbled biscuits (plain or slightly salted). This will suit anyone who often finds cake too sweet. If you have a sweet tooth you may prefer to use sponge fingers or butter biscuits. The base is then topped with a creamy curd cheese mixture and plenty of fresh fruit.

Butter biscuit slices with chocolate cream

These cakes are inspired by the chocolate cream biscuits which are so popular with anyone with a sweet tooth and with children in particular. They are a sweet and rich combination of cream filling and biscuits. We have improved the cream here and combined it with biscuits to make a sort of cake.

Crumble cake with fruit curds

1 tablespoon peanut butter

100g/4oz butter, at room temperature

75g/3oz caster sugar

300g/11oz lightly salted biscuits

For the creamy topping:

250g/9oz low-fat curd cheese

5 tablespoons caster sugar

250ml/8floz double cream

500g/18oz mixed fruit to decorate (raspberries, blackberries and blackcurrants)

1. Cream the peanut butter, butter and sugar with an electric hand whisk.
2. Coarsely crumble the biscuits and stir in.
3. Transfer the mixture to a small greased and floured (18-cm/7-in) springform tin and press down. Place the tin in the refrigerator.
4. Meanwhile press out the curd cheese in a tea-towel and beat with the sugar in a mixing bowl.
5. Whip the cream until stiff and gently fold in.
6. Spread the creamy mixture over the base. Chill again for 2 to 3 hours.
7. Shortly before serving wash, hull and dry the fruit and pile on top of the cake.

Butter biscuit slices with chocolate cream

Makes 12:

125g/4½oz butter, at room temperature

125g/4½oz brown sugar

75g/3oz plain chocolate, melted

24 oblong butter biscuits

3 tablespoons chopped almonds

3 tablespoons grated chocolate

1. Cream the butter and sugar using an electric hand whisk until light and fluffy.
2. Add the chocolate and mix well.
3. Cover the base of a greased and floured shallow tin with 8 biscuits placed side by side.
4. Spread with half the buttercream.
5. Cover with 8 butter biscuits, placed directly above the original 8 and spread with the remaining butter cream.
6. Sprinkle with almonds and grated chocolate and top with the last 8 biscuits.
7. Chill for at least 1 hour in the refrigerator.
8. When the cake is firm, cut into twelve. Use a sharp, preferably saw-edged knife to prevent the biscuits crumbling.

Crisp and light – cream waffles

Waffles are not expensive to make at home if you have a waffle iron. The batter is quick to mix and the cooking is a pleasure in which everyone can share, get the children to help. Waffles are at their best eaten in the kitchen straight from the waffle iron.

Trifle – a tempting mixture of sponge, fruit and cream

Trifle is an excellent way of using up leftover pieces of cake or biscuits. Any type of fruit can be used, and sometimes jelly is added to the fruit. Top with custard and cream, if liked or just a thick cream topping.

Makes 10:

125 g/4½ oz butter,
at room temperature
6 eggs, separated
150 g/5 oz caster sugar
grated rind and juice
of 1 orange
250 ml/8 fl oz single cream
200 g/7 oz plain flour
2 tablespoons butter for
the waffle iron
icing sugar for dusting

1. Whisk the butter and egg yolks for 3 to 4 minutes until frothy.
2. Add 100 g/4 oz sugar with the grated orange rind and juice and whisk for a further 2 minutes.

3. Whisk the egg whites with the remaining sugar until stiff.
4. Stir half the whisked whites into the yolk mixture with the cream and flour.
5. Finally gently fold in the remaining egg whites.
6. Brush the hot waffle iron with butter. Place 2 to 3 tablespoons of the mixture in the centre for each waffle. Cook until light brown according to the manufacturer's instructions.
7. Dust with icing sugar while still hot and serve immediately with whipped cream, stewed fruit, ice cream or fresh fruit.

Serves 4:

250 g/9 oz Madeira or
sponge cake
50 g/2 oz praline
3 tablespoons brandy
250 ml/8 fl oz sherry
250 g/9 oz sliced peaches
500 ml/17 fl oz double
cream
1–2 tablespoons caster
sugar
1 tablespoon vanilla sugar

1. Cut the cake into squares and place in a basin or straight-sided soufflé dish.
2. Keep 2 tablespoons of the praline on one side to decorate, and scatter the rest over the sponge. Soak the mixture generously in brandy and sherry.

3. Cover with the sliced peaches.
4. Whip the cream until stiff and sweeten to taste with sugar and vanilla sugar.
5. Either spread the cream over the top, lifting it into peaks, or pipe it on decoratively as illustrated.
6. Leave the trifle to stand for 1 to 2 hours in the refrigerator and then serve scattered with the rest of the praline.
Note: If you are making a trifle for children, replace the brandy and sherry with some orange or other type of fruit juice.

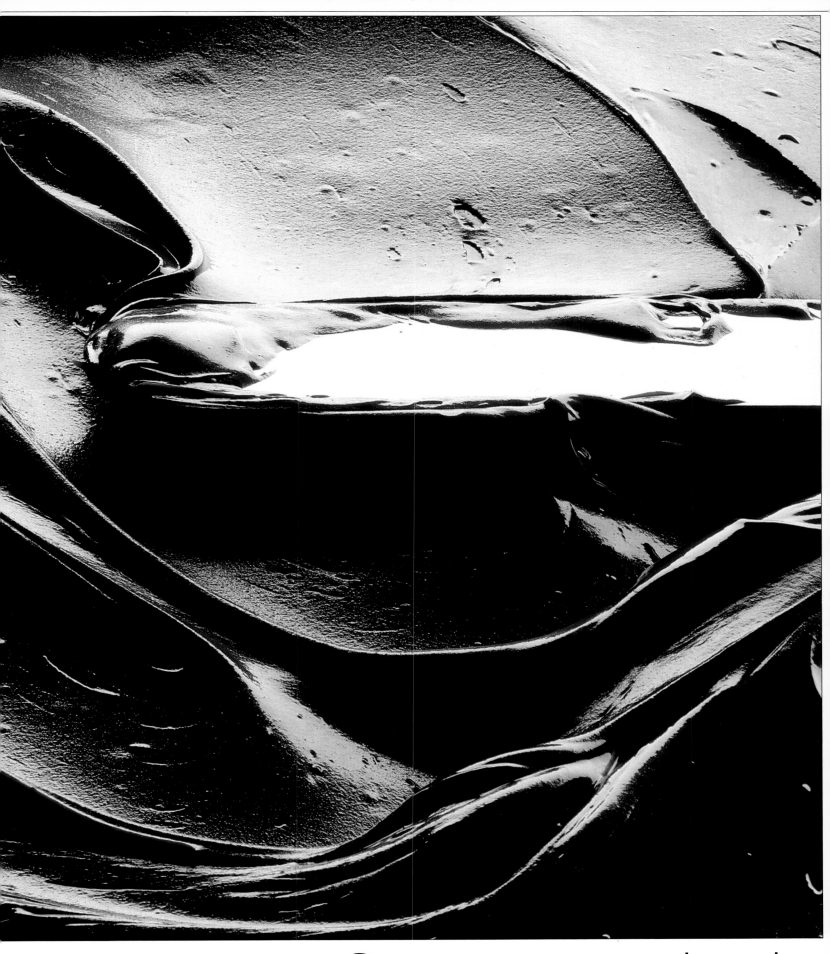

Creams to soothe the
palate and the soul

A delicious cream filling

Buttercream is a well blended mixture of liquid, fat and air. This makes it one of the most difficult processes to perfect in the whole art of cake making. But the effort is worthwhile for a perfect buttercream is simply unbeatable.

Buttercream – four different types

1. *Rich buttercream* (illustrated bottom right) The most elegant of the four types with a delicate balance of egg yolks and butter. It is based on a custard. The hot custard must be whipped long enough to thicken but must not be allowed to boil or the egg yolks will start to separate.

2. *French buttercream* (illustrated top right) This is the smoothest of the buttercreams but also the most time-consuming. Whole eggs and sugar are whisked over hot water to give a smooth cream. You will need patience here and once the mixture is out of the water, you have to go on whisking the egg mixture until cool.

3. *German buttercream* This is very similar to Rich buttercream but it varies because it has a flour-based custard (see page 237) which is whisked into the lightly whipped butter. Take care with blending in the butter. The custard and butter must be at the same temperature, so make the custard a day in advance to make it more stable.

4. *Italian buttercream* This is the easiest one to make, but it contains a lot of air. It is made with meringue (see pages 222–3), which is simply mixed with the creamed butter. The egg whites can be a problem as they must be whisked until firm enough to combine well with the butter, so follow the basic meringue recipe exactly.

Tips on butter

☐ Success depends on the quality of the butter. It must be fresh and very good quality.
☐ The butter should be at room temperature but not warm enough to begin to melt.
☐ When creaming the butter you will need patience (and a good food mixer – with a hand whisk you will get tired too soon). The creamed butter is ready when it looks like thick cream.
☐ Perfect buttercream is melting, airy and light and this depends on creaming the butter properly.

Tips on the basic custard

☐ Custard and butter must be at the same temperature, ie room temperature. If the custard is too hot the butter melts and loses its texture. If it is too cold the butter separates and solidifies into tiny flakes, preventing it binding with the custard.
☐ Never try to add all the custard at one go. Work it into the butter a little at a time.
☐ Work in gently with a hand whisk to avoid beating out all the necessary air.
☐ When piping with buttercream keep the bag as cool as possible.
Note: If despite all your care the buttercream looks likely to separate, quickly beat in an egg yolk working gradually outwards from the centre. In a sealed container buttercream will keep for several days in the refrigerator. Before using you will have to let it return to room temperature for about 3 to 4 hours.

Preparation

1. Measure the ingredients and place ready.

2. Break the eggs into a large metal bowl.

3. Whisk the eggs with an electric hand mixer for about 2 minutes.

4. Then slowly add the sugar, whisking continuously.

5. Place the bowl in hot, but not boiling, water.

6. Whisk for a further 4 to 5 minutes until the mixture is creamy.

7. Take the bowl out of the water. Whisk until cold.

8. Place the butter in a second bowl.

9. Beat until pale and the consistency of cream.

10. This takes about 15 minutes. On no account try to rush it.

11. Cut the vanilla pod open lengthways using a knife.

12. Scrape out the soft black pith.

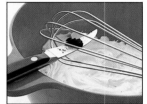

13. Scrape the pith off the knife with a whisk and whisk into the butter.

14. Once the custard is at room temperature, whisk into the butter.

15. Use the French buttercream immediately.

Preparation

1. Measure the ingredients and place ready.

2. Slowly bring the cream to the boil over a moderate heat.

3. Slit the vanilla pod and leave to steep in the cream.

4. Meanwhile separate the eggs. Place the yolks in a metal basin.

5. Add the sugar to the yolks and whisk in.

6. Add the hot cream, whisking vigorously.

7. Pour the mixture back into the pan and place on a low heat.

8. Heat slowly, stirring continuously with a rubber spatula.

9. Pour the thickened custard into a sieve.

10. Press through the sieve and leave to cool to room temperature.

11. Place the butter, also at room temperature, in a mixing bowl.

12. Beat on the highest setting for 15 minutes until thick and creamy.

13. The butter should be creamy white like thick cream.

14. Gradually beat the custard into the butter.

15. Transfer the Rich buttercream to a basin and use quickly.

Buttercreams from chocolate-brown to pistachio-green

Tips on buttercream

Regardless of which type of buttercream you choose (the four types are described in detail on page 230), you can vary the colour and flavour in a number of ways. Naturally, you have to work as carefully here as in making the basic cream. Buttercream is extremely delicate and any haste or carelessness may cause it to separate. So note:

☐ Any flavourings which have to be heated, such as melted chocolate or nougat, should be cooled to room temperature before adding to the buttercream.

☐ Liquid ingredients, such as alcohol or essences, should be whisked in a few drops at a time.

☐ Solid ingredients, such as nuts, should be ground to a fine powder. Any lumps will spoil the smooth surface of the cake and clog the smallest nozzle of the piping bag.

Nougat buttercream

(illustrated outside left) Slowly stir 200 g/7 oz nougat in a heatproof bowl over hot water until completely dissolved. Cool to room temperature and gently whisk into the finished buttercream.

Buttercream is naturally a pleasant creamy-white colour, but it can be made to look quite different, by just adding a variety of ingredients to give flavour and colour. Buttercreams like this will turn any sponge into an impressive, mouth-watering gâteau.

Chocolate buttercream

(illustrated centre left) Melt 100 g/4 oz plain chocolate in a heatproof bowl over hot water. Cool to room temperature and mix thoroughly with the buttercream.

Mocha buttercream

(illustrated inside left) Stir 3 teaspoons instant coffee with 2 teaspoons rum and mix into the finished buttercream.

Raspberry buttercream

(illustrated centre right) Press 100 g/4 oz fresh raspberries through a fine sieve. Mix with 3 tablespoons raspberry liqueur. Whisk into the finished buttercream a tablespoon at a time, waiting until one is fully mixed in before adding the next.

Nutty buttercream

(illustrated inside right) Crush 150 g/5 oz nuts of your choice in a mortar or electric grinder and stir into the buttercream. Finally flavour with 3 tablespoons rum, stirred in a few drops at a time.

Pistachio buttercream

(illustrated outside right) Grind 150 g/5 oz peeled pistachios in an electric grinder to a fine powder. Beat into the buttercream. Finally work 3 tablespoons cherry brandy into the cream a few drops at a time for extra flavour.

Piping buttercream

It will take some time before you can pipe buttercream as artistically as the illustrations on this page. But – take heart – practice makes perfect! Piping creams with a piping bag is an acquired art, but once you've got the knack, there will be no holding you, although sometimes it might seem that a piping bag filled with cream has a mind of its own.

Patterns and tips on piping technique

First choose the right nozzle:

☐ The large fluted nozzle gives wide fluted stripes and whirls almost the size of a single portion (1st photograph, far left).

☐ The medium fluted nozzle makes a twisting stripe along each portion (2nd photograph).

☐ The small fluted nozzle makes small stars or whirls (3rd photograph).

☐ The most versatile nozzle is the medium one.

Photograph 4 shows snaking lines narrowing towards the centre. The 5th photograph shows four whirls zig-zagging into the centre. Around the edge the small nozzle is used to make a border.

These are only an example of what can be done, for with a little practice you can make the most unusual and decorative patterns.

☐ To fill the piping bag first insert nozzle, then fold the top half outwards. Hold the point of the bag firmly in your left hand and fill with cream. Fold up the top and twist to prevent leakage (see photographs page 25).

☐ For piping hold the top of the bag between thumb and index finger while the other fingers exert pressure on the bag. Guide the bag by holding the bottom in your left hand.

☐ There should be no air in the bag, so first pipe into a basin to compress the cream.

☐ When you have emptied part of the bag, squeeze the cream down into the point, just like a tube of toothpaste.

Canache cream

This is an exceptionally high-quality pâtisserie cream which is so easy to make. It is a light, melt-in-the-mouth cream made with fresh cream and chocolate, guaranteed not to go wrong provided you always use fresh cream. Canache cream (French 'Ganache') is used to fill and cover chocolate gâteaux (see pages 68–9 and 77), to fill profiterolles (see page 199) and meringues (see page 222–3), as a base for the fruit in a flan (see page 108) or just as it comes as a quick dessert.

500 ml/17 fl oz single cream
400 g/14 oz plain chocolate, chopped

1. Heat the cream in a saucepan. Before it comes to the boil add the chocolate.
2. Remove the pan from the heat and beat until the chocolate has melted.
3. Chill for about 2 hours.
4. Whisk the chilled mixture with an electric hand mixer for 10 to 15 minutes until thick and frothy.

Lemon cream

A completely different cream. It is thickened with a little cornflour and egg yolks and given volume by the whisked egg white which is folded into the hot cream at the end. It is this which gives firmness to the cooled cream. Lemon cream is used as a basis for fruit in a flan. If you want to use it as a cake filling, you will have to stiffen it with 15 g/½ oz powdered gelatine, soaked in water, stirred into the hot cream until dissolved.

juice of 3 lemons
250 ml/8 fl oz water
75 g/3 oz sugar
2 egg yolks
2 tablespoons cornflour
2 tablespoons water
2 egg whites

1. Bring the lemon juice, water and sugar to the boil in a saucepan.
2. Beat the egg yolks with the cornflour and 2 tablespoons water until smooth, then add the boiling lemon water. Boil up once, whisking continously. Then remove from the heat and pour into a mixing bowl.
3. Whisk the egg whites until stiff and fold into the hot mixture. Cool the cream before using.

The star creams –
the crème de la crème

English custard

The richest and most delicate of the creams. Made with cream and egg yolks with no other binding agent. It is the egg yolks that give the firmness. The cream must reach exactly the right temperature to thicken it. If the egg yolk separates there is no way you can rescue it and you will have to start again. For the method and ingredients see Rich buttercream, pages 230–1 (photographs 2–10). Custard is used for desserts, ice cream (page 214) or as the basis of Rich buttercream (see pages 230–1). As a cake filling or a dessert to turn out of a mould (eg Crème bavaroise) you will have to add about $15\,g/\frac{1}{2}\,oz$ powdered gelatine and $250\,ml/8\,fl\,oz$ whipped cream.

Vanilla cream

Also known as pâtisserie cream. It was on this mixture that the original blancmange powder was based some hundred years ago. Although blancmange powder does not compare with the cream for flavour, it has remained extremely popular.

Pâtisserie cream is not that simple to make and the ingredients are quite expensive. Unlike English custard, to which it is very similar, pâtisserie cream contains a little flour which makes it slightly firmer and prevents it collapsing. It is used to fill profiterolles (see page 199), meringues (see pages 222–3) and cream slices (see page 177), as a bed for fruit in shortcrust flans or as the basis of German buttercream. You can vary the flavour in a number of ways, as for buttercream (see pages 232–3).

500 ml/17 fl oz milk
1 vanilla pod
5 egg yolks
100 g/4 oz sugar
25 g/1 oz plain flour
pinch of salt

1. Bring the milk to the boil with the vanilla pod, scrape the pith from the pod and add to the milk.
2. Beat the egg yolks with the sugar in a basin until creamy, adding the flour.
3. Stir the boiling milk into the egg yolk mixture. Return to the pan, and boil up once over a low heat, beating continuously.
4. Strain the vanilla cream and leave to cool. If you sprinkle the top with sugar this will prevent a skin forming.

These are the classics of the art of baking. You will find them so useful as they are infinitely versatile. All these creams have one thing in common, they are heated to bind and thicken them. These cooked creams can either be served on their own or with fresh or stewed fruit as a dessert. They can serve as a basis for other more complicated desserts or as a soft and creamy filling for small cakes or gâteaux.

A light cake covering or a delicious dessert

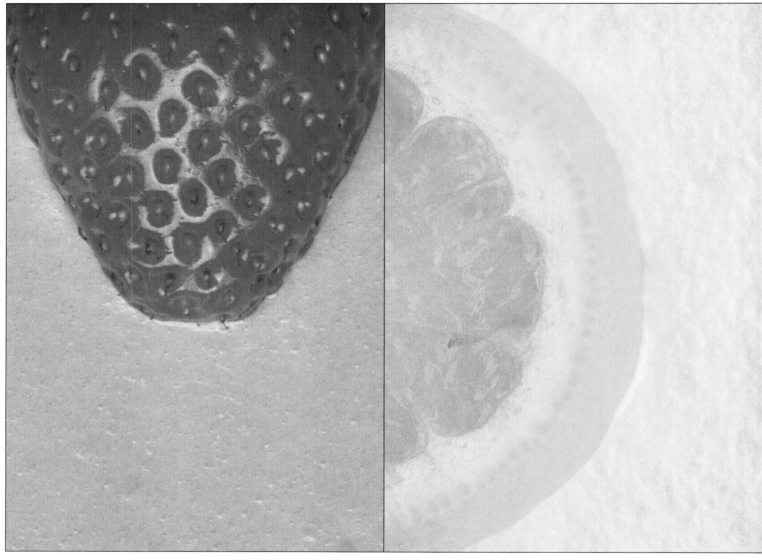

Basic recipe for strawberry cream

(illustrated left)

15 g/½ oz powdered gelatine

750 ml/1¼ pints single cream

500 g/18 oz strawberries, hulled

4–5 tablespoons icing sugar

1. Soak the gelatine, squeeze out well and dissolve in a heatproof bowl over hot water. Stir into the cream and chill.

2. Press the strawberries through a sieve or blend in a liquidiser and sweeten to taste.

3. As soon as the cream begins to jellify, whip with an electric whisk.

4. Fold the strawberry purée into the cream.

Whipped cream variations

From this basic recipe you can make a variety of whipped creams using different fruits or flavourings.

Here are five examples:

Lemon cream
Stir the juice of 1 lemon into the cream and gelatine, chill and then whip as in the basic recipe.

The trouble with whipped cream is that it will soon begin to fall no matter how well you whip it. So here is a trick which will not only improve the flavour but also ensure that it stays firm.

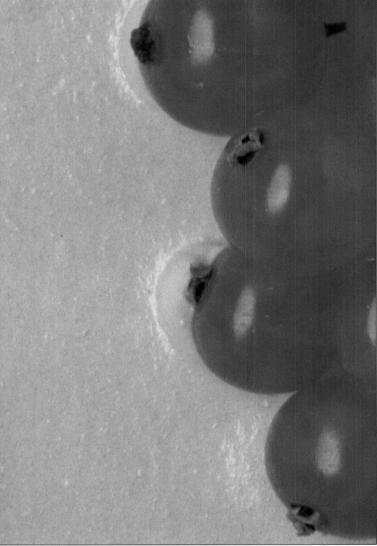

Blackberry cream
Proceed as in the basic recipe but replace the strawberries with 500 g/ 18 oz blackberries.

Red currant cream
Purée and strain 500 g/ 18 oz red currants. Proceed as in the basic recipe.

Curd cheese cream
(not illustrated)
Sweeten 250 g/9 oz drained curd cheese to taste, press through a sieve and fold into the whipped cream.

Mocha cream
(not illustrated)
Stir 5 tablespoons strong coffee into the cream and gelatine. Chill well and then whip as in the basic recipe.

Tips on whipped cream

☐ Always chill cream well before whipping and use a chilled metal basin as it holds the temperature well.
☐ Add the sugar towards the end or it will take longer to whip. It needs to dissolve quickly so it is a good idea to use fine icing sugar.

☐ Whipped cream without gelatine should be used immediately or it will fall.

It's amazing what you can do with butter

You can make light, fluffy creams for instance, for after all butter is nothing more than concentrated cream. If you replace the volume of water that has been taken out of it by beating in air, you get a superb rich cream. This is ideal if you haven't got all the ingredients you need to make a real buttercream. But don't think of this as a time-saving alternative – the longer and more patiently the butter is whipped, the creamier and lighter the final result will be.

Basic recipe for cherry butter

(illustrated bottom left)

100 g/4 oz glacé cherries

4 tablespoons cherry brandy

250 g/9 oz butter, softened

4 egg yolks

150 g/5 oz icing sugar

1. Coarsely chop the glacé cherries and in a basin soak in the cherry brandy.
2. In a large mixing bowl beat the butter with an electric hand whisk or in a food mixer for at least 10 minutes on the highest setting until it is white and fluffy.
3. Add the egg yolks and icing sugar. Beat vigorously for at least a further 5 minutes.
4. Finally fold in the steeped cherries using a rubber spatula.

Nougat cream

(illustrated top right)
Beat the butter until white and fluffy as in the basic recipe (see left). Replace the cherries with 300 g/11 oz nougat, gently dissolved over hot water and then allowed to cool. Beat again with the electric whisk until the cream is completely uniform.

Variations:
Into the creamed butter beat some glacé pineapple or marzipan, beaten until soft. Alternatively add some finely ground nuts such as almonds, pistachios or walnuts.

Chocolate butter

(illustrated top left)
Beat the butter until white and fluffy as in the basic recipe (see left) and instead of the chopped cherries work in 200 g/7 oz chocolate melted in a heatproof bowl over hot water, allowing it to cool before it comes into contact with the butter for it will lose its consistency if it becomes too warm.
Note: Always use absolutely fresh, good-quality butter.

Peanut cream

(illustrated bottom right)
Beat the butter until fluffy as in the basic recipe. Add 200 g/7 oz peanuts, ground very finely in a coffee grinder, together with 150 g/5 oz melted chocolate. (Alternatively you can chop the nuts and chocolate together in an electric grinder.) Or – easier still – mix a jar of creamed peanuts with the melted, cooled chocolate and work into the creamed butter.
Note: If the butter is to be flavoured with liquids (alcohol, fruit juice, etc) they should be added a few drops at a time so that the butter can bind with them properly to form an emulsion.

Gooseberry meringue flan

For the shortcrust base:

300 g/ 11 oz plain flour

200 g/ 7 oz ice-cold butter

100 g/ 4 oz sugar

1 egg

For the gooseberry cream:

500 g/ 18 oz fresh gooseberries, topped and tailed

500 ml/ 17 fl oz milk

1 vanilla pod, slit lengthways

pinch of salt

100 g/ 4 oz sugar

5 egg yolks

65 g/ 2½ oz plain flour

For the meringue:

4 egg whites

pinch of salt

200 g/ 7 oz caster sugar

1. For the shortcrust (see basic recipe page 103) quickly work the ingredients together with cold hands. Chill in the refrigerator for 30 minutes.

2. Roll the pastry out thinly to 5 mm/¼ in thick and cut a circle of 25 cm/ 10 in. in diameter. Bake in a moderately hot oven (200 C, 400 F, gas 6) for 15 minutes, or until cooked.

3. Blanch the gooseberries in boiling water for 2 minutes and then drain in a sieve.

Delicately concealed: gooseberry cream on a shortcrust base under light meringue

4. To make the cream, bring the milk to the boil in a saucepan with the vanilla pod.
5. In a basin beat the salt, sugar, egg yolks and flour. Stir in the boiling milk.
6. Return the mixture to the saucepan and stir over a moderate heat until it boils up. Remove from the heat immediately.
7. Strain the cream. Stir in the gooseberries and leave to cool.
8. Spoon the gooseberry cream over the shortcrust base to form a dome and chill in the refrigerator until set.
9. For the meringue, whisk the egg whites with the salt and 1 tablespoon sugar until stiff. Then slowly add the remaining sugar, continuing whisking until the meringue is firm and has a silky sheen.
10. Transfer the meringue to a piping bag with a large fluted nozzle. Using a decorative pattern of circles, whirls or lines, completely cover the gooseberry cream with meringue.
11. Place the flan in a very hot oven (240 C, 475 F, gas 9) until the surface of the meringue has browned.

Variations:
You can use almost any type of fruit, for example, red currants, bilberries, raspberries, Morello cherries, peaches, apricots or apples. Only firm fruit needs to be blanched before adding to the custard. It is not necessary for soft fruits. For further meringue recipes, see pages 222–3.

Used in this way meringue becomes a sort of cream. It is not dried at a low temperature, but baked quickly at a high temperature to make it a delicious brown on the outside while it remains soft and creamy inside. The meringue serves three purposes in one – it protects the gooseberry cream, makes the flan look attractive and provides a pleasant contrast of flavours.

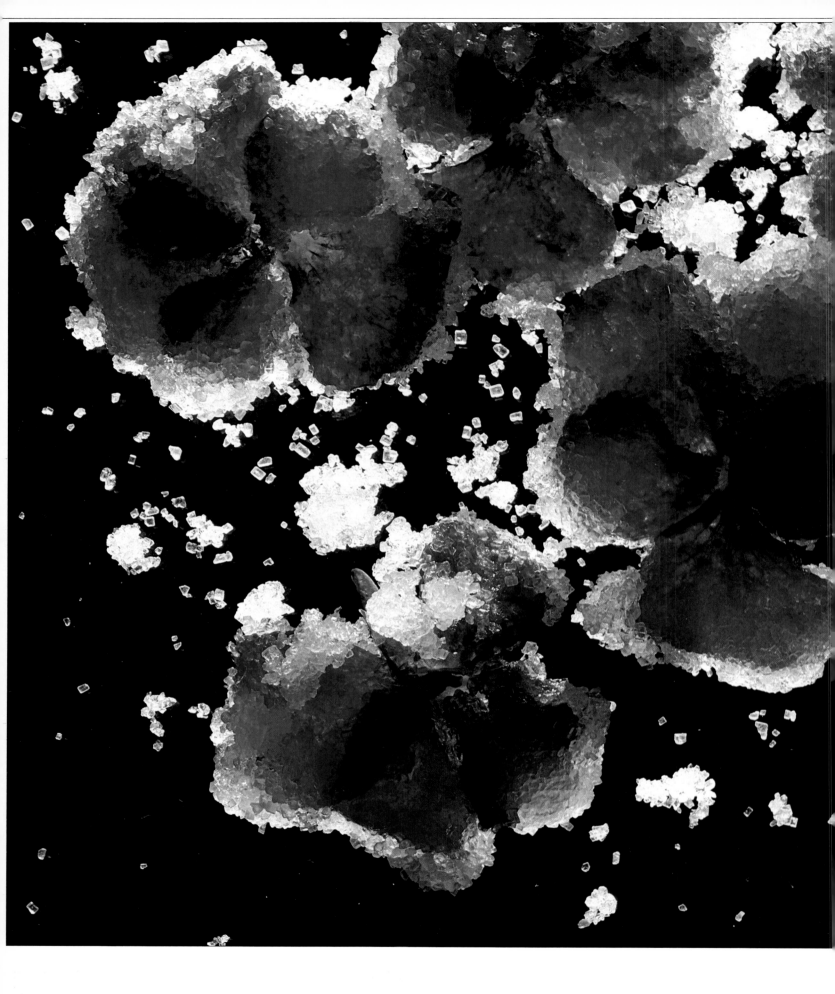

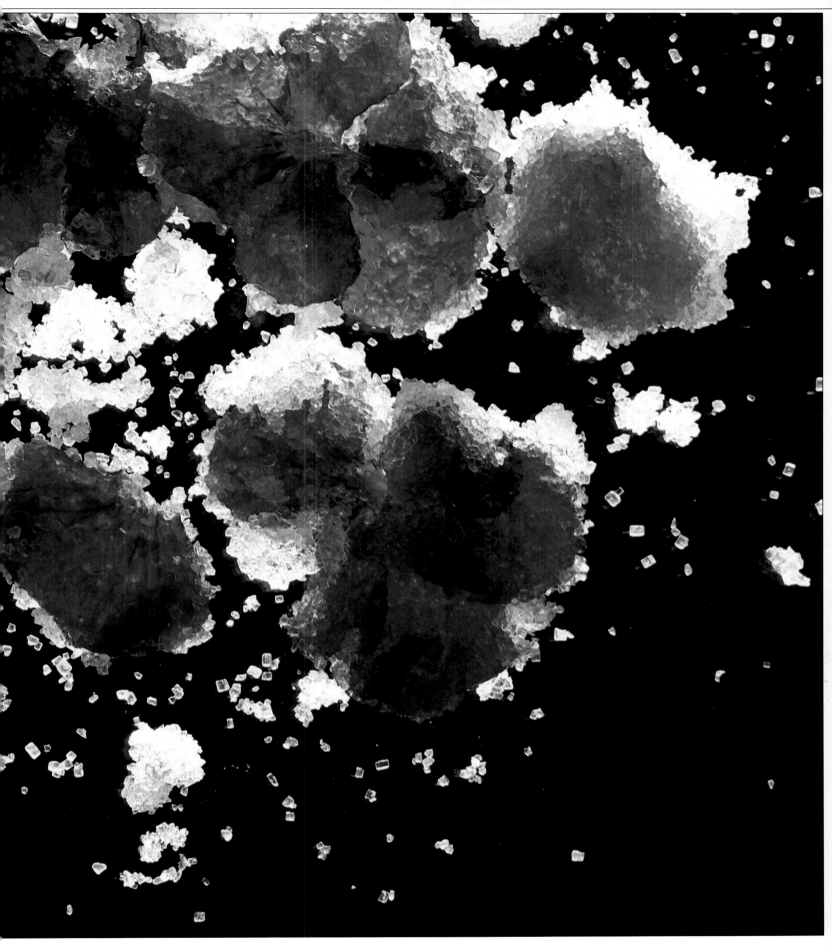

Decorating – all you need
to make gâteaux more attractive

Pink roses and chocolate leaves
– cake decorations

Preparation: chocolate

I. Get out a pan, bowl, rubber spatula, chopping board and the chocolate.

2. Coarsely chop the cooking chocolate with a large knife.

3. Place two-thirds of the chopped chocolate in a heatproof bowl.

4. Place in a saucepan half-filled with hot water.

5. Melt the chocolate, stirring with the rubber spatula.

6. Take the bowl out of the hot water.

7. Add the remaining chocolate to reduce the temperature.

8. Stir until it has melted. The chocolate should now be hand-hot (32C/90F).

9. To test the chocolate, dip a spoon into it and leave to dry.

10. The chocolate should set quickly and have a matt shine.

Preparation: chocolate leaves

I. Set the melted chocolate and washed leaves ready.

2. Lay the top of the leaves flat in the chocolate.

3. Wipe off excess chocolate on the rim of the bowl.

4. With the chocolate side uppermost bend over the handle of a wooden spoon.

5. When the chocolate has set, carefully peel away the green leaves.

Preparation: piped decorations

I. From baking paper cut a triangle.

2. With longest side away from you, begin rolling from the right-hand corner.

3. Fold the left side over pulling the point tight.

4. Cut a tiny piece off the point with scissors.

5. Fold the top over and use the piping bag to pipe delicate lines.

These should not be made by anybody who lacks patience. What you need here is plenty of time and a steady hand. Like any art, it is not easily mastered. One tip here on the difficult process of melting chocolate. To get a nice shiny covering chocolate, let it cool completely after the first melting and then warm slowly over hot water for a second time.

Preparation: marzipan roses

1. 6 tablespoons beetroot juice, 200 g/7 oz marzipan, 50 g/2 oz icing sugar.

2. Bring the juice to the boil in a saucepan over a moderate heat.

3. Boil the juice gently until reduced by half.

4. Sift the icing sugar over the marzipan.

5. Knead in thoroughly with your hands.

6. Spoon the reduced beetroot juice onto the marzipan.

7. Knead until the marzipan is a uniform pink colour.

8. Sprinkle the worktop with icing sugar and work the marzipan into a finger-thick roll.

9. Cut the roll into 1-cm/½-in lengths.

10. Make a wedge-shape centre for the rose.

11. To make the petals press the marzipan out until very thin.

12. Lift the petal off the worktop with a flexible palette knife.

13. Shape the petal over your fingertip and bend back the edges.

14. Place the petals around the wedge and press on firmly.

15. Leave to dry at room temperature for about 30 minutes.

Preparation: crystallised rose petals

1. Rose petals, 1 teaspoon gum arabic, 1 teaspoon caster sugar, water.

2. Stir together the gum arabic, sugar and water.

3. Using tweezers dip the rose petals into the liquid and allow to drain.

4. Dip in sugar to completely cover.

5. Dry on absorbent kitchen paper for several hours. These are for decoration only.

Icings to bring out the best or hide any faults

You can think of these as a form of make-up for your baking. Pale, uninteresting cakes can be livened up with icing to give an attractive shiny finish. And cakes that have come out of the oven too dark or not quite perfect in shape can be hidden under a sweet coating that not only looks good but also tastes delicious.

Royal icing

This gives a thick, dazzling white covering. It is used mainly for Christmas or wedding cakes (see pages 58–9, for example). Slowly whisk egg whites with an electric whisk until stiff and white, gradually adding icing sugar to make a firm, tacky mixture (500 g/18 oz icing sugar per egg white.)

The icing is spread on the cake using a palette knife or is piped in attractive patterns using a fabric or home-made paper piping bag. When dry royal icing sets very hard.

Apricot glaze

This has a host of different uses, giving a shine to sponge and pastries, preventing moist cakes such as Danish pastries, Madeira cake or savarins, from becoming dry, and to glaze flans.

450 g/1 lb apricot jam
3 tablespoons water
2 tablespoons sugar

Boil all the ingredients together in a saucepan over a high heat until the water has evaporated and the sugar has dissolved. The glaze should be spread hot on cakes and pastries, either spooned or brushed on.
Note: If the jam contains bits of fruit, strain the hot glaze through a sieve.

Use red currant jelly instead of apricot jam to glaze red fruit.

Glacé icing

This is the easiest way to decorate biscuits and can be made in several different colours.

100 g/4 oz icing sugar
1–2 tablespoons water

Sift the icing sugar to make it powder-fine. Stir in sufficient water to give a thick, spreading consistency. Instead of water you can use other liquids to add flavour: lemon or fruit juice, alcohol or coffee. To colour the icing use beetroot or spinach juice, saffron dissolved in water or artificial food colourings.

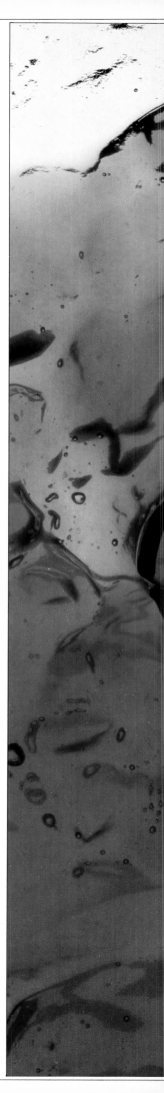

All about chocolate . . .

At the very mention of the word chocolate most people's eyes light up, their mouths begin to water and they lick their lips in anticipation . . . Chocolate is much more than a sweet: it is quite literally a food of the gods, for it is made from cocoa beans whose botanical name is Theobroma, food of the gods. What is more, the original drink made from cocoa beans, which were sacred to the ancient Aztecs . . .

Chocolate shavings

To decorate gâteaux and desserts for special occasions. To make them you need melted cooking chocolate (see page 246), a slab of marble (or glass, or other surface which is completely smooth and cool), a metal spatula and nimble fingers. Spread the liquid chocolate thinly on the marble. Cool until it just sets and then scrape it off the marble with the spatula. The firmer the chocolate, the narrower will be the shavings.
To make rolls of chocolate to decorate the top of a gâteau, the chocolate needs to be fairly pliable (see pages 68–9).

Cooking chocolate

This is a very waxy form of chocolate, which can be bought in large quantities for baking and which is much cheaper to buy than dessert chocolate. It is ideal in icings and making cake decorations.

. . . to make your mouth water

. . . must have been something quite terrible. Xococ (the origin of our word chocolate) means bitter/sour, so it must have been some sort of rather nasty sacrificial drink. Nevertheless, the Spanish conquistadors thankfully brought the brown bean back to Europe amongst their booty and inventive cooks were not slow to discover its potential. Right up to the present day chocolate is still considered the sweetest of all temptations.

Covering cakes in chocolate

The most tempting of all cakes are those covered in bitter-sweet chocolate. A marzipan base helps to even out any irregularities there might be. Roll the marzipan absolutely flat and then press or smooth on to the cake using a metal cake base (see page 16). Pour the melted chocolate (see page 246) into the centre and spread carefully with a palette knife, turning the cake as you go. There must be enough chocolate to completely cover both the top and sides. Leave until absolutely dry. It is a good idea to mark portions on the top with a warm knife before absolutely set. This prevents the chocolate breaking when you cut the cake (see pages 98–9).

Chocolate leaves

These are delightful with fresh raspberries to decorate a chocolate cake, as illustrated here. They make attractive and unusual chocolate shapes to serve with coffee or to make an inexpensive but impressive gift. Instructions for making chocolate leaves can be found on page 246. You can add variety by using a number of different leaves – if you feel ambitious, why not try to make a laurel wreath entirely of chocolate using bay leaves?

Marzipan fruits – lovely to look at and delicious to eat

Nothing is better than marzipan for modelling. Agile fingers can make true works of art which look almost too good to eat. They are always attractive however you use them, as a delightful gift, as a centrepiece for the tea-table or as decoration for a special cake. Of course, again you need patience and some artistic skill. If you are not artistic you can simply eat the marzipan. This may not help with the decoration, but it tastes delicious!

Marzipan – the various types

Marzipan consists of equal quantities of finely ground almonds and sugar, flavoured with a few drops of rose water and a dash of bitter almonds. It is quite easy to make: scald the almonds in hot water until the brown skin comes away easily. Then grind a little at a time with icing sugar in a coffee mill or mix to a firm paste in a food processor. Sprinkle with a little rose water and either add bitter almond flavouring or use a few bitter almonds with the almonds. Knead the marzipan vigorously. Wrapped in foil it will keep for several weeks. In principle this is no different from bought marzipan. This can be used as it comes or mixed with up to 50 per cent icing sugar to make it firmer and sweeter.

One type of marzipan can be uncooked. It is usually made into miniature loaves and coated in chocolate. Another type is cooked over a low heat to break down the protein in the nuts to give a more uniform consistency. This type of marzipan is usually made into hearts and lightly browned under a hot grill.

Tips for modelling with marzipan

☐ The marzipan should always be at room temperature, as it makes it easier to handle.
☐ Sprinkle the worktop repeatedly with icing sugar to prevent sticking.
☐ You will find modelling tools useful, and brushes in various sizes are essential. These are used for applying the colour, while you can use the pointed end to mark lines and dots, to make the eyes in potatoes or the indentation in a peach or plum.
☐ One trick to help you get an even orange peel effect is to stick mustard seeds to a piece of wood and roll the modelled orange backwards and forwards over them.
☐ If preferred, you can colour the fruit right through by working a little food colouring or coloured glacé icing into the marzipan. For an attractive effect work two pieces of marzipan of different colours together to give a marbled look. This makes really effective marzipan eggs for Easter.

How to make the fruit basket

(Clockwise from the left)
Mushroom: For the cap, stir cocoa powder with a little melted vegetable fat. For the stem thin the colour with a little extra vegetable fat.

Plums: Colour with strongly reduced beetroot juice (dark purple). Finally dust the plums with a little cornflour.

Peaches: Use red food colouring in varying strengths, paling to yellow on one side. Use the colour sparingly.

Lemons: Brush with yellow food colouring, toning to green at one end.

Cherries: Colour with a weak concentration of beetroot juice. Use real leaf stems as stalks.

Potatoes: Roll gently to and fro in a bowl of cocoa powder until lightly covered to look like earth. Brush off excess cocoa powder.

Carrots: Mix red and yellow food colouring. Shape carrots, mark with knife and brush with colour.

Orange: Mix red and yellow food colouring to the correct shade and apply in several coats.

Pears: Paint with saffron dissolved in hot water and add green tones with reduced spinach juice.

Bananas: Colour yellow with saffron and water. For the brown lines and flecks use cocoa powder stirred into a little melted vegetable fat.

253

The tools for piping

The usual fabric piping bag used for cake mixtures or creams is too clumsy for fine filigree work. So for fine decoration a small paper piping bag is used. You can make these yourself from greaseproof paper or baking parchment (see page 246) or simply buy them in kitchen shops. You throw them away after use. The smaller the hole in the point of the bag (cut with scissors), the finer the line you will be able to draw with it. So if you want to do a pattern involving several thicknesses, always do the thinnest lines first, followed by thicker spots, underlinings or initial letters.

The 'ink' for sugar writing

Glacé icing is easiest to handle, but it must be made thicker than usual. Mix icing sugar with only a few drops of liquid (water, alcohol, colouring) to make a thick but workable paste. It is a good idea to strain the icing to remove any small lumps that could clog the hole in the bag. The thin thread squeezed out of the bag must keep its shape and not run.

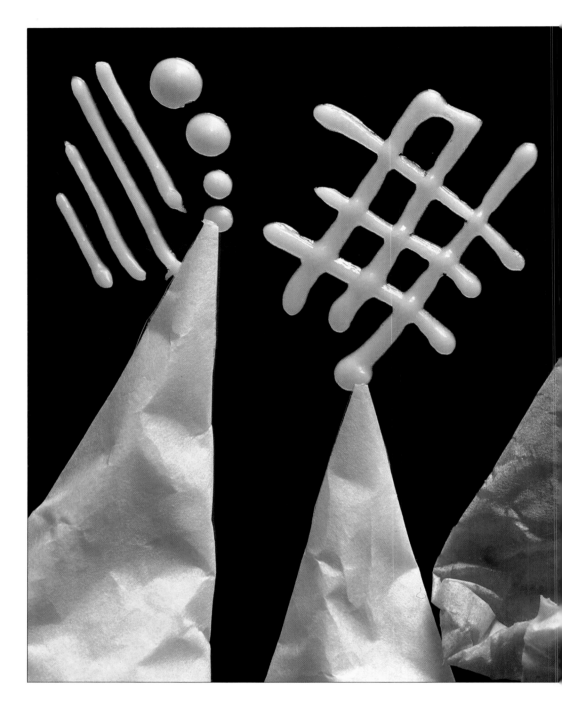

The art of piping with a greaseproof bag

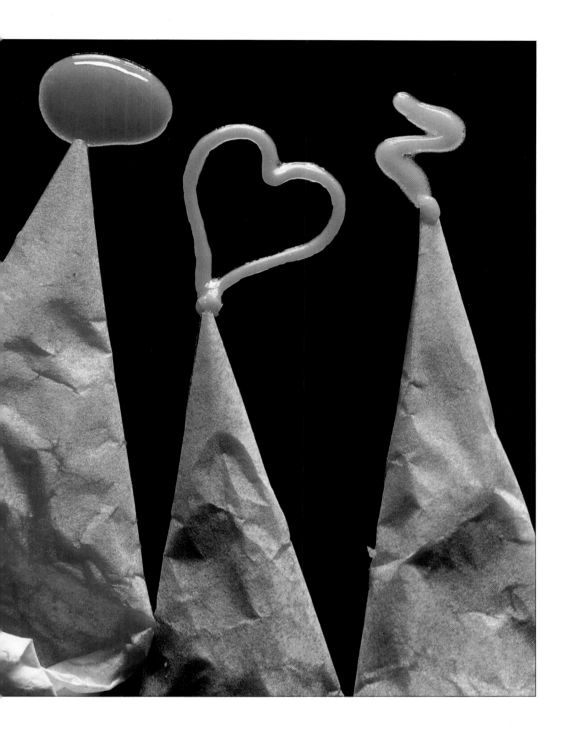

To decorate biscuits, cakes or sweets with fine lines and patterns, all you need is thick glacé icing and a small piping bag. And of course a steady hand. With a little practice you will be able to write a letter with it. A baking-tray sponge offers scope for a whole variety of messages to suit any occasion.

Chocolate writing

Thin lines of chocolate are a little more tricky. Melt a little cooking chocolate (see pages 246–7) and stir in a few drops of water or rum until it becomes viscous. Spoon quickly into the piping bag and use at once.

Tips on using a piping bag

☐ Always hold the piping bag at least 1 cm/$\frac{1}{2}$ in above the surface you are decorating. The higher you hold it, the more evenly you can draw with it.

☐ The thread of icing squeezed from the bag must be thick enough to be literally laid on the cake.

☐ For hair-thin lines place small cakes or sweets close together and move the bag quickly across them from right to left. The quicker you go, the thinner the lines.

☐ Work quickly and do not leave the full bag lying about or the point will dry and you won't be able to use it any more.

Coloured writing

You can use food colourings to make the white icing any colour you want. (They come in red, green, blue and yellow – and these colours can be mixed to produce others.) If you prefer natural colourings, you can use saffron for yellow, concentrated spinach juice for green or beetroot juice for red.

Flan cases in special shapes

— For flans you need a flan tin with a fluted rim. This gives the flan case a nice raised edge which prevents the fruit sliding or the glaze running over the edge.

— You can make the flan case in shortcrust, sponge or Genoese sponge to produce respectively a crisp, crumbly or light base.

— All three types can be baked in advance. In an airtight tin or plastic container they will stay fresh for up to a week.

Fruit filling

The fruit must look good as well as taste good, so try and choose fruits which contrast well in colour. Any fruit which is usually eaten cooked is suitable – hard fruits such as apples, pears or unripe peaches should first be braised in a little syrup or white wine. You can use the juice to make the glaze.

A practical flan filling is frozen berries which you can buy all the year round – raspberries, bilberries, blackberries, etc. Spread the frozen fruit in the flan case and cover with the hot glaze. This makes the fruit defrost more quickly and the glaze set more quickly.

Fruit flans for summer freshness even in winter

They can be made so quickly. Flan cases in shortcrust or sponge can either be bought or made in advance. You can use canned or frozen fruit and they are ready to serve as soon as the glaze has cooled. While it is cooling you get a chance to whip the cream and make the coffee.

Holds everything in place – the flan glaze

This gives the flan a nice shiny finish as well as extra flavour and prevents the fruit falling. Make the glaze using the jam of your choice, sugar and water (see page 248). Allow the glaze to set slightly before spooning on to the flan to prevent it running off the fruit and soaking into the flan. The best way is to paint it on thickly with a brush.

A covering of fruit jelly

Homemade glazes made with jelly have a better, more concentrated flavour. Choose a jelly which either harmonises or contrasts with the fruit – eg red currant, raspberry, apple, lemon, or orange. Bring to the boil with 1 tablespoon sugar. When cool this glaze is also firm and gives the flan a nice shine.

A bed of custard for the fruit

This is guaranteed to keep the flan fresh (if you have to make it the day before). Spread the flan case with buttercream or custard (see pages 231 and 237) before filling with fruit. This prevents the juice from the fruit soaking into the flan case too much.

Raspberry and bilberry flan

(illustrated top left) Fill a 25 or 28 cm/10 or 11 in cooked flan case with rings of raspberries and bilberries (500 to 575 g/18 oz–1¼ lb each) working outwards from the centre. Cover with a glaze or a fruit jelly.

Colourful fruit flan

(illustrated top right) Carefully arrange a 400-g/ 14-oz can mandarins around the edge of the flan case. Fill the centre with a 400-g/14-oz can apricot halves, rounded side uppermost. Use 200 g/7 oz fresh grapes to fill the gaps between them. Cover with a flan glaze made with the mandarin or apricot juice, or with fruit jelly.

Strawberry flan with pineapple

(illustrated bottom left) Place 4 or 5 canned pineapple rings in the flan case. Fill the spaces between them with fresh hulled strawberries. Cover with a glaze made with the pineapple juice.

Blackberry and red currant flan with kiwis

(illustrated bottom right) Peel 3 ripe kiwis and cut into 1-cm/½-in slices. Place the largest in the centre of the flan case and the rest in a circle around it. Fill the gaps with red currants and blackberries (250 g/9 oz each). Cover with a red currant jelly or a clear flan glaze.

30 ways to make your baking more attractive

1. Very thin *slices of orange* poached until soft in sugar syrup. These can be beautiful on a fresh-cream gâteau. Cover with apricot glaze to make them keep better.

2. *Marzipan roses* (see page 247) for wedding or similar special cakes.

3. *Truffles* coated in cocoa powder (see pages 266–7). Use to mark portions on a birthday cake covered with chocolate cream.

4. *Marzipan numbers* piped with chocolate dots. For an anniversary cake.

5. *Meringue crumbs* (see pages 222–3) make a nice crunchy coating for a cream cake.

6. *Cocktail cherries* to show the portions.

7. *Grated coconut* makes a nice edge for cream cakes or a coating for truffles.

8. *Coloured sugar balls* to decorate biscuits or a child's birthday cake.

9. *Walnut halves* used to mark portions on a gâteau covered with chocolate cream.

10. *Nut-nougat-cream* to cover a sponge or gâteau. Very attractive if applied in peaks.

11. *Spider's web pattern.* A very thin spiral of chocolate piped on to glacé icing and drawn from the centre outwards with the back of a knife or the tip of a cocktail stick. Beautiful for the top of a cake or to go on biscuits.

12. *Cocoa powder* to dust or coat sweets.

13. *Chocolate flower design* drawn with a paper piping bag. The flower is two quarters of a cocktail cherry. A really beautiful cake decoration.

14. *Raspberry jelly* for a bright red flan glaze.

15. *Marzipan rolls* to cover portions of gâteau. Cut to size exactly before placing on the cake.

16. *Whirls of cream with pineapple.* Stiffen the cream with gelatine (see pages 238–9) and pipe on to the cake.

Here at a glance you have a whole range of suggestions to choose from to turn the most ordinary cake into a masterpiece. They range from being childishly simple to needing a lot of skill. They cover baking for every occasion, from a plain cake for afternoon tea to the intricate wedding cake decoration with marzipan roses . . .

17. *Red currants* in fruit flans should be covered with a red glaze.

18. Homemade *chocolate shavings* on a cream gâteau (see pages 250–1).

19. A *nutty topping* is attractive and delicious on the sides of a gâteau. Can also be sprinkled into icing and used to cover sweets.

20. *Chocolate tiles* an unusual way of marking portions on a chocolate gâteau.

21. *Coloured sugar* for biscuits, buns or a child's birthday cake. Always sprinkle on wet icing to ensure that they stick properly.

22. *Wafer rolls* (ready bought) make an unusual crisp border to a cake.

23. *Baked meringue* for special fruit flans, desserts, etc. Lift the meringue into peaks and lightly brown in the oven.

24. *Strawberries in pink icing*. Beautiful marking portions on a cream gâteau. Half-dip fresh strawberries in pink glacé icing and dry well.

25. *Icing sugar* patterns. Place cardboard shapes on top of the cake and sift with icing sugar. Only use on dry surfaces.

26. *Crystallised or sugared violets*. Pretty decorations for a cream gâteau.

27. *Cinnamon sugar*. Not only looks nice but also adds flavour. To scatter or coat cakes and sweets.

28. *Lemon slice* and thin *zest* for lemon gâteau.

29. *Chopped pistachio nuts*. These look equally good on light or dark coloured cream cakes. Also around the edges.

30. *Coffee beans in chocolate*. To mark portions on any type of dark coloured cake.

Sweets and chocolates – little
nibbles full of sweetness

Tips on praline making

☐ Accuracy is most imporatant. Take great care over making the mixture and shaping and coating the sweets. Pralines should tempt you first because they look so pretty.

☐ Don't make them too large; you should be able to eat pralines at one bite.

☐ Use absolutely fresh ingredients.

☐ If you are new to the art of sweet-making, start with sweets that are coated in cocoa powder or a nutty topping. Coating them in chocolate needs some practice.

☐ When using chocolate follow the instructions on pages 246 and 250. To keep the chocolate at the right temperature throughout you will need a yogurt thermometer (available from kitchen shops).

☐ The melted chocolate should never rise above 32C/90F. The more frequently you cool and reheat it, the better its gloss will be.

☐ Do not try to get away with less chocolate for coating than given in the recipe. You will have a little over but it is impossible to work with less. You can easily use up any that is left over.

☐ Chocolate that has been overheated develops grey streaks as it dries. Keep it to use in another recipe for it is only the appearance that is affected, not the taste.

Pralines – sweets worth sinning for

As is so often the case with events of world importance, the invention of the praline was connected with a love story. According to legend the praline was the invention of the gallant Field Marshal Praslin. He is said to have pursued his affairs with women he loved with the help of these delicious sweets which now bear an adaptation of his name. If you would like to try his tactics for yourself, here is the basic recipe for you to try. But one word of warning – the better the pralines, the more seductive is their effect . . .

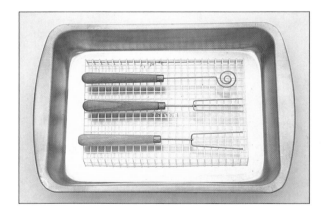

The right tools

If you enjoy making pralines it is a good idea to buy the right tools for the job. It makes the job much easier and (with a little practice) your sweets will look as good as any you can buy. You can buy a complete set, comprising a draining rack, tray (also used to set truffle mixtures) and three special implements from good kitchen shops.

A word on keeping sweets

Where possible sweets should be eaten within ten days to taste their best. Store them in paper cases (available from stationery shops) in a glass, tin or plastic container, separating the layers with paper or better still strong cardboard. Keep them cool but not cold. The ideal place is a cool room at around 18C/64F.

Rum truffles

Equipment
Measuring jug
Saucepan
Metal bowl
Whisk
Deep baking sheet
Knife
Rubber spatula
Sweet-making implements
Deep dish (see small photograph left)
Cling film
Paper cases

Ingredients:
Makes 60:

300 g/11 oz milk cooking chocolate
300 g/11 oz plain cooking chocolate
200 ml/7 fl oz single cream
6 tablespoons rum
100 g/4 oz creamed coconut
100 g/4 oz butter
For the coating:
500 g/1¼ lb milk cooking chocolate
500 g/18 oz caster sugar

Cooking times:
Preparation time:
30 minutes
Cooling and setting:
around 24 hours
Finishing off:
1 hour

Marzipan pralines

Equipment
Rolling pin
Knife
Saucepan
Metal bowl
Rubber spatula
Sweet-making implements
Draining rack
Paper cases

Ingredients:
Makes 40–50:

400 g/14 oz marzipan
icing sugar for worktop
For the coating:
575 g/1¼ lb plain cooking chocolate
100 g/4 oz whole peeled almonds

Cooking times:
Preparation time:
40 minutes
Drying:
10 minutes

Preparation: rum truffles

1. Measure the ingredients and place ready.

2. Slowly melt both types of chocolate in a bowl over hot water.

3. Heat the cream and rum but do not bring to the boil.

4. Add the creamed coconut and butter to the hot cream.

5. Remove the pan from the heat and allow the butter and fat to melt.

6. Stir the chocolate into the cooled, lukewarm mixture.

7. Whisk to a uniform cream.

8. Pour into a baking tray lined with cling film.

9. Cover with cling film and chill for 24 hours.

10. Turn the truffle mixture out of the tin and remove the cling film.

11. Cut the mixture into equal pieces.

12. With cool hands shape quickly into balls. Keep cool.

13. Melt two-thirds of the chocolate in a heatproof bowl to coat the balls.

14. Remove from the water, add remaining chocolate, stir to melt.

15. Get the truffle balls and sweet-making implements ready.

16. Using the spiral fork dip the balls in the chocolate.

17. Coat well, lift out on the fork and drain.

18. Tip the sugar into a deep dish and place the coated balls in the sugar.

19. Place all the balls separately in the dish and cover with sugar.

20. When the chocolate has set, place the truffles in paper cases.

Preparation: marzipan pralines

1. Measure the ingredients and place ready.

2. On the sprinkled worktop roll the marzipan out to 1 cm/½ in thick.

3. Cut very exactly into rectangular, bite-sized pieces.

4. Slowly melt two-thirds of the cooking chocolate in a bowl over hot water.

5. Stir in the remaining chocolate and melt.

6. Place the pieces of marzipan on a praline fork and dip into chocolate.

7. Cover completely and allow to drain slightly.

8. Place on a draining rack or paper and leave to set.

9. While the chocolate is still soft, top each with a peeled almond.

10. Place the finished marzipan pralines in paper cases.

Cutting the pralines

Fresh pralines from the store cupboard

You can keep the basic ingredients for these sweets in your store cupboard. You can buy marzipan and nougat in airtight packets and both will keep for a long time. Opened packets or mixtures bought loose should always be wrapped well in foil. In this way marzipan will keep in the refrigerator for three to four weeks and nougat for about two weeks. In an airtight wrapping, a homemade truffle mixture will keep for up to one week in the refrigerator. The only other thing you need is plenty of sugar. Be over generous with the sugar when rolling and cutting the sweets to ensure that they can't stick to the worktop, your hands or the knife.

Marzipan pralines

(illustrated top)
These are easiest of all to make. You can buy the marzipan and it is child's play to work with. It does not become too soft with repeated handling and, unlike nougat or truffle mixture, you do not need to keep putting it in the refrigerator after every stage to firm it up again. Sprinkle the work top generously with icing sugar and with a rolling pin (also sugared well to avoid sticking) roll out the marzipan to 1–1.5 cm/$\frac{1}{2}$–$\frac{3}{4}$ in thick. Using a sharp knife or sweet cutters, cut into diamonds, squares or rectangles. Cover with cooking chocolate and decorate to taste (see step-by-step photographs, pages 262–3).

Even if it is the very first time you have attempted the difficult art of sweet-making, you will be able to make beautiful confectionery by the end of this section. There is nothing that can go wrong here. All you need is a ruler and a knife that cuts cleanly.

Nougat pralines

(illustrated centre)
Nougat too is best bought ready-made. The nougat must be firm enough to cut cleanly, so always keep it wrapped in foil in the refrigerator. It goes soft easily and will only cut if it is well chilled. Sprinkle the worktop and rolling pin generously with icing sugar and roll the nougat. If it becomes soft, return it to the refrigerator until firm. Trim the edges of the nougat and cut into shapes as for the Marzipan pralines. Chill again before coating in cooking chocolate and decorating. (See Marzipan pralines page 263 and pages 266–7).

Pralines from truffle mixture

(illustrated bottom)
Make and chill the mixture as in the basic recipe on pages 262–3. Sprinkle generously with icing sugar and cut into squares, rectangles or diamonds or roll into balls.
Before making the balls, cool your hands in cold water and then work very quickly. At body temperature the mixture becomes soft and is impossible to shape. Dip your hands in icing sugar to prevent the truffles sticking. If you are working in a hot kitchen, put the balls in the refrigerator as soon as you have made them.

Dressing up the pralines

The right time for decorating

It is not easy to pick exactly the right moment to decorate. The chocolate coating must be firm enough not to be damaged when you decorate or coat the praline, but not so hard that the coating won't stick to it. The lighter the coating, the longer you can wait. Icing sugar or cocoa powder will stick to chocolate that is already too firmly set to take vermicelli or caster sugar.

Getting a perfect coating

Allow plenty of cocoa powder, sugar, icing sugar or vermicelli for coating. You should have enough to literally bury the sweets, so that rather than moving the sweets about, it is the coating that is piled over them. This sugar can be saved and used again.

Coating in chocolate vermicelli

(illustrated top left) Coat pralines in melted cooking chocolate and drain well. While still quite soft completely cover in vermicelli, and leave them in the vermicelli until set. When you lift them out, any excess will just fall off.

Icing sugar coating

(illustrated top right) Coat the sweets in cooking chocolate and drain. Coat immediately in plenty of icing sugar.

Cocoa powder coating

(illustrated bottom left) Dip the pralines in a bowl of milk cooking chocolate and drain. Coat immediately in icing sugar. Once coated, avoid handling the chocolates, to prevent dark stains.

Sugar coating

(illustrated bottom right) Coat the pralines in melted white chocolate. Drain and cool very slightly so that the chocolate is still quite soft. Cover completely with sugar. Do not lift the chocolates out until they are completely set.

When the pralines come out of the chocolate with their silky smooth coating, they still need something extra to decorate them. You will find some suggestions in the photographs on the right-hand page. Or you can use the chocolate coating as a soft base for cocoa powder, sugar or chocolate vermicelli.

Decorating with nuts

(illustrated top left)
— For marzipan chocolates use almonds, walnuts or pistachios.
— Hazelnuts go better with nougat chocolates.
— Press whole nuts into the chocolate while still very soft.
— Scatter chopped nuts on to the chocolate while still soft.

Piped decorations

(illustrated top right)
When piping on chocolates choose contrasting colours. Use milk or plain chocolate to pipe on to white chocolate. On plain chocolate use a white or milk chocolate. You can use criss-cross patterns, spirals, zig-zag lines, or small flecks. Always allow the icing to set hard before packing to avoid smudging. (See piped decorations pages 254–5).

Other decorations

(illustrated bottom left)
Chocolate shavings: Smooth milk chocolate coating topped with a fan of chocolate shavings (see pages 250–1).
Coffee beans: A coating of light milk chocolate topped with a coffee bean.
Lattice pattern: Coat in chocolate. Just before it sets firm, roll the sweet to and fro on the draining rack.

Decorating with candied fruit

(illustrated bottom right)
The colour contrasts here can be very pretty, eg white chocolate with a piece of candied lemon peel. Milk chocolate with a piece of dried apricot. Milk chocolate with half a date. Or white chocolate decorated with narrow strips of glacé pear.

What goes on top should also be inside

This is the basic rule when decorating chocolates. The decoration on the outside should tell you what is under the chocolate coating. Tips and ideas on varying the praline mixture can be found on the following page.

Pralines that just melt in the mouth

The pralines described in the first two sections had hard centres, but now we turn to the best chocolates of all, the ones with soft centres which cannot help but bring a smile to your lips as they melt deliciously in the mouth! The marzipan or truffle mixture has to be made soft and creamy. You can no longer cut them to shape, but will have to use a piping bag. The end result is described on this page.

Truffles

These chocolates contain a lot of cream and butter and so will not keep for very long, but eaten fresh they are really wonderful. Two different basic mixtures are used here: one based on the basic recipe (see pages 262–3) (photographs right-hand column) and the other a butter truffle mixture (photographs left-hand column). You can vary the flavour of both with different types of liqueur. Top quality fruit liqueurs such as raspberry, cherry, pear, plum or apricot are ideal.

Marzipan chocolates

The more liquid you work into the marzipan, the creamier it becomes. Use rum, Cognac or coffee liqueur, Amaretto, orange liqueur or strong concentrated coffee or espresso for flavouring. You can give the soft marzipan extra bite and flavour by adding ground nuts or pistachios. Whether you pipe the mixture or roll and cut it depends on the amount you add.

Pear liqueur truffles

(illustrated left-hand column, from bottom to top)
Makes 60:

60 foil cases

575 g / 1¼ lb plain cooking chocolate, melted

For the truffle mixture:

250 g / 9 oz soft butter

75 g / 3 oz creamed coconut

100 g / 4 oz icing sugar

250 g / 9 oz milk cooking chocolate, melted

4–5 tablespoons pear liqueur

50 g / 2 oz milk cooking chocolate, to decorate

1. Place the foil cases close together and fill with the melted chocolate.
2. Empty the cases by turning upside down on a draining rack over a bowl of chocolate.
3. To make the truffle mixture, vigorously whisk the butter, coconut (at room temperature) and icing sugar until light and thick, or use a food processor on the highest setting for about 10 minutes.
4. Add the melted, cooled chocolate. Stir in the pear liqueur a few drops at a time.
5. Using a plain nozzle, pipe the mixture into the prepared foil cases. Chill for several hours.
6. Dip the tops into the chocolate. When dry decorate with thin stripes of milk chocolate.

Butter truffles

(illustrated 2nd column from left, bottom to top)

1 pear liqueur truffle recipe

(see left) without alcohol

To decorate:

575 g / 1¼ lb milk cooking chocolate, melted

500 g / 18 oz caster sugar

1. Make the truffle mixture as described in the pear liqueur truffle recipe (see left).
2. Using a plain nozzle, pipe in balls on to a baking tray covered with baking parchment.
3. Chill overnight.
4. Cover with the melted chocolate, roll in sugar and leave to set.

Cognac truffles

(illustrated right-hand column, bottom to top)
Prepare 60 foil cases as in the pear liqueur truffle recipe (see left) but using milk cooking chocolate instead of plain.
1. Make the basic rum truffle mixture (see pages 262–3) using Cognac instead of rum and when cold, whisk with an electric whisk until light. Using a fluted nozzle pipe the truffle mixture into the prepared cases and chill overnight.
2. Dip the tops in melted milk cooking chocolate and chill until the chocolate has firmly set.

Pistachio pralines

(illustrated 2nd column from right, bottom to top)
Makes about 40:

400 g / 11 oz marzipan

75 g / 3 oz ground pistachios

4–5 tablespoons rum

500 g / 18 oz plain cooking chocolate

50 g / 2 oz milk cooking chocolate

20 pistachios, halved, to decorate

1. Mix the marzipan with the pistachios, adding sufficient rum to give the creamy consistency shown in the photograph.
2. Using a medium fluted nozzle, pipe on to a baking tray covered with baking parchment.
3. Leave to dry for 24 hours at room temperature.
4. Dip in plain chocolate, drain well and dry on the baking sheet.
5. Decorate with thin stripes of the milk chocolate and pistachio halves.

Petits fours are a type of confectionery. Made with light sponge, marzipan or cream, covered in thick icing and decorated as beautifully as you are able. The name means literally 'little ovens'. In France all bite-sized confectionery is referred to as petits fours even when it requires no baking, such as pralines or fruit in jelly (see pages 218–9 and 262–9).

Basic recipe for petits fours

Makes around 50 bite-size sweets:

½ sheet Genoese sponge (see page 82)
4 tablespoons apricot jam
400 g/14 oz marzipan
500 g/18 oz icing sugar
6 tablespoons water
For coloured icing:
6 tablespoons fruit juice or, as in step-by-step photographs, beetroot juice to make a bright pink colour
25 shelled pistachios, halved to decorate

Decorations for petits fours

Here you can give full rein to your artistic talents. There are no set rules for petits fours. They can consist of several layers of sponge sandwiched with marzipan, jam or a cream. They can be triangular, round, oval or star-shaped. The main point to remember is to bake the sponge on the previous day so that it will cut more easily without crumbling and is slightly flatter. This is important if you intend to sandwich several layers together. You can leave the icing white or colour it with food colourings or natural ingredients. Here are a few different ideas on how to decorate them:

1. Spread the sponge with jam and trim the edges.

2. Roll out the marzipan, place over the sponge and cut into squares.

3. To make the icing, stir the beetroot juice into the icing sugar.

Petits fours –

4. The icing should be thick but still be able to run off a spoon.

5. Place the sponges on a rack and pour on the icing.

6. Decorate with pistachio halves before the icing dries.

Large photograph left-hand page, left to right
For these petits fours the icing has not been coloured with beetroot juice.

1. Using a paper piping bag pipe a delicate flower shape in dark chocolate. Fill in the outline with milk chocolate. Pipe a blob of white icing into the centre.

2. Pipe two long stripes of icing. Decorate with a crystallised violet and half a pistachio.

3. Pipe a flower stem in chocolate. Use a crystallised rose petal for the flower and pistachio halves for leaves.

4. Fill a flower of coloured marzipan with candied lemon peel stem. Decorate with lines of chocolate.

5. Try decorating with a delicate tracery of chocolate lines and quarter of a cocktail cherry sprinkled with ground pistachios.

6. Stick a piece of glacé pineapple into the wet icing and decorate with a chocolate pattern.

7. Use a walnut half for decoration, dipped half in chocolate and then in ground pistachios.

8. Pipe a delicate lattice of diagonal chocolate lines and then place a coffee bean in the centre.

9. Use a crystallised violet petal, a chocolate stem and pistachio leaves to decorate.

Large photograph right-hand page, left to right
10. Try making a marzipan flower with a centre of coloured sugar.

11. Pipe a pattern with chocolate lines, a cocktail cherry, and pistachios.

12. Use candied lemon peel leaves, a marzipan flower and piped chocolate lines.

13. Pipe a chocolate flower and fill the centre with icing.

14. Use crystallised violet petals to decorate.

15. Piece of candied orange peel decorated with chocolate stripes.

16. Place a small glacé cherry in the centre and surround with tiny dots of chocolate.

17. Use a hazelnut half dipped in chocolate, then surround with ground pistachios.

18. Pipe geometric chocolate lines and add a coffee bean.

pretty and delicious

Caramel bonbons

I orange	
5 sugar cubes	
300g/11oz granulated sugar	
50g/2oz honey	
5 tablespoons water	
250ml/8floz single cream	
40g/1½oz butter	
neutral flavoured or almond oil to grease foil or baking parchment to line tin	

1. Rub the orange peel against the sugar cubes so that they absorb the volatile oils.
2. Fast boil the cube and granulated sugars, honey and water over a high heat for 2 to 3 minutes. Remove from the heat.
3. Bring the cream to the boil in a large saucepan (use a 2-litre/3½-pint pan as the mixture spits). Add the caramelised sugar. Boil, stirring continuously, until the mixture browns.
4. Now stir in the butter and remove the pan from the heat. To test if the caramel will set or needs cooking longer, drip a little on to a cold plate.
5. Pour the mixture into a tray covered with oiled foil or paper. Cool until lukewarm.
6. Turn out of the tray and peel off the foil. Using an oiled knife, cut into strips and then into bite-sized pieces.
7. Wrap the cooled caramels in cellophane.

Hard and crunchy, soft and melting, sweets for children's treats

Children can have the greatest fun possible in making their own sweets. But never leave them on their own. Boiling sugar has its obvious dangers for it reaches extremely high temperatures. So impress upon your children that they should always use a wooden spoon.

Ingredients:	Sugar	Brown sugar	Glucose or honey	Corn or maple syrup	Canned or fresh milk	Fresh cream	Butter	Water	Oil	Instant coffee
Sugar bonbons	250g 9oz		25g 1oz					7 Tbls		
Butter bonbons	500g 18oz						50g 2oz	10 Tbls	2 Tbls	
Soft butter bonbons	450g 1lb				250ml 8floz		50g 2oz	4 Tbls	2 Tbls	
Soft coffee caramels	250g 9oz		75g 3oz			250ml 8floz				2 Tbls
Soft chocolate caramels	250g 9oz		75g 3oz			250ml 8floz				
Hard chocolate caramels	250g 9oz		50g 2oz			100ml 4floz				
Soft caramels	250g 9oz		75g 3oz			250ml 8floz				
Russian caramels	250g 9oz	50g 2oz		50g 2oz		7 Tbls	75g 3oz	6 Tbls	2 Tbls	
Hard coffee caramels	250g 9oz					100ml 4floz				2 Tbls

Which sweets do your children prefer?

There are crunchy sweets which shatter when you bite on them – for your teeth's sake these are best sucked! Then there are light, melting sweets which can be chewed. The consistency of sweets depends on how long you boil the sugar and whether you add cream, butter or milk to the mixture. The chart lists the ingredients needed and the quantities for each type of sweet.

The method in each case is the same as the basic recipe.

What equipment do you need

In each case, a saucepan to boil the sugar, preferably with a long handle which is easier to get hold of than a small round handle when you need to move the saucepan quickly off the heat. The saucepan should be heavy-based and of a good conductive material (stainless steel or even copper).

A small tray with a raised edge covered with baking parchment in which the mixture sets. You can also use a rectangular baking dish or a plate covered with a double layer of aluminium foil raised at the edge to form a rim which will prevent the mixture running over the edge.

Praline

This nutty topping is very easy to make and will keep for weeks in a jar or tin, with a close-fitting lid. So you can always have some to hand every time you want to decorate the sides of a gâteau or cake or make a nice crunchy topping for a dessert.

10 tablespoons sugar	
4 tablespoons water	
100g/4oz whole, unpeeled almonds	

1. In a heavy-based saucepan, quickly bring the sugar and water to the boil.
2. Fast boil until the sugar thermometer shows 156C/312F and the sugar is pale brown (see pages 208–9) in colour.
3. Add the almonds and stir until fully coated in sugar.
4. Turn out on to an oiled marble sheet or greased baking tray and cool slightly.
5. Crush with a rolling pin until the mixture resembles fine crumbs.

A sweet coating for fresh fruit

The highlight of a visit to the fair for the kids is to eat bright red
toffee apples with their unnatural-looking glossy coating of toffee.
It cracks and splinters when you bite into it and tastes wonderfully
sweet in contrast with the sour juiciness of the fresh apple hiding
beneath the crystal coating of sugar. Or for something completely
different how about cherries, dark and silky, deliciously coated in
velvety chocolate . . .

Toffee apples

The sugar coating should be clear as glass and shiny, so the sugar has to be boiled to exactly the right point. You will need to buy a sugar thermometer to measure it exactly.

For toffee apples you need fairly sour dessert apples of a similar size and with unmarked skins. Golden Delicious are ideal for they keep their shape best in the heat of the sugar.

6 dessert apples
6 toffee apple sticks
550 g/19 oz sugar
5 tablespoons water
1 teaspoon red food colouring
1 teaspoon vinegar

1. Wash the apples, dry very thoroughly, remove the stalks and push a stick into the stalk end of each.
2. Get a baking tray ready, sprinkle it evenly with 4 tablespoons sugar.
3. Quickly bring the remaining sugar, water, colouring and vinegar to the boil in a heavy-based saucepan.
4. Fast boil until the sugar thermometer reaches 156C/312F.
5. Remove the pan from the heat immediately. Dip in the apples one after the other and stir in the syrup until completely covered.
6. Place on the prepared bed of sugar in the baking tray and leave to cool.

Variations:
Instead of apples you can cover other fruits with toffee. Grapes are excellent, so are sliced pears, oranges or firm peaches.

Chocolate cherries

Use perfect, large cherries. They should be crisp and firm and the stem still fresh and green, for the stems are important to the look of these sweets (see pages 260–1).

500 g/18 oz cherries
250 ml/8 fl oz brandy
575 g/1¼ lb plain cooking chocolate

1. Carefully wash the cherries, but do not remove stalks.
2. Place in a tall, narrow jar and pour on the brandy. Leave in the refrigerator for about 2 weeks to steep, making sure that the cherries are completely covered with alcohol throughout.
3. Drain the cherries. Dry on a thick layer of absorbent kitchen paper.
4. Gently melt the cooking chocolate several times (see page 246).
5. Make sure the cherries are completely dry and, holding each one by its stem, dip into the chocolate. Dry on a wire rack or on baking parchment. For a thicker layer of chocolate, repeat the process several times.

Glossary of Cooking Terms and Techniques

Baking Blind

This is a technique of par-baking unfilled pastry cases for flans or quiches to make sure that the pastry base is thoroughly cooked through in the finished item. The base of the pastry case is pricked all over with a fork, then a piece of greaseproof paper is placed loosely in the middle. Dried beans or peas are sprinkled over the paper to prevent the pastry from bubbling up during baking and to prevent the sides of the unfilled case from falling in. The pastry is baked for 10–15 minutes, the paper and beans are removed and the filling is added ready to be cooked completely.

The dried peas or beans can be stored when cool for repeated use. Ceramic 'beans' are also available for this purpose. (See also page 24.)

Bain Marie

This is a water bath in which delicate items are cooked. A roasting tin or similar is used and half filled with hot water. The dish or bowl containing the food is placed in the tin of water and cooked in the oven or, in some cases, on top of the hob. This is used for custards or any other light mixtures which are likely to curdle if they are exposed to fierce heat.

Base Line and Grease

This is a method of preparing cake tins before baking. For light cake mixtures, if there is any danger that the cake may stick to the base of the tin then a circle of greaseproof paper is cut to the same size as the tin and placed in the base. This must be well greased along with the sides of the tin. This will ensure that the cake turns out easily when it is cooked. The paper is peeled off the bottom of the cake before it is cooled.

Beating

This is a vigorous mixing method used for batters or similar mixtures. A wooden spoon is used and the intention is to incorporate air into the mixture, at the same time removing any lumps to give a smooth consistency. An electric food mixer can be used.

Blanching

This is a technique of submerging ingredients in boiling water, bringing rapidly back to the boil and draining immediately or cooking very briefly before draining. In some cases boiling water is poured on to the ingredients then drained off after a short standing time. This latter method is used when peeling fruits like tomatoes and peaches. The boiling water loosens the skin after about 30–60 seconds, making it easy to peel away.

Blanching is also used as a method of briefly cooking foods which are then incorporated into salads or used in more complicated dishes (for example quiches) where they will not have adequate opportunity to cook completely without this blanching. The technique can also be used for taking the edge off the flavour of strong ingredients, such as onions or garlic, if they are to be combined with delicate items.

Chopping

Cutting into very small pieces. Foods may be finely or coarsely chopped but the pieces should not be large chunks and the result should be even.

To chop an onion easily, cut it in half and place one half cut side down on a board. Cut into slices, then cut across into small pieces. Cut the second half in the same way. Other whole vegetables can be cut in a similar way by first cutting strips, then cutting these across into small pieces.

A food processor can be used to carry out most chopping operations to the required degree. Small electric choppers are available for herbs and these are similar to liquidisers.

Clarify

This is a clearing process used for stocks which can be used in soups and sauces or as a glaze for savoury dishes. The stock is cleared by adding stiffly whisked egg white to the simmering liquid, then cooking very gently for about 15 minutes. The stock is strained through fine muslin to remove the egg white and to produce a clear result.

Creaming

This is a method of combining ingredients or softening individual items. Fat and sugar are creamed together to form the base for certain cake mixtures. A wooden spoon is used to beat the fat and sugar in a circular motion until the mixture becomes pale and soft. Air is incorporated into the mixture during this process. An electric food mixer can be used.

In some instances, butter may be creamed to soften it before it is used in a recipe. In this case, the fat is beaten until it is creamy in texture, but not necessarily light or pale.

Deep Frying

This is a method of cooking food by immersing it in very hot fat. Before cooking, the food must be protected in some way – fruit can be coated in batter, certain foods can be coated in egg and breadcrumbs or other items can be coated with flour. The fat used can be lard, dripping or, more popularly, oil. It is important that the fat is hot enough before the food to be cooked is added. If the fat is not hot, then the food will not be sealed immediately on the outside and the result may be greasy. A thermometer should be used to measure the temperature of the fat and it should read 180 C/350 F or slightly higher. It is equally important that the fat does not overheat and burn during cooking as this will taint the food with an unpleasant flavour. During cooking the temperature should be as constant as possible. The temperature of the fat can be tested by adding a small cube of day-old bread to the pan. If the fat is hot enough the bread will brown in 1 minute. For safety the pan should be no more than two-thirds full of fat when deep frying.

The food should be lowered carefully into the hot fat, then drained thoroughly on absorbent kitchen paper when cooked. Certain mixtures which are normally baked can be deep fried. For example, choux pastry and puff pastry can both be cooked by deep frying and yeast dough is deep fried to make doughnuts. (See page 189)

Dicing
Cutting food into small even-sized cubes. The size may vary and food can be finely diced into very tiny pieces, or the pieces can be slightly larger but they should not be large cubes or chunks.

Dusting
Cooked items are sometimes dusted with sugar (icing or caster). The sugar can be put in a small sieve or tea strainer or a sugar sifter can be used. Cake tins are sometimes dusted with sugar or flour before the mixture is put in them, see *grease and flour*.

Folding In
This is a method of incorporating an ingredient into a very light mixture, for example flour or melted fat into a mixture of whisked eggs.. and sugar. For this a large metal spoon is used and the ingredients are added in small batches, with the mixture being carefully lifted and folded in a figure of eight motion to incorporate the ingredients without knocking out any of the air. It is important that the mixture is not stirred or beaten at all or the air will be lost.

Glazing
Foods are brushed with a glaze for different reasons. Breads, pastries and scones can be brushed with a little milk or beaten egg before cooking to produce a nice brown result. This is known as glazing. Alternatively, the term can be used to describe the process of brushing cooked items or fillings for flans with a glaze which will give a shine and at the same time form a protective coating (to prevent drying out). For this a thickened fruit glaze is used or warmed jam can be sieved and slightly thinned before brushing over the fruit.

Grease and Flour
This is a method of preparing baking tins. The tin is first greased, then a small amount of flour is spooned into the tin and it is tilted and tapped until the flour completely coats the inside of the tin. Excess flour is tipped out.

Light cake mixtures are baked in greased and floured tins to ensure a good rise. The airy mixture slightly clings to the prepared surface of the tin as it cooks and this gives the cake a surface to adhere to as it rises.

Infuse
This is a method of imparting the flavour of a particular ingredient to a liquid. For example, a vanilla pod is allowed to stand in hot milk for a length of time until it gives up its flavour to the liquid. Fruit rind, spices and other ingredients can be infused in liquid in this way, then strained out before the liquid is used.

Kneading
This is a technique used in the preparation of bread dough or similar yeasted mixtures. The dough is stretched and pounded with the intention of developing the gluten in the flour to make a smooth, elastic mixture. As the yeast works within the dough, the elastic nature of the mixture traps the bubbles of gas which are given off to make the dough rise and to give a light result. To achieve the correct result, dough is kneaded for about 10 minutes to ensure that the yeast is evenly distributed and that the dough mix becomes tough enough to hold the gas and rise adequately. A dough hook can be fitted on an electric food mixer to knead the dough or this can be done in a food processor.

Knock Back
This is the technique of lightly kneading dough after the first rising process to knock out all the gas which has been incorporated. It is not a lengthy kneading operation but should be just enough to flatten the dough ready for the second rising.

Macerate
Soaking fruit in liquor with the intention of combining or accentuating the flavours. The ingredients can be allowed to stand overnight or for several hours until the flavour is brought out to the full. In some cases the intention is to impart the qualities of a liqueur or particular alcoholic liquor to the food.

Paring
Thinly peeling off the rind of citrus fruit. The idea is to take off the rind without having any of the sharp white pith. This is used to flavour or decorate a variety of dishes, both sweet and savoury.

Prove
This is the process of rising yeast dough. The kneaded dough is covered and placed in a warm place to prove until it has doubled in size. This process is usually carried out twice when making dough.

Purée

This is the term used to describe a fine pulp prepared from fruits or vegetables. Foods can be puréed through a sieve, by pressing the mixture through several times, or by blending them in a liquidiser or food processor.

Resting

A period of resting should be allowed for when preparing pastry goods. The rolled out, finished pastries should be set aside in a cool place for 15–30 minutes before they are baked. This allows time for the mixture to settle down after being rolled and prevents it from shrinking during cooking. It also promotes a better texture in the finished item.

Rolling Out

Pastry should be rolled out on a surface dusted with a very light covering of flour. Excess flour used at this stage will spoil the balance of the mixture. The pastry should be rolled with very light strokes in one direction only. The pastry can be carefully turned around during rolling but it should not be turned over. Rolling pins of various types are available but a clean empty wine bottle can also be used.

Some types of icing and almond paste are rolled out to be used on cakes.

In this case a light dusting of icing sugar is used to prevent the mixture from sticking to the work surface.

Rubbing In

This is a method of incorporating fat into dry ingredients. It is used in the preparation of various pastries and some cake mixtures. The key to success is using a light touch to rub the fat into the flour. Only the tips of the fingers should be used and the mixture should be lifted into the air as it is worked. When the fat is incorporated sufficiently the mixture should resemble very fine breadcrumbs. The fat should be chilled and you should keep your hands as cool as possible while rubbing the fat into the flour.

Shredding

Cutting into very fine, even strips. This is used for candied fruit rinds, fresh fruit rinds and other fresh ingredients for both sweet and savoury purposes. To achieve best results, the food should be finely sliced first, then cut into thin shreds.

Sieving

This is the process of pressing ingredients through a sieve to remove unwanted fibres and to reduce the mixture to a smooth purée.

Sifting

Passing dry ingredients, for example flour, through a sieve. The sieve is tapped or shaken to encourage the ingredients to pass through. This process removes any lumps and lightens the flour.

Tempering

A process of working melted chocolate before it is used to coat items or to make sweets. The melted chocolate is poured on to a marble slab and moved with a palette knife, by scraping it in towards the middle, folding it over and then returning it to the basin to be heated gently again.

Whisking

This is used to incorporate air into ingredients and to combine certain items. A metal whisk is specially designed to incorporate air. A food mixer with a whisk attachment can be used.

Zesting

The zest is the outer rind of a citrus fruit and this can be removed in fine strips using a zester – a specially designed tool which is scraped over the outside of the fruit. The zest is used to flavour or decorate a variety of dishes.

Index

281